HOSPITALITY AS

The issues in this book will be recognised as crucial by anyone who wants to achieve a more satisfying grasp of the relation to each other of Christian ethics and moral philosophy, and by anyone who wants to understand what makes for fruitful exchanges between interlocutors who really do hold opposing views. Bretherton's clear and engaging text reaches beyond mere analysis and criticism to the development of a model of dialogue in terms of 'hospitality'. I commend this book strongly and without reserve.
Nigel Biggar, Regius Professor of Moral and Pastoral Theology,
Oxford University

Bretherton's book is quite brilliant: elegant in its structural composition, tightly argued, lucidly written, erudite, nuanced and urbane, and relentlessly theological.
Gavin D'Costa, Professor of Catholic Theology,
University of Bristol, in Theology (2008)

We live amid increasing ethical plurality and fragmentation while at the same time more and more questions of moral gravity confront us. Some of these questions are new, such as those around human cloning and genetics. Other questions that were previously settled have re-emerged, such as those around the place of religion in politics. Responses to such questions are diverse, numerous and often vehemently contested.

Hospitality as Holiness seeks to address the underlying question facing the church within contemporary moral debates: how should Christians relate to their neighbours when ethical disputes arise? The problems the book examines centre on what the nature and basis of Christian moral thought and action is, and in the contemporary context, whether moral disputes may be resolved with those who do not share the same framework as Christians. Bretherton establishes a model – that of hospitality – for how Christians and non-Christians can relate to each other amid moral diversity.

This book will appeal to those interested in the broad question of the relationship between reason, tradition, natural law and revelation in theology, and more specifically to those engaged with questions about plurality, tolerance and ethical conflict in Christian ethics and medical ethics.

For Gabriel

Hospitality as Holiness

Christian Witness Amid Moral Diversity

LUKE BRETHERTON
King's College London, UK

ASHGATE

© Luke Bretherton 2006
First published in paperback 2010

All rights reserved. No part of this publication may be reproduced, stored in a retrieval system or transmitted in any form or by any means, electronic, mechanical, photocopying, recording or otherwise without the prior permission of the publisher.

Luke Bretherton has asserted his right under the Copyright, Designs and Patents Act, 1988, to be identified as the author of this work.

Published by
Ashgate Publishing Limited
Wey Court East
Union Road
Farnham
Surrey, GU9 7PT
England

Ashgate Publishing Company
Suite 420
101 Cherry Street
Burlington
VT 05401-4405
USA

www.ashgate.com

British Library Cataloguing in Publication Data
Bretherton, Luke
 Hospitality as holiness : Christian witness amid moral diversity
 1. Hospitality – Religious aspects – Christianity 2. Christian ethics 3. Witnessbearing (Christianity) 4. Evangelistic work
 I. Title
 241.6'71

Library of Congress Cataloging-in-Publication Data
Bretherton, Luke.
 Hospitality as holiness : Christian witness amid moral diversity / Luke Bretherton.
    p. cm.
 Includes bibliographical references and index.
 ISBN 0-7546-5372-2 (hardcover : alk. paper)
 1. Hospitality—Religious aspects—Christianity. 2. Witnessbearing (Christianity)
3. Evangelistic work. 4. Christian ethics. 5. Church and the world. 6. Holiness. I. Title.

  BV4647.H67B76 2006
  241'.671—dc22
                                                                        2005012748

ISBN 9780754653721 (hbk)
ISBN 9781409403494 (pbk)

Printed and bound in Great Britain by
MPG Books Group, UK

Contents

Preface	*vii*
Acknowledgements	*viii*
List of abbreviations	*ix*

Introduction	**1**

PART I   THE PROBLEM OF MORAL PLURALITY

1 Alasdair MacIntyre's diagnosis of the contemporary context	**9**
The incoherence of contemporary moral debates	9
Virtue, tradition and the recovery of moral reason	17
Truth, Thomism and discerning the moral order	20
Natural law and the conditions for free and just relations	25
Incommensurability and the resolution of moral disputes	26
Summary	30
2 Germain Grisez and the shared rationality of all moral traditions	**34**
Whose Justice? Which Thomism?	34
Grisez and the new natural law account of ethics	36
Grisez and MacIntyre compared	39
The challenges Grisez poses to MacIntyre	47
A critique of Grisez and the new natural law theory	51
Summary	56
3 Oliver O'Donovan and the distinctiveness of Christian ethics	**61**
Modernity: the apostate child of Christianity	61
O'Donovan's evangelical ethics	64
O'Donovan and MacIntyre compared	69
Ad hoc commensurability or a clash of traditions?	74
MacIntyre's openness to theological specification	80
Incommensurability and the resolution of moral disputes revisited	87

PART II   THE NATURE AND SHAPE OF CHRISTIAN HOSPITALITY

4 Local politics, ecclesiology and resisting modernity	**95**
Local politics and resisting modernity	96
MacIntyre's conception of relations between Christians and non-Christians	99

	Ecclesiology and resolving ethical disputes	101
	Eschatology and the nature of Christian distinctiveness	110
	Summary	115
5	**The practice of hospitality**	**121**
	Hospitality, tolerance and Christian witness	121
	Hospitality and the shape of relations between Christians and their neighbours	126
	A theologically specified account of hospitality	128
	Hospitality and tolerance contrasted	147
	Summary	150
6	**Hospitality, hospice care and euthanasia – a case study in negotiating moral diversity**	**160**
	Defining euthanasia	161
	The practice of medicine and euthanasia	165
	Philosophical defences of euthanasia	168
	Relating autonomy, death and suffering within a theological account of good care	172
	MacIntyre's response to the care we owe the suffering-dying	178
	Grisez's understanding of the care we owe the suffering-dying	180
	Hospice care as an embodiment of Christian hospitality	183
	Conclusion	**196**
	Bibliography	199
	Index	211

Preface

This book is a revised version of a doctoral dissertation submitted to the University of London, and I am grateful to my examiners, Nigel Biggar and Robert Song, for their critical feedback on the thesis. I would like also to thank Michael Banner, my doctoral supervisor, for his great patience, foresight and guidance, and without whom, what shards of light there are in this book would be too obscured to see; Andrew Walker for starting me off in my research and guiding my first tentative steps; the late Colin Gunton and the Institute for Systematic Theology weekly seminars at King's College London for constantly opening up new theological horizons to me and Crispin Fletcher-Louis for guiding my reading in New Testament scholarship. I owe a debt of appreciation to Tim Summers, Chris Roberts and Philip Barnes for help in editing earlier drafts of the book.

I am grateful for the financial support I received from the Ecclesiastical Insurance Group, the Whitfield Institute, the Grubb Institute, and the variety of organizations (especially the St Ethelburga's Centre for Reconciliation and Peace) who employed me over the duration of the doctoral research and so contributed towards the practical support of this project.

For personal support throughout the period of its writing I would like to thank Ashley Meaney for his prayers, constant encouragement and healing wisdom; and Charlie Colchester, Marsh Moyle, Juraj Kusnierik, Milan Čičel, Sára Miklós, András Visky, and all of those with whom I worked in Central and Eastern Europe for first raising the questions I seek to address in this book and inspiring the search for answers. My greatest thanks must go to my wife, Caroline, for sustaining and abiding with me throughout the years of study.

Luke Bretherton
Epiphany, 2005

Acknowledgements

Parts of Chapter 5 have been taken, with revisions, from an article that appeared in *Studies in Christian Ethics*, volume 17, number 1 (2004) under the title of 'Tolerance, Hospitality and Education: A Theological Proposal'. This is reprinted by permission of Sage Publications Ltd.

The Scripture quotations contained herein are from the New Revised Standard Version Bible, copyright © 1989 by the Division of Christian Education of the National Council of the Churches of Christ in the USA, and are used by permission. All rights reserved.

List of abbreviations

ANF	*Ante-Nicene Fathers*
AV	Alasdair MacIntyre, *After Virtue: A Study in Moral Theory*, 2nd edn (London: Duckworth, 1994).
CMP	Germain Grisez, *The Way of the Lord Jesus: Christian Moral Principles*, 3 vols (Chicago: Franciscan Herald Press, 1983), I.
Desire	Oliver O'Donovan, *The Desire of the Nations: Rediscovering the Roots of Political Theory* (Cambridge: Cambridge University Press, 1996).
DRA	Alasdair MacIntyre, *Dependent Rational Animals: Why Human Beings Need the Virtues* (London: Duckworth, 1999).
LCL	Germain Grisez, *The Way of the Lord Jesus: Living a Christian Life*, 3 vols (Quincy, IL: Franciscan Press, 1993), II.
NPNF	*Nicene and Post-Nicene Fathers*
RMO	Oliver O'Donovan, *Resurrection and Moral Order: An Outline for Evangelical Ethics* (Grand Rapids: Eerdmans, 1986).
SCE	*Studies in Christian Ethics*
TRV	Alasdair MacIntyre, *Three Rival Versions of Moral Enquiry: Encyclopaedia, Genealogy, and Tradition* (London: Duckworth, 1989).
WJ	Alasdair MacIntyre, *Whose Justice? Which Rationality?* (London: Duckworth, 1988).

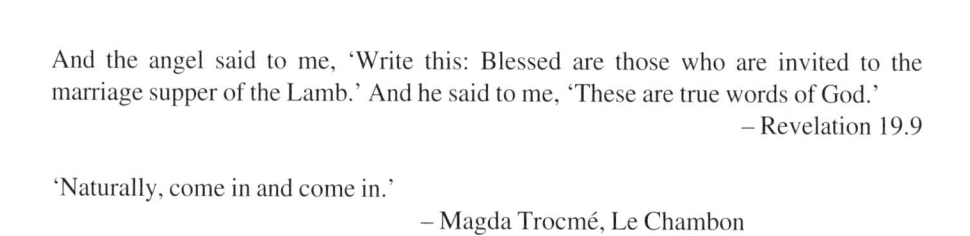

And the angel said to me, 'Write this: Blessed are those who are invited to the marriage supper of the Lamb.' And he said to me, 'These are true words of God.'
– Revelation 19.9

'Naturally, come in and come in.'
– Magda Trocmé, Le Chambon

Introduction

The lumbering Chinook helicopter carried us from Skopje, over the mountainous border and across the central, arable plain of Kosovo. As dusk encamped around us we could see many charred houses and a few which had recently been set alight. This jarred with the sight of whole families joyously waving as we passed overhead. Seated beside me were a number of Anglican Bishops, part of an official delegation invited by the Serbian Orthodox Church to begin efforts at reconciliation between Britain and Serbia. We arrived on 9 July, 1999, exactly a month after NATO's last air strike.

By the time we reached Peć, in north-west Kosovo, it was pounding with rain. Our British Army escorts met us and drove us to the monastery that is the seat of the Serbian Patriarchate. Driving through the town we saw the devastation from bombs and burning. Italian soldiers clustered together on street corners. A few vegetable stalls were set up and one or two cafes had opened. An Italian armoured personnel carrier was stationed outside the monastery itself. At the gates of the monastery a monk greeted us and led us past a clod of women huddled in the entrance. We were taken to view the medieval churches of the Holy Apostles, the Holy Virgin and Saint Nicholas. These churches form a single building inside the walled monastery grounds. Vespers was in progress and the sound of prayer and chanting followed us as we looked at the darkened frescos and the salvaged remains from recently destroyed churches in the region.

Here we were, members of an established church from a *de facto* secular liberal democracy, whose government had been at war with the government of this country and whose troops now occupied part of it. We were in a medieval Serbian Orthodox monastery surrounded by nominally Catholic soldiers, who, as part of a secular 'humanitarian' military force, were now protecting the Serbs from nominally Muslim and nationalist Albanians who were still, *de jure* at least, Serbs, and who had themselves, until a few weeks previously, been the object of racist and nationalist inspired ethnic Serbian violence.

The temptation is to categorize the situation just described as exceptional or foreign, as something far removed from our own experience, that is, from the experience of those of us who live in Western liberal democratic societies. Certainly few situations involve the level of deadly conflict as that witnessed in the Balkans. Nevertheless, a similar dynamic can be seen in disputes about globalization, abortion, animal welfare, genetic modification of plants, building new airports or roads, nuclear weapons and immigration. Relations between different groups are often hostile or even violent and there seems to be no shared criteria by which to decide who is right. Determining the identity of the conflicting parties, their motives, and the justice and truth of their claims is hard and often confusing. Who tells the truth and whose narrative frames the 'truth' are hotly contested. At the same time, new and complex moral problems increasingly confront us. Some of these moral problems arise because of developments in science and technology, those around human cloning and genetics, for example. Other problems that were presumed settled have emerged as in need of re-negotiation, such as the relationship between religious and political authorities in determining the common good.

This book seeks to address the problem of how Christians should relate to their neighbours when ethical disputes arise within the context just described. Addressing this problem involves first, mapping the contemporary context in which Christians and non-Christians encounter each other; second, determining the significance of the differences between Christian and non-Christian moral judgements; and finally, establishing a framework for how Christians and non-Christians should relate to each other.

The issues I address in this book were provoked initially by working with local churches in Central and Eastern Europe from 1992 to 1997. These churches were adjusting to a radically new situation. Their context was one in which state socialism clashed with consumerism; Christianity jostled with nihilism, new religious movements and a myriad of other faiths; and nationalists raged alongside communists and liberals in a complex weave of political power grabbing. Amid the ruins of the European Marxist project, it was, ironically, Marx's dictum that 'all that is solid melts into air' which seemed most fitting.[1] The very newness of this situation – and its instability – raised important questions for Christians: how should they negotiate with others in an ethically plural and vehemently contested social, economic and political context; can Christians and non-Christians settle their ethical differences; and does the historical context affect the possibility of resolution or not?

During this period in Western Europe and in America faith in capitalist, liberal democracy reigned. Those forces that resisted this 'end' to history were seen as atavistic survivals from a barbarian past that would soon wither. The role of religious traditions in national and international affairs was largely ignored. However, the myopia surrounding the religious dimension of domestic and international politics is increasingly recognized as a mistake, especially since the Al-Qaeda attacks on New York and Washington, DC in September 2001. From debates about abortion and euthanasia, to campaigns for debt relief for poor countries, to the political impact of developments within Islam, some account is needed of the continuing role of religious traditions.[2] Yet secularist assumptions still dominate political and social debates. The suggestion is that common ground must be found between everyone in a plural society and for this to happen 'private' convictions must be left behind. Some form of agnostic 'public reason', through which shared deliberation can be processed and consensus reached, is endorsed. But strategies for resolving ethical disputes that focus on either common ground or an agnostic 'public' language of arbitration face a key problem: they often fail to interact with the most deeply held beliefs and important social practices that inspire and shape people. It is these beliefs and practices that constitute particular traditions and unless we take seriously the claims of a particular tradition in terms of its own frames of reference, real understanding and agreement are not possible. We need to pay sufficient attention to the particular presuppositions of a tradition, neither judging a tradition in terms alien to it nor demanding it become something it is not. Failure to do this means we try to enter a conversation shaped decisively by one side and so, in effect, ignore what the other is actually saying and doing. The result is misunderstanding and ill-judged actions. In addressing the current context of deep moral and cultural diversity this book attempts to take the theological presuppositions of Christianity seriously and outline a form of engagement with other moral views that neither seeks common ground nor demands the adoption of a 'foreign' language in order to generate consensus.

Alasdair MacIntyre provides an influential account of the contemporary situation. For MacIntyre contemporary Western society is characterized not just by a plurality of traditions (a situation common to all historical epochs), but an extreme form of plurality wherein coherent traditions have broken down into fragments that co-exist in a confused *mélange*.

The result of this fragmentation of traditions for MacIntyre is that, today, justice is what the strong make it. In MacIntyre's view it is capitalist corporations and the bureaucracies of the nation-state that are strong. Thus, it is capitalist corporations and the bureaucracies of the nation-state that determine what counts as justice. Furthermore, because of the fragmentation of traditions, public debate has become civil war carried on by other means. According to MacIntyre, this is the contemporary context in which Christians live and work and carry on relations with their neighbours.

MacIntyre develops a first order account of how ethical thought and action is constituted by a tradition and how such a tradition is incommensurable with other rival traditions. When MacIntyre uses the term 'incommensurable' he means that when two or more traditions encounter each other at a particular moment in time, there is no common standard of measurement to judge between their respective conceptions for determining what is rational and moral. MacIntyre, however, does not see incommensurability as either inevitable, or a permanent condition, or impossible to overcome. He sets out a second order meta-theory for how different traditions can, over time, resolve disputes. His meta-theory seeks to steer between the Scylla of relativism and the Charybdis of positing some universally human and culturally neutral grounds for adjudicating between incommensurable traditions. What troubles MacIntyre is that the fragmentation of traditions existent in the contemporary context severely hinders the process he sets out from being undertaken effectively. Such fragmentation makes conflicts between traditions, which at heart are conflicts about the criteria to evaluate what is just (that is, they are debates about what is due to each member of the community) extremely difficult to resolve.

MacIntyre's first order account of what constitutes a tradition and his second order meta-theory of how different traditions relate forms the basis of his constructive response to the contemporary context. He argues that particular traditions should form communities in which the practices and rationality of a tradition are embodied and the dominant, incoherent patterns of the contemporary context resisted. By doing so, communities of resistance engage in a form of local politics that is just and rational. This type of local politics allows for the kind of conversation that MacIntyre views as crucial to resolving ethical disputes between incommensurable traditions.

In order to test MacIntyre's diagnosis and constructive proposal I shall compare and contrast it with the work of two contemporary moral theologians: Germain Grisez and Oliver O'Donovan. The comparison will focus on Grisez and O'Donovan's respective understanding of the degree of difference between Christianity and other traditions and whether traditions are incommensurable. The comparison with Grisez assesses whether MacIntyre overemphasizes the difference between Christianity and other moral traditions while the comparison with O'Donovan assesses whether MacIntyre underemphasizes it.

For Grisez, there is greater congruence between Christians and non-Christians than MacInyre allows. Grisez holds that faithful witness to Jesus Christ, as understood and defined by the Magisterium of the Roman Catholic Church, is the identifying feature of Christian action. However, Grisez argues that Christians and non-Christians share a self-evident, tradition-free set of criteria for evaluating what is just and good; it is these that enables them to resolve disputes in a relatively unproblematic fashion. By contrast, O'Donovan does not think Christianity can resolve disputes either on the basis of a tradition-free set of criteria or via the kind of process MacIntyre sets out. For O'Donovan, the moral knowledge that Christians possess – that the created order is fallen, reconciled, and redeemed – can be known only through the revelation given in the Christ-event. The comparison with O'Donovan serves the additional purpose of demonstrating whether MacIntyre's conception is open to further theological specification.

O'Donovan, while largely sharing MacIntyre's diagnosis of the contemporary context, has a conception of Christian thought and action and how it relates to non-Christian thought and action that is explicitly formulated in response to the revelation of God given in Jesus Christ. While acknowledging the role tradition plays in enabling people to know revelation O'Donovan understands there to be more involved than just tradition. For him an account of the church is needed when assessing relations between Christians and non-Christians. Crucially, the church is more than a tradition. The terms 'the Christian tradition' and 'the church' cannot be used as synonyms for each other. Rather, the term 'tradition' is an epistemological category, whereas 'the church' is an ontological one: 'the church' of which Christians are a part, makes a claim to be a way of being. O'Donovan helps us negotiate the relationship between Christian ethics and ecclesiology, for his ecclesiology relates directly to his conception of Christian ethical thought and action and how it is distinct from non-Christian action. A theological analysis can then be given of how Christians relate to non-Christians, and thus how MacIntyre's model of such relations is parallel or contrary to it.

In the second half of the book I give a constructive account of how Christians should, in terms of their own criteria of evaluation, engage with non-Christians when confronted by ethical disputes or common moral problems. I argue that the theologically specified motif of 'hospitality' constitutes a fuller account than MacIntyre's meta-theory of how Christians and non-Christians may relate with regard to ethical disputes. As a social practice hospitality has been central to shaping relations between the church and its neighbours and has taken many forms in the Christian tradition. Care for the sick and the poor, hospitality to strangers, educational initiatives, and peace-making endeavours are all examples of ways in which the church hosts its neighbours and at the same time, bears faithful witness to Jesus Christ. In order to explicate the nature, shape and the implications of the practice of hospitality, hospitality and tolerance are contrasted. The notion of tolerance provides an important comparison because, within the contemporary context, tolerance is the most common way of conceptualizing relations with an 'other' with whom one disagrees. I argue that hospitality constitutes a better way of framing relations with strangers than tolerance.

An analysis of the debate over euthanasia in the final chapter provides a test case of the arguments in the book as whole. The dispute over euthanasia constitutes a paradigmatic instance of the difficulty Christians have in resolving ethical disputes with their neighbours when there is no common ground to which appeal can be made. After a critique of the debate, and an assessment of MacIntyre and Grisez's response, I analyse why hospice care is an instance of Christian hospitality and why it constitutes the best Christian response to care for the suffering-dying.

In short, the aim of this book is to develop, in dialogue with contemporary moral philosophy and theology, a constructive account of how the practice of hospitality constitutes the way in which Christians should respond to moral disputes in a context of deep diversity.

Notes

1 Karl Marx and Friedrich Engels, *The Communist Manifesto*, trans. Samuel Moore (London: Penguin, 1967), p. 83.

2 On this see Scott Thomas, 'Taking Religious and Cultural Pluralism Seriously: The Global Resurgence of Religion and the Transformation of International Society', *Millennium: Journal of International Studies*, 29.3 (2000), 815–41.

PART I
THE PROBLEM OF MORAL PLURALITY

CHAPTER 1

Alasdair MacIntyre's diagnosis of the contemporary context

The purpose of engaging with Alasdair MacIntyre's work is to use MacIntyre as a dialogue partner in the attempt to formulate a conception of how Christians are to engage with non-Christians, which is both rooted in the Christian tradition and attentive to the reality of the contemporary context. As noted in the introduction, MacIntyre offers an account of the contemporary context as distinct from ages past in its inability to resolve ethical disputes. In addition he gives an account of Christian ethical thought and action as constitutive of a tradition that has no immediately available or obvious common measure by which it can resolve ethical disputes with other, non-Christian, traditions. But the question is, is MacIntyre's diagnosis correct? To answer this question it must be discerned whether MacIntyre paints an accurate picture of the contemporary context of moral debate, whether his substantive theory is sufficiently open to theological development, and whether a conception of relations between Christians and non-Christians shaped by MacIntyre's moral philosophy can at the same time be faithful to the presuppositions of Christianity.

In this chapter I outline MacIntyre's diagnosis of the contemporary context. His diagnosis is situated within an assessment of MacIntyre's first order theory of tradition-guided rationality and his second order meta-theory of how different traditions resolve disputes. Included in the discussion of his meta-theory is an analysis of why MacIntyre believes Thomism is the optimal instance of a tradition and an account of his understanding of incommensurability.

The incoherence of contemporary moral debates

MacIntyre's position is that, even though different traditions are incommensurable in their conceptions of truth and justice, these traditions can, over time, resolve ethical disputes between themselves. However, according to MacIntyre, the development of liberalism involves, simultaneously, the development of individualism and bureaucratic rationality. These elements – liberalism, individualism and bureaucratic rationality –fragment traditions and the structures of community central to creating a just and rational society. Consequently, the fragmentation of traditions makes resolving disputes between those holding different viewpoints extremely difficult, so that public debate on moral problems is now interminable, highly conflictual (sometimes deadly), and stifles rational deliberation between contending parties.

MacIntyre's critique of contemporary moral debate is derived directly from his first and second order substantive theories. For MacIntyre, what is rational and just demands some conception of practical rationality at work within a particular tradition's conception of the common good. An example of this in practice is MacIntyre's critique of the modern way of achieving translatability and rational debate. He notes that it involves translating all traditions into international English and decontextualizing the tenets of a particular tradition and hence removing the very ground – its social practices, community and history – which make any tradition coherent and rational.[1] Indeed, MacIntyre criticizes contemporary modes of reasoning and notions of justice because they lack the necessary conditions to be rational and just. These modes of reasoning lack the necessary conditions because they are based on conceptions of *jus* as a property (or *dominium*) of the individual, whereby rationality becomes the justification of the preference (or will) of such an individual, or of a particular interest group.[2] Given this situation, social co-operation breaks down, society is highly conflictual, and there is an inability to resolve fundamental disputes. In effect, justice becomes what the strong make it. In contemporary society the strong are the bureaucracies of nation-states and the management of capitalist corporations, both of which inherently tend towards the manipulation of people solely in pursuit of the 'goods of effectiveness'; that is, profit, power and status.

MacIntyre uses two literary devices to illustrate the process by which he believes this situation came about. The first is a parable of catastrophe and the second is to draw a parallel with anthropological accounts of the Polynesian concept of 'taboo'. At the opening of *After Virtue* MacIntyre invites us to imagine that the natural sciences suffered a catastrophe: scientists are lynched, science teaching stops, laboratories are destroyed, and books are burned. After a time, people try to reinvent science. However, all they possess are fragments detached from any knowledge of the contexts that gave them significance. They have bits of theories, instruments whose real use is forgotten, single pages of articles, and half-chapters of books. As a result, they might do 'chemistry', or 'physics', or 'astronomy', in the sense that they would argue about good and bad theories, or debate the theory of relativity, but what they could not do would be real science: for there would be no overall conception of what the point of science was. The crux of the parable is simple. MacIntyre states:

> The hypothesis which I wish to advance is that in the actual world which we inhabit the language of morality is in the same state of grave disorder as the language of natural science in the imaginary world which I described. What we possess ... are fragments of a conceptual scheme, parts which now lack those contexts from which their significance derived. We possess, indeed, simulacra of morality, we continue to use many of the key expressions. But we have very largely, if not entirely lost our comprehension, both theoretical and practical, of morality.[3]

The implication of the 'disquieting suggestion' that modern morality is in chaos is that we lack the resources even to recognize the full extent of the disorder, much less extricate ourselves from it.

The process by which this situation came about, and its implications, becomes even clearer in MacIntyre's discussion of the Polynesian word 'taboo'. In the journal of his third voyage Captain Cook records how the Polynesians strictly prohibited certain practices, such as men and women eating together, and yet could offer no clear explanation for their prohibition. Forty years later, King Kamehameha II abolished taboos in Hawaii with no apparent social consequences. MacIntyre notes that anthropologists draw a variety of conclusions from this. Mary Douglas suggests that, initially, taboo rules were embedded in a context which conferred intelligibility upon them, much in the same way that Deuteronomy presupposes a certain cosmology and taxonomy to make sense of its prohibitions.[4] Once deprived of this context and background belief the taboo rules appeared to be a set of arbitrary prohibitions, which were then eventually abandoned. For the rules had been gradually deprived of any status that could secure their authority. In the absence of the status conferred by their original context and background, and of any possible meaningful re-evaluation, such rules resisted both interpretation and justification. For when the resources of a culture are too meagre to carry through the task of reinterpretation, the task of justification becomes impossible too.

MacIntyre holds that this is exactly the position of liberal attempts at justification of contemporary moral norms. According to MacIntyre, analytic philosophy sought to justify our own contemporary taboos without reference to any wider context, but failed. It presupposed that morality is an autonomous field of study that does not require an overall context to make sense of it. In *Three Rival Versions of Moral Enquiry* MacIntyre traces a stage in the process of growing incoherence to late Victorian 'encyclopaedic' thinking, as propounded by Henry Sidgwick, Adam Gifford and others. He discusses how the misunderstanding of taboos by such thinkers reveals their own confusion. According to MacIntyre, they misunderstood taboo rules as primarily negative prohibitions, rather than as merely the negative side of enabling prescriptions. He states: 'They were unable ... to envisage the possibility that both morality and rationality ought to be understood in a way which would make much of what they took to be morality appear as irrational and as arbitrary as the taboo customs of the Polynesians appeared to them.'[5] For MacIntyre, modern moral utterance and practice can only be understood as a series of fragmented survivals from an older past. So for example, the deontological character of moral judgements is the ghost of conceptions of divine law, which are alien to the metaphysics of modernity. The insoluble problems which these ghosts generate for modern moral theorists will remain insoluble until their history and context is properly understood. MacIntyre states that the only true story

> will be one which will both enable us to distinguish between what it is for a set of taboo rules and practices to be in good order and what it is for a set of taboo rules

and practices to have been fragmented and thrown into disorder and enable us to understand the historical transition by which the latter state emerged from the former.[6]

The task MacIntyre undertakes in *After Virtue* and his subsequent work is to narrate what he considers to be the true story.

The loss of teleological modes of moral reasoning

The loss of any sense of rational enquiry into morality as taking place in a wider context or framework means we have no criteria by which to judge the gap between what we are and what we ought to be. According to MacIntyre's account of history, what was eliminated by the eighteenth century was any concept of 'man-as-he-could-be-if-he-realised-his-telos'. This left an apparently unbridgeable gap between the notion of morality having a definite content, and a certain notion of human nature in its basic or primitive state: that is, there was no way to relate coherently existing moral imperatives to the notion of human nature as it naturally existed because the teleological framework to relate them was abandoned. The ethical injunctions were supposed to nurture and educate human nature into its *telos*, and so these injunctions could not be derived in reverse from an appeal to the reality of human nature. Yet this is precisely what was attempted. MacIntyre writes:

> The eighteenth-century moral philosophers engaged in what was an inevitably unsuccessful project; for they did indeed attempt to find a rational basis for their moral belief in a particular understanding of human nature, while inheriting a set of moral injunctions on one hand and a conception of human nature on the other which had been expressly designed to be discrepant with each other.[7]

In his book analysing MacIntyre's critique of modernity and capitalism in particular, Peter McMylor concurs with MacIntyre on this point. He comments that the upshot of jettisoning any notion of 'man-as-he-could-be-if-he-realised-his-telos' was that: 'No moral argument could move from factual premises to moral and evaluative conclusions. This is unsurprising since the intellectual material for such a move had been removed.'[8]

The abandonment of teleology lies at the heart of contemporary moral philosophy, which asks not 'What sort of person am I to become?' but 'What rules ought we to follow and why ought we to obey them?' As outlined in the taboo parallel, the lack of any coherent rational justification leads to a set of rules and principles that appear arbitrary. This is compounded by the lack of any historical context in debates about morality, for history is judged irrelevant to what are conceived of as abstract universal principles. Morality is thereby reduced to a set of rules and principles lacking context and it is in this form that it falls prey to the critics, notably Nietzsche, who argues that appeals to moral objectivity are in fact expressions of subjective will. MacIntyre depicts Nietzsche as a European Kamehameha II who dismisses all attempts to base morality on conscience, the categorical imperative, or moral sentiment, and abolishing natural rights and utility as fictions no longer worthy of being told.[9] For Nietzsche, morality can be only what the individual will creates. Far from being able to make judgements about what we are and what we ought to be, we can only properly say that morality is whatever passes for morality; that is, justice is what the strong make it. Thus, the contemporary question – 'what rules ought we to follow and why ought we to obey them?' – allows no criteria for agreeing a resolution. The central problem of contemporary debate is its simultaneous and inconsistent treatment of moral argument as both an exercise of rational powers and mere expressive assertion.[10]

Strength as the determining factor in contemporary morality

We can see that for MacIntyre the parables of the destruction of science and of taboo rules in Polynesia portray a situation that arises precisely when the conditions MacIntyre demands for rational deliberation no longer exist, either within a tradition or between traditions. As far as MacIntyre is concerned, when any society loses its modes of tradition-guided rationality, and in particular a shared belief in some conception of an ultimate human good, then three important consequences ensue. First, participants in that society are deprived of any shared standard of judgement in debates over particular moral and evaluative issues. This is the case in contemporary society, wherein more and more substantive moral issues are contested. Second, this development, reinforced by doubts as to the trustworthiness of those with whom one enters into moral disagreement, strengthens the tendency to construe appeals to principle as nothing more than masked expressions of desire, preference and will. Thus, distinguishing between genuine rational debate and its parody becomes increasingly difficult. Third, in MacIntyre's words 'a new need would arise for norms whose central purpose would be protective: to defend each person from becoming merely an instrument for the achievement of someone else's desires, preferences and will'.[11] The result of the three elements, taken together, is that:

> Justice could no longer be understood exclusively or even primarily as a matter of sustaining and repairing the breaches in an order in which allocations were in respect of contributions to a good, in shared allegiance to which social co-operation found its warrant.[12]

Rather, justice would be transmuted into the defending of each against all. MacIntyre traces the genealogy of this transformation of justice from Aquinas, through Hobbes, Hume, Kant, Nietzsche and others to its present incoherent and essentially defensive conception in the rhetoric of rights. He summarizes his conclusion as follows:

> What I have argued, then, is that we inhabit a culture in which disagreements, and more especially fundamental disagreements, about rights cannot be rationally debated, and indeed that it was in key part because those beliefs and

> commitments which must be shared if a particular society is to be capable of rational debate were at an earlier stage no longer widely enough held, that the modern conception of rights developed in the way that it did. It follows that it is seriously imprudent, if one not only cares about advancing, sustaining, and protecting the goods of human life, but also counts rationality, theoretical and practical, as central among those goods, and believes that only rational modes of achieving one's social and moral ends are justifiable, to adopt the contemporary idiom and rhetoric of rights.[13]

Given his critique of the 'rhetoric of rights' it is hardly surprising that MacIntyre does not see liberal democracy as in the vanguard of human freedom. Rather, he sees the politics and practices of liberal democracy as intrinsically unjust. He describes the modern state as 'a large, complex and often ramshackle set of interlocking institutions, combining none too coherently the ethos of a public utility company with the inflated claims to embody ideals of liberty and justice'.[14] He condemns its democratic aspects as a charade.[15] For MacIntyre, the societies of advanced Western modernity are run by 'oligarchies disguised as liberal democracies'.[16] The range of what is open to be discussed and changed is severely curtailed, so that no substantive issues about ways of life can be raised.[17] Such debate as occurs is the antithesis of serious intellectual enquiry, prohibiting as it does systematic rational analysis. Instead, policies and decisions emerge 'from a strange *mélange* of arguments, debating points and the influence of money and other forms of established power'.[18] It would be wrong, however, to characterize MacIntyre as specifically anti-modern, for he sees such problems as possibilities in all societies. For example, in 'Natural Law as Subversive: The Case of Aquinas' MacIntyre discusses how Aquinas's thirteenth-century contemporaries, Emperor Frederick II and King Louis IX of France, both attempted to pursue the goods of effectiveness, over and against the goods of excellence, in their legal and political administration.[19] However, MacIntyre does see the modern predicament as particularly acute, especially since it is characterized by 'a politics from whose agendas enquiry concerning the nature of that politics has been excluded, a politics thereby protected from perceptions of its own exclusions and limitations'.[20] It is this situation which is distinctive.

MacIntyre's critique of liberalism

MacIntyre perceives the acuteness of the contemporary situation as rooted in problems intrinsic to the primary discourse of contemporary moral philosophy: liberal individualism. As briefly noted above, the inability to provide justification for moral principles develops out of a conception of rationality as universal and without social context. By contrast, MacIntyre believes there can be no spectators' gallery from which a pure, abstract rationality 'free' from tradition, history, and social context can look down upon and evaluate all others. All forms of rationality are protagonists *within* the play, each claiming they have the true script. They encounter each other as actors upon a single stage. MacIntyre's complaint is that the principles which inform the theory and practice of justice within a liberal polity claim to be, but are not, neutral with respect to rival and conflicting theories of the human good. He states that where these principles are in force:

> they impose a particular conception of the good life, of practical reasoning, and of justice upon those who willingly or unwillingly accept the liberal procedures and the liberal terms of debate. ... The starting points of liberal theorizing are never neutral as between conceptions of the human good; they are always liberal starting points.[21]

In MacIntyre's understanding, rational enquiry into morals is inherently tradition-bound and must take account of its social context. MacIntyre follows Aristotle in holding that humans require some kind of a *polis*. He states:

> Aristotle gave us excellent reasons for believing that both rational enquiry in politics and ethics and rationality in action require membership in a community which shares allegiance to some tolerably specific overall conception of the ultimate human good. ... What such a shared understanding provides is precisely the kind of standard independent of, not only individual desires, preferences and will, but also of the interests of particular groups within the community, by appeal to which rational debate on practical questions can be carried on.[22]

This rational debate, which is founded on the movement towards a more explicit and detailed understanding of the ultimate human good, is an essential condition for justice to be secured. In MacIntyre's view, the securing of justice requires that each member of the community can receive what is her due in respect of her contribution to the ultimate human good (as conceived by the particular tradition in which she is situated).[23] Consequently, as the understanding and specificity of the ultimate good increases, so the ability of a society to give each person her due increases, and thus that society is increasingly just.

MacIntyre's conception of the relationship between justice and rationality seems to stand opposed to that of liberalism. MacIntyre cites the work of John Rawls and Robert Nozick as examples of how liberal conceptions of rationality and justice contrast with his account. MacIntyre writes:

> Rawls and Nozick articulate with great power a shared view which envisages entry into social life as – at least ideally – the voluntary act of at least potentially rational individuals with prior interests who have to ask the question 'What kind of social contract with others is it reasonable for me to enter into?' Not surprisingly, it is as a consequence of this that their views exclude any account of human community in which the notion of desert in relation to contributions to the common tasks of that community in pursuing shared goods could provide the basis for judgments about virtue and injustice.[24]

However, it could be argued that, far from excluding the kind of account of human community MacIntyre seeks, liberalism is just such an account. For example, Brian

Barry contends that liberalism could be presented as a self-conscious tradition, with Rawls's *A Theory of Justice* as an equivalent to Aquinas's *Summa*.[25] MacIntyre has come, in his later work, to concur with those, like Barry, who make this point. Yet instead of constituting a reason for praising liberalism, the fact that liberalism functions like a tradition is for MacIntyre a failure of liberalism. In *Whose Justice? Which Rationality?* MacIntyre notes that liberalism, in seeking some neutral, tradition free standard of rational justification, to which appeal could be made on issues of morality, contradicts itself by becoming a tradition: one partly defined by the interminability of the debate over what such neutral principles might consist of.[26] A further contradiction resides in the fact that, contrary to its own claims, liberalism has an evident conception of the good. Although every individual is equally free to propose and to live by whatever theory of the good he or she proposes, derived from whatever theory or tradition he or she may adhere to, that conception of the good must not involve reshaping the life of the rest of the community in accord with it. This qualification demonstrates liberal individualism's own broad conception of the good and also the severe limitation in its toleration of rival conceptions of the good in the public arena. As MacIntyre states:

> The overriding good of liberalism is no more and no less than the continuing sustenance of the liberal social and political order. Thus liberalism, while initially rejecting the claims of any overriding theory of the good, does in fact come to embody just such a theory.[27]

Hence, although liberalism seems to contradict MacIntyre's conception of rationality as tradition guided enquiry, in practice it mirrors it. According to MacIntyre, liberalism, in acting like a tradition, not only contradicts its own basic presuppositions, but is also, in practice, oppressive: it is engaged in imposing its conception of the good politically, legally, socially, and culturally wherever it has power to do so.[28]

MacIntyre directly opposes the premise of liberalism that we are not merely choosers, but are essentially isolated choosers, of our own good. The conception of human beings as isolated choosers is, in MacIntyre's view, the root of our present anomic, atomized and alienated condition. MacIntyre's Aristotelian conception, wherein excellence is directly linked to the nature of one's society, correspondingly sets limits to the ability of individuals to 'create' their own conceptions of the good. For MacIntyre, the fruit of liberalism is an increasingly fragmented society which increasingly inhibits the ability to make appropriate choices as there is less and less society to be a part of. Hence, liberalism is incapable of securing justice and ensuring that morality is not what the strong decide.

In this context, where each is against all, anarchy does not ensue because the structures and forms of governance control and rationalize society to their own ends. For MacIntyre, this control is exercised by the bureaucratic and management practices both of the administrative structures of the modern nation-state and of capitalist corporations. These systems embody 'bureaucratic rationality'. As defined by Weber, this rationality involves being engaged in a competitive struggle for scarce resources, both human and non-human, and in seeking to direct these resources as effectively as possible to specified ends.[29] Thus, according to MacIntyre, not only is public life and moral discourse in disarray, it is also oppressive because the quest for justice is replaced by the demand for managerial effectiveness.

MacIntyre holds that the values and morals of every culture assume embodied expression in the social world through certain archetypes or characters.[30] The primary moral representatives of contemporary culture, who illustrate the character of its moral disarray and injustice, are: the aesthete (whose primary evaluative criteria is pleasure and the avoidance of boredom); the manager (whose key criteria for evaluation is effectiveness in matching means to a predetermined end: which is nothing more than successful power); and the therapist (who is like the manager seeking effectiveness, not of an organization, but of the individual).[31]

In summary, the development of liberalism, from the Enlightenment period on, involves, simultaneously, the development of individualism and bureaucratic rationality. These core elements of modernity – liberalism, individualism and bureaucratic rationality – have together led to the fragmentation of traditions and the structures of community central to creating a just and rational society. The injustice of the present context and the fragmentation of traditions make resolving disputes between different viewpoints extremely difficult, so that public moral discourse is now highly conflictual and often violent; for example, the contemporary debate over the morality or otherwise of fox hunting is often characterized by physically violent conflict. This is both the context in which Christians must relate to their neighbours and the malaise that affects Christianity itself as one tradition that is itself subject to the forces of fragmentation.

Virtue, tradition and the recovery of moral reason

MacIntyre's diagnosis of the contemporary context is founded on his first order substantive theory of tradition-guided rationality and his second order meta-theory of how different, incommensurable moral traditions relate. Many commentators fail to take full account of MacIntyre's substantive theory. They focus instead on his critique of contemporary moral discourse. However, his critique cannot be understood properly except in the light of his substantive theory. This theory centres around MacIntyre's conception of practices, virtues internal to practices, the narratives that enable the proper ordering of such practices, and the tradition which is constituted over time by a particular constellation of narratives, practices and virtues. I will assess MacIntyre's conception of practices, virtue and tradition. However, MacIntyre's use of 'narrative' will not feature in the discussion because it no longer plays any major role in his substantive theory. The shift came about because MacIntyre stopped arguing from sociological premises and began arguing from philosophically derived first principles.[32]

Practices and virtues

MacIntyre defines a practice as:

> Any coherent and complex form of socially established co-operative human activity through which goods internal to that form of activity are realized in the course of trying to achieve those standards of excellence which are appropriate to, and partially definitive of, that form of activity, with the result that human powers to achieve excellence, and human conceptions of the ends and goods involved, are systematically extended.[33]

He cites chess, football, farming, architecture, and the creation of political communities as examples of practices. The central feature of MacIntyre's understanding of a practice is that it implies a standard of excellence internal to that practice. To play football well, a player must heed the standards which define the playing of football. Not just anything counts as playing football well, and those features that do count are defined by the practice, not by the player. MacIntyre understands morality as a practice. The criteria for being moral, or acting well, are defined by the kind of practice in which we are engaged, not by the decision or preference of the individual. This conception of morality gives a central place to the virtues (which are the goods internal to the practice) rather than to general rules or abstract principles.

For MacIntyre, the virtues are the means by which we fulfil the various practices that constitute our life. They are also necessary to enable us to seek the good life. They are:

> Those dispositions which will not only sustain practices and enable us to achieve the goods internal to practices, but which will also sustain us in the relevant kind of quest for the good, by enabling us to overcome the harms, dangers, temptations and distractions which we encounter, and which will furnish us with increasing self-knowledge and increasing knowledge of the good. The catalogue of the virtues will therefore include the virtues required to sustain the kind of households and the kind of political communities in which men and women can seek for the good together and the virtues necessary for philosophical enquiry about the character of the good.[34]

Thus the virtues are central to the formation of personal identity and the very pattern and shape of life together in society.

As indicated in the quotation, the virtues are central to sustaining practices. However, practices must become institutionalized in some form if they are to survive for any length of time. This process of institutionalization is, in MacIntyre's view, good and necessary. However, there is, for MacIntyre, an inherent tension between practices and institutions. Institutions are primarily concerned with external goods. For example, the practice of medicine developed the institutional form of the hospital; yet the goals of a hospital, in contrast to the goals of medicine, are to acquire the necessary money and resources to sustain the hospital. The ideals and creativity of a practice are always vulnerable to the competitiveness of its institutional form. Therefore, without the virtues (for example, of justice, courage, and truthfulness) practices could not resist the corrupting power of institutions.[35]

MacIntyre does not claim that there is one catalogue of virtues fixed for all time. He notes how different social and historical contexts emphasize different virtues. For example, he contrasts the catalogue of virtues in Homer with those of the New Testament pointing out that humility, a primary virtue in the latter, is counted a vice in the former. Following Aristotle, MacIntyre believes changes in what is considered a virtue are determined by changes in how the good for humans is conceived. Thus Homer's teleology – his conception of the good life – was very different from the teleology of the New Testament. It should be noted that in Homer virtue is secondary to and dependent upon a clear concept of social role, whereas in Aristotle (and related accounts) it depends on what the good life for man, as the *telos* of human action, is defined as. However, all the catalogues of the virtues that MacIntyre gives an account of, from Homer to Benjamin Franklin, require for their application some prior account of certain features of social and moral life in terms of which the virtues can be defined and explained. As previously noted, in his later work MacIntyre endeavours to give a Thomist account of what the pattern and shape of life together should consist of, and thence what virtues should be cultivated. He summarizes this account as follows:

> In order to flourish, we need both those virtues that enable us to function as independent and accountable practical reasoners and those virtues that enable us to acknowledge the nature and extent of our dependence on others. Both the acquisition and the exercise of those virtues are possible only insofar as we participate in social relationships of giving and receiving, social relationships governed by and partially defined by the norms of the natural law.[36]

Tradition

Practices and the exercise of the virtues presuppose a wider social and historical context: a tradition. To enter a practice is to enter into a relationship not only with its contemporary practitioners, but also with those who have preceded us in and extended the practice. MacIntyre states: 'It is thus the achievement, and *a fortiori* the authority, of a tradition which I then confront and from which I have to learn.'[37] A tradition is constituted by a set of practices and is the medium by which such practices are shaped and transmitted across generations. Mulhall and Swift note that, for MacIntyre, 'Traditions may be primarily religious or moral (for example Catholicism or humanism), economic (for example a particular craft or profession, trade union or manufacturer), aesthetic (for example modes of literature or painting), or geographical (for example crystallizing around the history and culture of a particular house, village or region).'[38]

For MacIntyre, it is traditions that are the repositories of standards of rationality, which in turn enable appropriate moral deliberation and action. A tradition is an ongoing rational conversation in which the best hypotheses so far achievable are examined, tested, refined, and ultimately surpassed by succeeding formulations. It is only through this kind of cumulative process that significant progress in inquiry can be made. It is only by participation in the dialectical discipline of a particular tradition that human beings are able to refine and advance their understanding of a given subject matter.

MacIntyre's understanding of tradition lies at the heart of his moral and epistemological theory. For MacIntyre, the narrative of an individual's life is to be understood against the background of the wider social context within which that individual finds herself. This wider social context consists of sets of practices that serve to define the virtues, and those practices, in turn, sustain and are sustained within a tradition that provides the resources with which the individual may pursue her quest for the good. Thus, the individual does not decide to join a tradition, but is inducted into a particular tradition and, through that tradition, into a way of reading the world. MacIntyre writes:

> The intending reader has to have inculcated into him or herself certain attitudes and dispositions, certain virtues. So a pre-rational reordering of the self has to occur before the reader can have an adequate standard by which to judge what is good reason and what is not.[39]

Herein lies the epistemological dimension of traditions. It is traditions that are the repositories of standards of rationality, which in turn enable appropriate moral deliberation and action in accord with the natural law.

While MacIntyre understands practical rationality as socially embodied in a myriad of cultural forms he identifies its generic structure as Aristotelian, and Thomism as the best account of practical rationality yet articulated. For Aristotle, to be human is to act rationally in society with others. This involves identifying a good to be pursued and identifying the action most likely to secure that good under present circumstances. Action is undertaken for the sake of some good, lesser goods being pursued for the sake of greater goods, the greatest good being that of the good life. There are four implications to this view. First, both ends and means are subject to reason; second, reasoning itself cannot be solely instrumental because reason and action are themselves partially constitutive of the end for which they are undertaken; third, practical reasoning necessarily results in action; and last, rationality can be articulated in ways that are no longer simply cultural and conventional but also philosophical and critical.

Truth, Thomism and discerning the moral order

Central to MacIntyre's view is the contention that while standards of truth and rationality are inseparable from a particular, historical tradition, truth is the goal of all inquiry. We advance towards this truth by degrees, error being attributed to the mind's inadequate grasp of its object. MacIntyre has thus come to change his position in his later work, moving from the implicit relativism in *After Virtue* to committing himself to a Thomist conception of truth. This includes the espousal of natural law grounded in a conception of the ultimate good as friendship with God as defined by Christian theism.

Philosophy, for MacIntyre, should be a journey towards the discovery of first principles and to embark on such a journey presupposes an end – meaning both completion and *telos* – to that journey.[40] He holds that contemporary schools of philosophy and the wider culture of modernity deny the possibility that any principle is or can be first.[41] MacIntyre argues that first principles are essential in order to guide the mind to its *telos*. However, this presupposes there is such a thing as a *telos* and that this *telos* is fixed and finite.[42] Such a presupposition is not obvious to the contemporary universe of discourse, which, according to MacIntyre, has no place within it for any conception of fixed ends that can be discovered; instead, all ends are decided upon or invented or relative to a particular social context. MacIntyre points out that, by contrast,

> Genuinely first principles ... can have a place only within a universe characterised in terms of certain determinate, fixed and unalterable ends, ends which provide a standard by reference to which our individual purposes, desires, interest and decisions can be evaluated as well or badly directed. For in the practical life it is the *telos* which provides the *arche*, the first principle of practical reasoning.[43]

Thus, the *telos* provides the first principle, and the two stand or fall together. This realist view constitutes the acceptance, by MacIntyre, of natural teleology.[44]

Thomism as the optimum account of how to discover truth

MacIntyre has moved beyond saying that rational enquiry demands a tradition: instead, he holds that Aristotelianism represents the best theory of what makes a tradition rational and Thomism is the best instance of such a tradition. Thus he states: 'For it is indeed a Thomist thesis that all practical reasoners, often unwittingly and often very imperfectly, exhibit in significant ways the truth of the Thomist account of practical reasoning by how they act.'[45]

For MacIntyre, the articles of the *Summa*, with their constant engagement with other viewpoints and positions, are the exemplary instance of tradition-constituted enquiry that seeks truth. MacIntyre argues that through this dialectical process Aquinas successfully synthesized Aristotle and Augustine. Aristotle gave Aquinas that which Augustine could not: that is, a comprehensive analysis of practical rationality, the virtues, and the nature of moral enquiry. However, MacIntyre sees Aristotle's work as ultimately tragic because, in its conception, only the gods can achieve the happiness which Aristotle sees as ordering the *telos* of the moral life.[46]

Aquinas, on the other hand, drew from Augustine and the Bible the ultimate end of practical rationality and the conditions for the possibility of achieving such an end. Thus for Aquinas, revelation complemented Aristotle by supplying a more adequate characterization of the nature of the end of practical rationality, and providing a formulation for achieving this ultimate end.

In addition to its formulation of the ultimate end, Aquinas also drew from the Augustinian tradition the notion of the perverted will. MacIntyre understands the perverted will, or *mala voluntas*, within the Augustinian tradition, to mean 'a rooted tendency to disobedience in the will and distraction by passion, which causes obscuring of the reason and on occasion systematic cultural deformation.'[47] This concept of sin and the perverted will disturbs the Aristotelian moral framework completely, for it claims that at some point no amount of virtue or training will enable one to progress towards the ultimate good. Acting against our best interests is, according to MacIntyre, inexplicable within the framework of a strictly rational account of human nature. Moreover, MacIntyre recognizes that sin, as defined by Augustine, affects not only our ability to achieve the good, but also human knowledge of the good.[48] For MacIntyre, once the notion of sin is introduced a radically new vision of action and agency becomes necessary. To know and do what is good requires radically new qualities of character, infused by the free grace of a good God, whereby we may pursue our ultimate end. In Aquinas's account, these new qualities of character are the freely given gifts of faith, hope, and charity. For MacIntyre, the Augustinian notion of the perverted will does not derail the Thomist appropriation of Aristotle but complements it.[49] However, it does relativize Aristotle's account of the virtues because grace becomes the necessary complement to practical rationality.[50] On MacIntyre's reading of the Thomist synthesis, it is precisely because of Aristotle's analysis of practical rationality as involving the virtues that something like grace is required: if we need to be a particular kind of person in order to move towards knowledge of the truth about the human good, but we cannot become this kind of person in our strength alone (because our will is perverse), then we need the grace and revelation of God to continue on our quest to the human good (that is, friendship with God). It is important to note, however, that MacIntyre thinks basic knowledge of the natural law is possible 'to any plain person's unclouded moral apprehension'.[51] To move beyond this basic knowledge requires excellence in virtue and the disclosure of revelation. In MacIntyre's estimation, Aquinas's use of the concept of the perverted will completes, rather than overthrows, a tradition of enquiry initiated by Plato.[52]

MacIntyre's Thomist account of truth

Following Aquinas, MacIntyre understands humans to be fallible, fallen, and finite. Thus the scope of human discourse is limited so that, in MacIntyre's view, humans must advance to truth incrementally. Only by subjecting the views of one's tradition to dialectical testing can one attribute reasonableness to the tradition. Success in such encounters grants warrant to the truth-claims and assertions of a tradition. Through dialectical testing, error is attributed to the mind's inadequate grasp. Discovery of limitations is the source of progress not despair. MacIntyre couples this conception of warranted assertability with a conception of truth as timeless and universal. He states:

> The concept of truth is timeless. To claim that some thesis is true is not only to claim for all possible times and places that it cannot be shown to fail to correspond to reality ... but also that the mind which expresses its thought in that thesis is in fact adequate to its object.[53]

In his discussion of types of first principles MacIntyre justifies a limited degree of self-evidence; for example, the statement that 'every whole is greater than its parts' is obviously self-evident. However, most first principles are understood as evident only in the context of a larger conceptual framework. First principles are embedded within traditions and one must be 'wise' to grasp them; that is, one must have become a certain type of person to reason rightly and so be able to discover the truth. MacIntyre understands this to be a Thomist conception of truth that he summarizes as follows:

> My mind or rather my soul is only one among many and its own knowledge of my self qua soul must be integrated into a general account of souls and their teleology. Insofar as a given soul moves successfully toward its successive intellectual goals in a teleologically ordered way, it moves toward completing itself by becoming formally identical with the objects of its knowledge, so that it is adequate to those objects, objects that are then no longer external to it, but rather complete it. ... The mind, actualised in knowledge, responds to the object as the object is and as it would be, independently of the mind's knowledge of it.[54]

The above quotation is indicative of MacIntyre's realist view of truth. However, MacIntyre maintains that we can only gain access to the truth within a particular tradition. He argues that only certain kinds of experiences will provide adequate premises for sound practical reasoning. Furthermore, MacIntyre states that:

> Only a life whose actions have been directed by and whose passions have been disciplined and transformed by the practice of the moral and intellectual virtues and the social relationships involved in and defined by such practice will provide the kind of experience from which and about which reliable practical inferences and sound theoretical arguments about practices can be derived.[55]

However, this does not imply any form of relativism with regard to moral enquiry, for even though practical reason is tradition guided, its operation within a rational tradition presupposes there is a *telos* for human beings which it is the object of moral and political enquiry to discover.[56]

In developing this line of argument MacIntyre recognizes that while the pursuit of truth is relative to a particular tradition the truth that tradition seeks is independent of any particular tradition. In his positive assessment of the Papal encyclical *Veritatis Splendor* MacIntyre states that the projects and goods we seek as individuals, communities and institutions, and what means there are for achieving these goods, will vary from culture to culture. However, what is universal is twofold: 'The need for a presupposed understanding that such goods will contribute to the achievement of *the* human good and the need for recognition of a set of requirements which enable human beings to benefit from the disciplines of learning.'[57] For MacIntyre, these are the preconditions for a rational conversation and for justice to be secured. These universal preconditions are 'definitive therefore of what human beings share with one another by nature, as rational beings. And they are in fact the requirements imposed by the precepts of the natural law'.[58] Thus, while humans necessarily seek the truth from a particular perspective by virtue of being fallible, finite and fallen, and this quest inevitably draws on the resources of a particular culture (thus truth-claims are relative to particular traditions), humans do seek a truth which is independent of their particular perspective. MacIntyre states:

> What *is* required is that truth should be understood to be something other and something more than warranted assertability. What we take to be warrantedly assertible is always relative to the standards of warrant upheld in our particular time and place, in our particular culture. But in asserting that something is true we are not talking about warrant or justification, but claiming rather that this is in fact how things are, not from the point of view of this or that culture, but as such.[59]

The very nature of this quest for truth, and the reality of such culture-transcending truth, means that humans are able to transcend their particularity. As MacIntyre puts it:

> Just as we are not to be explained as wholly determined by our physical and biological make-up, so we are not merely products of our cultural environment, but actual or potential creative shapers of it, precisely insofar as we can evaluate its perspectives in terms that are nonperspectival, the terms of truth.[60]

MacIntyre recognizes that his account of truth is inherently theological. He points out that thinkers such as Nietzsche and Derrida, whom he calls 'genealogists', have realized that such an ultimate and final and true account has hidden within it some view of the relation of contingent beings to some ground beyond contingent being. MacIntyre states: 'The genealogical accusation is not just that theism is in part false because it requires the truth of realism, but that realism is inherently theistic.'[61] MacIntyre considers Thomism to provide sufficient ground for holding that some ground beyond contingent being does indeed exist and that this ground must be thought of in terms of Christian theism.[62] MacIntyre states:

> The only type of teleologically ordered universe in which we have good reason to believe is a theistic universe. Hence, moral progress of the plain person

towards her or his ultimate good is always a matter of more than morality. And the enacted narrative of that progress will only become fully intelligible when it is understood not only in terms of metaphysics but in an adequate theological light, when, that is, the particularities of that narrative are understood to embody what is said about sin and about grace in the IaIIae of the Summa as well as what is said about law and the virtues. The moral progress of the plain person is always the beginnings of a pilgrim's progress.[63]

Natural law and the conditions for free and just relations

MacIntyre's line of argument constitutes a justification for natural law based not on intuition or inherent conscience, but on what constitutes the basis of rational deliberation about moral action and how it is inherently teleological unless negated by other institutions.[64] Thus MacIntyre states:

> When I discover that my life is, as a matter of biological and social fact, partially ordered by regularities which give expression to these primary tendencies towards particular ends, I have it in my power to make these ends mine in a new and secondary way by self-consciously directing my activities to these ends and, insofar as I have rightly understood my own nature, it will be rational for me to do so. The rules to which I will have to conform, if I am so to direct my activities, are those expressed by the precepts of the natural law. What was mere regularity become rule-governedness.[65]

With Aquinas, MacIntyre holds that human beings 'are indeed by our specific nature directed toward certain hierarchically ordered ends, and it is not in our power to have ends other than these.'[66] We can decide whether or not to engage in rational decision making and to direct our actions to those ends or not. However, MacIntyre warns that the 'virtues of independent rational agency' which enable humans to transcend their animal nature need for their adequate exercise to be accompanied by 'the virtues of acknowledged dependence'.[67] Thus human flourishing requires a certain kind of society, one whose common good takes account of human vulnerability and interdependence. Natural law articulates the necessary conditions for humans to direct their actions towards appropriate ends. Thus MacIntyre states: 'So natural law is discovered not only as one of the primary objects of practical enquiry but as the presupposition of any effective practical enquiry.'[68] As such, adherence to the natural law is the necessary condition for justice to be secured and for social relations to be moral.

It is important to realize that MacIntyre is not proposing some form of natural theology. Even though he seeks to defend the view that 'we have a knowledge of justice prior to and independently of our knowledge of divine commands,'[69] this does not entail the claim that: 'Any appeal to a standard of truth or goodness, established independently of our knowledge of God's revealed Word and will, is and must be an appeal to something external to that Word and will.'[70] Rather, the claim is made that we can know of some basic form of justice prior to knowledge of revelation, and that such knowledge is the precondition for the reception of revelation, only because this is how God has so ordered things. MacIntyre states that by progressing beyond our initial conceptions of justice, by which we evaluate and accept the Divine claims as just,

> we discover, as our analogically and historically ordered concept of justice develops, that the standards by which we judged God is itself a work of God, and that the judgments which we made earlier were made in obedience to the divine commands, even although we did not and could not have recognized this at that earlier stage. God, it turns out, cannot be truly judged by something external to his Word, but that is because natural justice recognized by natural reason is itself divinely uttered and authorized.[71]

MacIntyre warns elsewhere that progression beyond our initial conceptions of justice is not inevitable. He states: 'Unless, unlike the rich young man, we respond to God's offer of grace by accepting it, we too shall be unable to fully understand and to obey the law in such a way as to achieve that ultimate good which gives to such understanding and obedience its point and purpose.'[72] And such a failure in turn leads to a radical loss to and of the self, for it is the loss of that to which we are ordered. Thus simply discerning and conforming to the natural law makes us neither free nor fully human. Rather, it is a minimum condition for such freedom and fullness to be possible, 'but without understanding of and obedience to God's law, we become self-frustrating beings.'[73]

Incommensurability and the resolution of moral disputes

MacIntyre differentiates truth from 'rational justification [which] can only be internal ... and relative to ... each particular standpoint'.[74] Truth, in contrast, is not relative to a standpoint but is the *telos*, the final end, of all versions of veritable enquiry, so that 'progress in enquiry consists in transcending the limitations of such particular and partial standpoints in a movement toward truth'.[75] However, this position raises the issue of how one tradition may relate to another. MacIntyre accepts that a neutral account of near universal features of human life can be drawn up; however, such an account will be equally compatible with far too many rival bodies of theory to be of any use in adjudicating between them.[76] Equally, though,

> any account which is rich enough in its identifications and characterizations to be genuinely relevant to the evaluation of a set of theoretical claims concerning the virtues will in fact turn out already to presuppose in those identifications and characterizations some one such theoretical stance regarding the virtues, rather than its rivals.[77]

Therefore, to use Michael Walzer's term, any genuinely 'thin' theory will be so thin it would not be of use, and any 'thick' theory is too thick.[78] This still leaves room for working out some genuinely rational way of rival traditions engaging with one another as rival traditions.

To address this issue MacIntyre develops a second order theory. Kelvin Knight points out that while this second order theory cannot provide a solution to the problem of relativism, it can establish that the problem is solvable in principle: a claim already implicit in MacIntyre's first order theory. As Knight puts it: 'Only a substantive theory might, according to MacIntyre's meta-theory of traditions, solve the problem by demonstrating its superiority over its rivals.'[79] MacIntyre takes Thomism to be just such a substantive theory. This still leaves the issue of how MacIntyre understands rival traditions to adjudicate which one best approximates the truth they seek without recourse to some external criteria.

As noted above, his basic starting point is that all good traditions attempt to articulate some notion of the truth. Truth here is conceived of in terms of the mind's correspondence to its object; that is, there is an external reality to be conformed to. While rival traditions may share a similar structure, or conception of the virtues, or overlapping modes of practical rationality, or even 'penultimate' ends, they are at root 'incommensurable'. MacIntyre summarizes what he means by describing two or more traditions as being 'incommensurable' when he states:

> During such a stretch of time it will be the case that those who inhabit each of the two or more rival schemes of thought and practice embody them in their beliefs, actions, judgments, and arguments in such a way that it is both the case that the members of the two or more rival parties can agree, each from their own point of view, that they are referring to, characterizing, and conducting their inquiries about what is indeed one and same subject matter, and yet also in their characterizations of and questions about that subject matter employ, to some large and significant degree, concepts whose applicability entails the non-applicability, the vacuousness, of the conceptual scheme or schemes employed by their rivals. It is not that what is according to the one scheme true is according to its rival false; it is rather that the standard or standards which determine how the true–false distinction is to be applied are not the same. And there is, during this stretch of time at least, no higher standard yet available to judge between these rival standards.[80]

In short, when MacIntyre uses the term 'incommensurable' he means that, when two or more traditions encounter each other at a particular moment in time, there is no common standard of measurement to judge between their respective conceptions for determining what is rational and moral. As Michael Fuller argues, MacIntyre is not referring to incommensurability of meaning, rather, MacIntyre's use of the term incommensurability refers to how different traditions are incommensurable (or at least partially so) in terms of truth and justification.[81] This is to say that Aristotle and Confucius, with sufficient attention, may be able to understand what each other means, but they have no way, in the first instance, of agreeing the truth and justification of their respective moral frameworks. What MacIntyre seeks to address is how, despite their incommensurability, rival traditions might develop a means of adjudicating between themselves. It is important to realize that MacIntyre does not see incommensurability as either inevitable or a permanent condition. The element of time is important: conceptual schemes and social practices can change over time and become compatible due to both internal and external changes.

MacIntyre's conception of incommensurability is based on his view that standards of judgement regarding morality and rationality are internal, and peculiar to, a particular tradition such that each set of standards excludes the possibility of application to key predicates of those in another tradition. Furthermore, the use of predicates in a particular tradition will give expression to distinctive modes of observation, of seeing and or imagining, as well as of reasoning. Another dimension of the incommensurability between rival traditions relates to their differing conceptions of the ultimate good. For it is the vision of the ultimate good held by a particular tradition that provides that tradition with its overall unity of vision and its ordering of the virtues. Thus, according to MacIntyre, different visions of the ultimate good lead to different conceptions of the moral life.

MacIntyre argues that over time rational debate is possible between incommensurable traditions as long as a certain process is followed and certain criteria are met. The first stage is that protagonists from each tradition must learn the language of their rivals' tradition, enriching their own vocabulary where necessary. MacIntyre holds that when profound differences between different traditions occur this does not preclude all mutual understanding. However, understanding is only possible for those adherents of one tradition who are able to learn the language of the other as a 'second first language'.[82] By inhabiting both standpoints they will be able to recognize what is and what is not translatable from one language to the other. MacIntyre states: 'It is they therefore who will be able to understand what would have to be involved by way of an extension and enrichment of their own language-in-use if it were to be able to accommodate a representation of the other.'[83] MacIntyre cites the examples of Cicero translating between Greek philosophy and Latin and the Jesuits translating between Confucianism and European languages as instances of this process.[84] One tradition undergoes a process of enrichment, achieving for itself the partial translatability of the other tradition. Partial translatability makes possible rejection instead of incomprehension. Prior to such translatability, MacIntyre contends, incomprehension is inevitable, as the foreign schema is still evaluated solely in terms alien to it. However, translatability, and the consequent option of rejection, make possible the second stage in the conversation between rival traditions. The second stage involves each rival giving an account or history of the other in terms defined by the other, thus demonstrating that it properly understands the other within the other's own criteria of evaluation. MacIntyre states:

> Insofar as each of these two incompatible and incommensurable bodies of theory and practice has passed beyond the initial stage of partial incomprehension and

partial misrepresentation of the other, by so enriching its linguistic and conceptual resources that it is able to provide an accurate representation of the other, it follows that accurate representation will be of the other as a historically developing body of theory and practice, succeeding or failing at each stage, in the light of its own standards, in respect of the difficulties or problems internal to it.[85]

MacIntyre then asks: 'To what might the construction of such histories lead?'[86] He answers this question by setting out the third stage in his meta-theory of how different traditions may negotiate their incommensurability.

The third stage involves each tradition evaluating itself in the light of its rival and judging whether its own account of the truth is inferior to that offered by its rival. For this to take place MacIntyre believes two conditions must be met. He states:

> The first [condition] is that [a tradition's] own history, as narrated in the light of its own standards, the standard internal to it, should lead in the end to radical and, so far as it is possible to judge, irremediable failure, perhaps by reason of its sterility and resourcelessness in the face of some set of problems which its own goals require it to solve, perhaps because, in trying to frame adequate solutions to its problems and an adequately comprehensive account of the subject matter with which it deals, it lapses into irreparable incoherence. ... And those external to that standpoint, who have incorporated within their own structures of understanding an accurate representation of that standpoint and its history, may on occasion be able to recognise such a condition of failure, even when it has gone unacknowledged by the adherents of the tradition of inquiry which has failed.[87]

The second condition which must be satisfied, in order that adherents of one tradition may be justified in acknowledging that some alternative, incompatible, and rival tradition is rationally superior, is as follows. The adherents of this alternative rival tradition must be able to provide the resources to explain to the other tradition's adherents why that other tradition failed by its own standard of achievement and,

> more precisely, why it succeeded and why it failed at just the points and in just the ways in which by those same standards it did succeed and fail. Moreover, the resources for such explanation must not be available in anything like the same way within the body of theory and practice whose failure is being explained.[88]

MacIntyre concludes: 'When both of these conditions are satisfied, then it is rational for the adherents of the tradition of inquiry which has failed to transfer allegiance to that which has provided the explanation of failure.'[89] In other words, if these conditions are met, then adjudication between the rival traditions can take place.[90] For if each gives an account of the other and irresolvable problems are seen in either of the traditions that the rival can explain, or give a solution to, then it is rational, according to MacIntyre, for the 'loser', within the terms of reference of their own tradition, to accept their rival's criteria of evaluation. Thus, as MacIntyre puts it, 'Incommensurability ... does not after all preclude rational debate and encounter.'[91]

Three Rival Versions of Moral Enquiry constitutes MacIntyre's most extensive attempt to follow the process outlined above.[92] For MacIntyre it is Thomism that is vindicated above its contemporary rivals. As MacIntyre puts it:

> It is ... precisely because and in so far as Thomist Aristotelianism enables us to achieve an adequate understanding both of our history and of that of others ... [that] it vindicates its claim to have identified the standards by appeal to which all practices and traditions are to be evaluated.[93]

In short, MacIntyre thinks incommensurability does not exclude rational debate nor the eventual resolving of disputes about ethics, and that, when debate between traditions is entered into, Thomism will be vindicated as the bearer of standards by which to evaluate the morality of all other traditions.

Summary

The analysis presented here of MacIntyre's substantive theory clarifies why he believes the contemporary context of moral discourse differs to ages past and why he holds that in contemporary Western societies justice is what the strong make it. His substantive theory provides the lens through which he is able to bring into focus what is wrong with present moral debate and, as we shall see, it furnishes him with a vision for its remedy.

For MacIntyre Christianity is necessarily incommensurable with other ethical traditions. Moreover, the contemporary context in which Christians encounter those outside its tradition is unjust, oppressive, and detrimental to rational debate between Christians and non-Christians. According to MacIntyre, Christians will often be incoherent to their neighbours and their moral positions viewed by non-Christians as mere plays for power. However, it is still possible for Christians to engage with their neighbours in ethical disputes in a rational way. The possibility of rational engagement with rival traditions depends on a Thomistic account of ethics. MacIntyre contends that a Thomistic account of ethics can adjudicate and resolve disputes with those who follow its two predominant, contemporary rival traditions: that is, liberals and genealogists.

The account of MacIntyre's work given here both clarifies the parameters of the problem of moral plurality and establishes a way to address this problem. I shall now assess MacIntyre's account of contemporary moral debate, his conception of the differences between Christians and non-Christians, and his account of how Christians might resolve disputes with non-Christians. In the first instance this is done by comparing and contrasting his account with that of the contemporary Roman Catholic moral theologian, Germain Grisez.

Notes

1 Alasdair MacIntyre, *Whose Justice? Which Rationality?* (London: Duckworth, 1988), pp. 384–86; hereafter referred to as WJ.

2 Alasdair MacIntyre, 'How Can We Learn What *Veritatis Splendor* Has to Teach', *The Thomist*, 58 (1994), p. 182.

3 Alasdair MacIntyre, *After Virtue: A Study in Moral Theory*, 2nd edn (London: Duckworth, 1994), p. 2; hereafter referred to as AV.

4 Ibid., p. 112.

5 Alasdair MacIntyre, *Three Rival Versions of Moral Enquiry: Encyclopaedia, Genealogy, and Tradition* (London: Duckworth, 1989), p. 29; hereafter referred to as TRV.

6 AV, p. 113.

7 Ibid., p. 55.

8 Peter McMylor, *Alasdair MacIntyre, Critic of Modernity* (London: Routledge, 1994), p. 89.

9 AV, pp. 113–14.

10 Ibid., p. 11.

11 Alasdair MacIntyre, 'Community, Law and the Idiom and Rhetoric of Rights', *Listening*, 26 (1991), p. 101.

12 Ibid.

13 Ibid., p. 106.

14 Alasdair MacIntyre, 'Politics, Philosophy and the Common Good', in *The MacIntyre Reader*, ed. Kelvin Knight (London: Polity Press, 1998), p. 236.

15 Alasdair MacIntyre, *Dependent Rational Animals: Why Human Beings Need the Virtues* (London: Duckworth, 1999), p. 131; p. 142; hereafter referred to as DRA.

16 MacIntyre, 'Politics, Philosophy and the Common Good', p. 237.

17 Ibid., p. 238.

18 Ibid., p. 239.

19 Alasdair MacIntyre, 'Natural Law as Subversive: The Case of Aquinas', *Journal of Medieval and Early Modern Studies*, 26 (1996), 61–83.

20 MacIntyre, 'Politics, Philosophy and the Common Good', p. 239.

21 WJ, p. 345.

22 MacIntyre, 'Community, Law and the Idiom and Rhetoric of Rights', p. 99.

23 Alasdair MacIntyre, 'Which God Ought We To Obey and Why?', *Faith and Philosophy*, 3.4 (1986), p. 367.

24 AV, p. 251.

25 Brian Barry, 'The Light That Failed', *Ethics*, 100.1 (1989), p. 165.

26 WJ, p. 335.

27 Ibid., p. 345.

28 For a critique of MacIntyre's notion that liberalism has itself become a tradition see: Jeffrey Stout, 'Homeward Bound: MacIntyre on Liberal Society and the History of Ethics', *Journal of Religion*, 69 (1989), 220–32 (p. 229). Cf., Jean Porter, 'Openness and Constraint: Moral Reflection as Tradition-guided Inquiry in Alasdair MacIntyre's Recent Works', *Journal of Religion*, 73 (1993), 514–36.

29 AV, pp. 25–26.

30 Ibid., p. 28.

31 Ibid., p. 30.

32 For an account of this shift see: Kelvin Knight, 'Introduction', in *The MacIntyre Reader*, p. 15; Cf., DRA, pp. 8–9. For an account and critique of MacIntyre's use of narrative see: Gregory Jones, 'Alasdair MacIntyre on Narrative, Community, and the Moral Life', *Modern Theology*, 4 (1987), 53–69.

33 AV, p. 187.

34 Ibid, p. 219.

35 Ibid, p. 194.

36 DRA, pp. 155–56.
37 AV, p. 194.
38 Adam Swift and Stephen Mulhall, *Liberals and Communitarians* (Oxford: Blackwell, 1992), p. 90.
39 TRV, p. 82.
40 WJ, p. 175.
41 Alasdair MacIntyre, 'First Principles, Final Ends and Contemporary Philosophical Issues', in *The MacIntyre Reader*, pp. 172–73.
42 Ibid., p. 172.
43 Ibid., pp. 173–74.
44 See DRA, p. x. For a critique of MacIntyre's lack of natural teleology in AV and the implications of this see Russell Hittinger, 'After MacIntyre: Natural Law Theory, Virtue Ethics, and Eudaimonia', *International Philosophical Quarterly*, 29 (1989), p. 454; and Jean Porter, *The Recovery of Virtue: The Relevance of Aquinas for Christian Ethics* (London: SPCK, 1994), p. 83.
45 MacIntyre, 'How Can We Learn What *Veritatis Splendor* Has to Teach', p. 174.
46 TRV, pp. 137–38.
47 Ibid., p. 140.
48 Ibid., p. 141
49 Ibid., p. 140.
50 DRA, p. xi.
51 TRV, p. 141.
52 For positive assessments of MacIntyre's account of Aquinas see: Thomas Hibbs, 'MacIntyre, Tradition and the Christian Philosopher', *The Modern Schoolman*, 68 (1991), 211–23; and Christopher Thompson, 'Benedict, Thomas, or Augustine?: The Character of MacIntyre's Narrative', *The Thomist*, 59 (1995), 379–407. For a critical assessment see John Haldane, 'MacIntyre's Thomist Revival: What Next?', in *After MacIntyre: Critical Perspectives on the Work of Alasdair MacIntyre*, eds John Horton and Susan Mendus (London: Polity Press, 1994), pp. 91–107.
53 WJ, p. 363.
54 MacIntyre, 'First Principles, Final Ends and Contemporary Philosophical Issues', p. 176.
55 Ibid., p. 177.
56 For MacIntyre's argument against relativism see: WJ, pp. 366–69.
57 MacIntyre, 'How Can We Learn What *Veritatis Splendor* Has to Teach', p. 184.
58 Ibid.
59 Ibid., p. 187. Cf., WJ, p. 363.
60 MacIntyre, 'How Can We Learn What *Veritatis Splendor* Has to Teach', p. 188.
61 TRV, p. 67. For MacIntyre's discussion of Derrida see: 'First Principles, Final Ends and Contemporary Philosophical Issues', pp. 178–80.
62 For a more extended account by MacIntyre of his argument see: WJ, pp. 349–69; and TRV, pp. 127–48.
63 Alasdair MacIntyre, 'Plain Persons and Moral Philosophy: Rules, Virtues and Goods', in Knight, *The MacIntyre Reader*, p. 152.
64 For a discussion of the deleterious impact of institutions on the ability of persons to reason rightly see: AV, p. 194.
65 MacIntyre, 'Plain Persons and Moral Philosophy', p. 139.
66 Ibid.
67 DRA, p. 120.
68 WJ, p. 180.
69 MacIntyre, 'Which God', p. 359.
70 Ibid., p. 366. This point is made in explicit reference to Barth's critique of attempts to construct such a defence of knowledge of justice independent of knowledge of revelation.
71 Ibid., p. 370.
72 MacIntyre, 'How Can We Learn What *Veritatis Splendor* Has to Teach', p. 190.

73 Ibid., p. 194.
74 Alasdair MacIntyre, 'Moral Relativism, Truth and Justification', in Knight, *The MacIntyre Reader*, p. 203.
75 Ibid., p. 207.
76 Alasdair MacIntyre, 'Incommensurability, Truth and the Conversation between Confucians and Aristotelians about the Virtues', in *Culture and Modernity: East–West Philosophic Perspectives*, ed., Eliot Deutsch (Honolulu: University of Hawaii Press, 1991), p. 105.
77 Ibid.
78 Michael Walzer, *Thick and Thin: Moral Argument at Home and Abroad* (Notre Dame: University of Notre Dame Press, 1994).
79 Knight, 'Introduction', in *The MacIntyre* Reader, p. 16.
80 MacIntyre, 'Incommensurability, Truth and the Conversation between Confucians and Aristotelians about the Virtues', pp. 109–10.
81 Michael Fuller, *Making Sense of MacIntyre* (Aldershot: Ashgate, 1998), p. 113.
82 MacIntyre, 'Incommensurability, Truth and the Conversation between Confucians and Aristotelians about the Virtues', p. 111.
83 Ibid.
84 Ibid.
85 Ibid, p. 117.
86 Ibid.
87 Ibid.
88 Ibid, p. 118.
89 Ibid.
90 In addition, MacIntyre has two necessary conditions for this kind of rational debate between traditions to be possible. These are that both traditions admit they are fallible, and both admit there is not some external point of reference. Ibid., p. 121.
91 Ibid., p. 118.
92 MacIntyre gives a further account of this process in the article 'Moral Relativism, Truth and Justification', in Knight, *The MacIntyre Reader*.
93 Alasdair MacIntyre, 'A Partial Response to my Critics', in Horton and Mendus, *After MacIntyre*, p. 300.

CHAPTER 2

Germain Grisez and the shared rationality of all moral traditions

Whose Justice? Which Thomism?

This chapter analyses the manner in which Germain Grisez contests MacIntyre's diagnosis of the contemporary context and MacIntyre's conception of the incommensurability between Christian and non-Christian ethical action. According to Grisez, all traditions, despite great variation of culture, and the problems of sin, share a general, or universal, ethic based on practical reason. Thus, for Grisez, what MacIntyre identifies as the central problem of contemporary moral discourse – namely, the fragmentation of particular moral traditions – is not the devastating problem that MacIntyre takes it to be.

It is worth stating that Grisez and MacIntyre do share a common project: both attempt to re-formulate and re-accommodate natural law theory in a modern context. Their common project is born in part out of a similar sense that the concept of the natural law, and Aquinas in particular, represents a vital resource for addressing the dysfunctional character of contemporary moral discourse. Thus, while having a very different response in the contemporary context to MacIntyre, Grisez is sympathetic to MacIntyre's critique of it. Indeed, Grisez is himself a vehement critic of liberalism, utilitarianism and proportionalism.[1] Hanink notes that Grisez's first formulations of his natural law ethics were as part of his response to changes in legislation regarding abortion that were justified on grounds of individual freedom.[2] Grisez rejected the radical individualism the policy presupposed, perceiving it to be a denial of the human community of trust basic to the bearing and nurture of children.[3] He was appalled that human rights, which formed the intellectual foundations of the policy, could become restricted to the strong and the self-sufficient. Thus, like MacIntyre, his critique of liberalism forms part of a deeper concern that justice must not be what the strong make it. MacIntyre's concern for this was outlined in the last chapter. Grisez's concern for it is indicated by his theory of the goods. We see in his theory essentially the same project as Plato's: how can we say that the goods of excellence supersede and define the goods of effectiveness, so that justice is not simply what the strong make it? Grisez reveals this concern in relation to the contemporary context when he quotes *Centesimus Annus*:

> 'It must be observed in this regard that if there is no ultimate truth to guide and direct political activity, then ideas and convictions can easily be manipulated for reasons of power. As history demonstrates, a democracy without values easily turns into open or thinly disguised totalitarianism.'[4]

As Nigel Biggar comments: 'Grisez notes – as Alasdair MacIntyre and Charles Taylor have done before him – that this moral 'relativity' ... leaves no objective basis for resolving moral conflicts, makes force the only arbiter, and so undermines social order.'[5]

Grisez's reformulation of natural law is referred to as the 'new natural law theory'. After his initial engagement with Aquinas, Grisez developed the philosophical foundations of this new natural law theory in two works: *Beyond the New Theism: A Philosophy of Religion* and *Free Choice: A Self Referential Argument*.[6] His approach to natural law was further developed by collaborative work with John Finnis and Joseph Boyle.[7] Although there are slight differences between Grisez, Finnis and Boyle, for the purposes of this chapter their views can be taken as interchangeable. Where their differences are pertinent, they will be made explicit. The parallels between the new natural law theorists and MacIntyre are drawn out by Pauline Westermann who states (in relation to Finnis and MacIntyre):

> Both men, different as they may appear, assume that we should return to the happier times of Aristotle and Aquinas, in order to bring moral theory to a more inspiring level than it is nowadays. Both men criticise modernity for its stress on the individual as a right-holder, and its emphasis on procedures rather than virtues. Both thinkers stress the importance of the community, in which citizens can participate and in which moral discourse is guided by a practical orientation on the good life. Both criticise the distinction between private and public and the modern tendency to relegate morals to the private domain only.[8]

However, as Westerman goes on to comment, what distinguishes the new natural law theorists from MacIntyre is that they explicitly refuse to underpin their approach with any significant criticism of the essentially modern programme in which reason is given priority over nature.[9] This difference is drawn out sharply in the different approaches Grisez and MacIntyre have to Aquinas.

MacIntyre notes that many modern readers of Aquinas tend to read questions 90–97 of the *Summa* Ia–IIae, with its discussion of law, in isolation from the rest of Aquinas's writings. However, MacIntyre argues that the disputes over the meaning of the *principium* of the natural law indicate that questions 90–97 are not self-interpreting. Rather, Aquinas's discussion of these questions must be read within the wider context of his work, notably his natural teleology and the development of the debate between Augustinians and Averroists in questions 1–89.[10] This observation by MacIntyre prompts Keith Pavlischek to ask whether Grisez's approach to natural law enables a genuine congruence of faith and reason which is the hallmark of Catholic philosophy or 'whether it leads to an emasculation of the theological tradition to fit the philosophy.'[11] I shall address this issue later on. Meanwhile, it should be noted that MacIntyre thinks Grisez approaches Aquinas in an essentially modern way.[12] He states: 'Germain Grisez interprets the *principium* in the light of a post-Humean fact-value distinction.'[13]

Grisez would not deny this charge by MacIntyre. The 'new' natural law theory explicitly seeks to take account of modern moral philosophy, and specifically the proposition that one cannot derive an 'ought' from an 'is'. According to Porter this contradicts what Aquinas believed. Porter states: 'For [Aquinas], there is no final distinction between what an agent ought (morally) to do and what is in that agent's true self-interest.'[14] Hence, according to Porter, moral claims have a motivational force for Aquinas because they are in the agent's self-interest: that is, what they ought to do relates to what they are in reality. Porter goes on to say: 'Anyone who understands that his own true good lies in acting in accordance with these claims [about what he is] will necessarily be motivated to act upon them. Of course someone who does not understand that will not be so motivated.'[15] What Porter articulates as Aquinas's perspective is exactly the position MacIntyre now takes. In MacIntyre's analysis: 'Evaluative judgments are a species of factual judgment.'[16] This is the opposite of the view taken by Grisez, who, following Hume, does not see a direct relationship between what someone is and what they ought to do.[17] This contrast between MacIntyre and Grisez in relation to the 'post-Humean fact-value distinction' will be assessed at greater length below.

While some, like John Haldane, question whether MacIntyre is a true Thomist, he is closer to Aquinas than Grisez with regard to the relationship between metaphysics and practical rationality.[18] Grisez would probably agree. However, the nature of the relationship between metaphysics and practical rationality does raise a central point of contention between Grisez and MacIntyre, one which will be analysed in this chapter: that is, in contrast to MacIntyre, does Grisez's approach to natural law, and his essentially modern account of moral decision making, provide both a better way to address the question of whether Christians and non-Christians can resolve ethical disputes (and if so how can this be done), and a better account of how Christians might respond to the dysfunctional nature of contemporary moral discourse?

Grisez and the new natural law account of ethics

For Grisez, our capacity for reflective freedom is part of our bearing God's image and is central to our ability to realize the whole range of basic goods open to us. These basic goods are divided into two kinds. There are *substantive* goods: these are prior to and apart from our choices. There are also *reflexive* goods that can be instantiated only in and through the choices by which one acts towards their attainment. Choice enters into their very definition; they cannot be realized or participated in except by choosing to realize or participate in them.[19] This leads to Grisez's axiology: our natural inclinations point us to these goods, and each of these goods is a dimension of what it means to be human; so that each of these basic goods is a constituent of human flourishing or integral fulfilment. This fulfilment is our *telos* so that we do not aim merely to fulfil certain roles or skills but to develop a kind of human excellence. It is reason that directs our free responses to the basic goods, enabling us to pursue them in a creative way. But we are limited in our ability to pursue and fulfil these goods.

At this point Grisez claims that these goods are incommensurable: there is no common measure enabling us to say that one good is more valuable than another, and one cannot replace one good for another. For example, the good of friendship cannot be compared with the good of religion, and if one loses one's faith, friendship may compensate for the loss, but it cannot replace or act in religion's stead. But how are we to proceed, given the existence of a plurality of incommensurable and non-fungible goods? For Grisez, the moral course is to remain open to all of the goods and co-operate with others so that the community, if not the individual, can realize the fullest range of goods. It is this that constitutes the common good. This gives rise to Grisez's first principle of morality, which he formulates as follows: 'In voluntarily acting for human goods and avoiding what is opposed to them, one ought to choose and otherwise will those and only those possibilities whose willing is compatible with a will toward integral human fulfillment.'[20] This first principle is natural not because it is deduced from some prior theoretical or metaphysical account of human nature, but rather because precisely by one's originally practical understanding of these aspects of human flourishing and fulfilment one comes both to realize (make actual in practice) and reflectively and theoretically to understand the nature of the sort of being (the human person) who is fulfilled through seeking these basic goods.[21]

On the basis of this brief summary (which will be elucidated over the course of this chapter) we can see why Grisez does not accept that different moral traditions are incommensurable. For Grisez, practical rationality provides a tradition-free and universal means of settling ethical disputes between different traditions. Indeed, Grisez's understanding of ethics implies that Christians can resolve ethical disputes with non-Christians on the basis of a shared rationality and a general ethics. What is especially significant for resolving ethical disputes is that, for Grisez, there is no substantive body of Christian knowledge.

The differences between the moral knowledge of Christians and non-Christians

For Grisez, there are no substantive differences between the moral knowledge of Christians and non-Christians; thus, according to Grisez, Christians and non-Christians can resolve ethical disputes on the basis of practical reason. Grisez holds that the Christian faith deepens both the epistemic and axiological level of his account of practical rationality. Thus, Scripture underscores and clarifies what reason can discern and our covenant relationship with God sets the basic goods within a broader and deeper context. For example, from the perspective of unaided reason alone, friendship, and its distinctive expression in marriage (sexual community), are great goods. Understood in the light of Scripture, however, their significance as part of integral human fulfilment is intensified for they point to our friendship with God.[22] As regards concrete moral judgements the Christian can arrive at decisions of conscience different from those dictated by reason alone, but not contradictory to reason. For example, to respond to deadly aggression non-violently instead of reacting in self-defence (which entails the use of violent force) is to go beyond the dictates of reason alone. Only a deepened understanding of the nature of reality could make a more demanding principle appear reasonable or purposeful. Grisez envisages the Christian virtues of faith, hope and charity to bring this deepened understanding. He states:

> The modes of responsibility [are] transformed by faith (which tells us how to live a good life in a fallen world), by hope (which supplies the confidence in God required to make the effort), and by charity (which gives one the power to really live in this way).[23]

Therefore, Grisez believes there is such a thing as Christian ethics (that is to say, the Gospel does make a difference to our moral knowledge); however, Christian ethics is only formally and not substantively different from an ethic derived from right reason. This is because, as far as he is concerned, revelation neither changes the basic goods in any way nor brings to bear on morality any distinctively new moral knowledge. Grisez states: 'The teachings of faith neither conflict with any of the general principles of morality nor add principles to them. Yet faith does generate specific norms proper to Christian life.'[24] Grisez elucidates further:

> In taking the actual human condition into account, divine revelation proposes specific norms, which can be derived from the general norms of human morality, yet are unknowable without the light of faith. Christian norms add to common moral requirements from within, by specifying them, not from without by imposing some extrahuman demand upon human acts. Rather than ignoring or violating the general requirements of human morality, one who lives by Christian faith fulfils them.[25]

Grisez's position is clarified by Oliver O'Donovan's analysis of the work of John Finnis. O'Donovan notes that Finnis, and also, I contend, Grisez, do have a 'Christian' ethics, but not a theological ethics. For Grisez and Finnis, there are no distinctive moral inferences to be made from the evangelical proclamation; that is, there are no Christian first principles to supplant the first principles of natural law. Rather, the Christian sees the world and its potentialities more accurately because through the revelation of Jesus Christ the world acquires an enhanced intelligibility. O'Donovan states:

> There is no evangelical content to [their] moral reasoning. The difference between Finnis and myself, then, seems to amount to this: while I believe that a distinct behaviour is demanded by the resurrection of Jesus, he believes that the same behaviour is demanded which was demanded anyway, but that the demand is clearer and more cogently perceived.[26]

Truly to fulfil morality requires Christian faith, but there is nothing *new* to such fulfilment. Therefore, there is no moral knowledge that is in principle unknowable by non-Christians. Hence, within Grisez's system, moral disputes can, in theory, be resolved by practical reason without recourse to revelation (although in practice this may be required). Furthermore, for Grisez, while there is Christian action (derived from the moral law further specified by revelation) this action cannot, in any substantive way, be said to be unique or distinctive to moral knowledge available apart from revelation. The implications of this view in relation to how Grisez conceives the depth of difference between Christians and non-Christians on moral questions are manifold. These implications will be assessed by comparing and contrasting MacIntyre and Grisez.

Grisez and MacIntyre compared

Grisez's account of ethics contrasts directly with MacIntyre because for Grisez practical rationality is universal and not situated within a tradition. In other words, Grisez rejects MacIntyre's view that all knowledge is tradition-situated, and has a very different conception of practical rationality and truth. It is important to untangle this cluster of key differences between MacIntyre and Grisez.

In summary, for Grisez, moral knowledge is not based on theoretical knowledge, but practical knowledge. In contrast to MacIntyre, Grisez believes morality is not derived from some prior reality, discerned by theoretical knowledge. Rather, Grisez posits a universal and self-evident practical rationality through which morality is discerned. Unlike theoretical or metaphysical knowledge that is necessarily arrived at through a particular tradition, any reasonable person anywhere can arrive at practical knowledge. Thus knowledge of morality is not necessarily situated within a particular tradition. I will now examine Grisez's explanation of his position in order to understand how and why his account of ethics is radically divergent from MacIntyre's.

Grisez's account of the foundation and nature of ethics

Central to Grisez's moral theory is the distinction between first principles of practical reasoning and the first principles of morality. According to Grisez practical reasoning has two stages. The first is concerned with what might be done, the second with what ought to be done.[27] Everyone, whether moral or not, uses the principles of the first stage of practical reasoning in considering what they might do. Following Aquinas, Grisez identifies as the first principle of practical reason that '*the good is to be done and pursued: the bad is to be avoided*'.[28] This principle directs action and does not distinguish between moral good and evil: 'good' here refers to what is intelligibly worthwhile, while 'bad' refers to whatever is considered to be a privation of intelligible goods.[29] Thus for Grisez, there is an intrinsic relationship between human goods and appropriate actions bearing upon them.[30]

The first principles of practical reason This first principle of practical reasoning is specified by identifying the basic forms of human flourishing which are the goods that are to be pursued and done. Unlike Aquinas, Grisez argues that we can identify a specific list of goods: for Grisez, there are eight.[31] These basic goods, having been grasped by practical reason, serve as the principles of practical reasoning; that is, they provide the framework for thinking about what to do. Grisez states: 'One way the basic goods function as principles of actions is through being *known* as ultimate rational grounds (principles of practical reason) for proposing actions to be done for certain benefits (anticipated instantiations of those goods).'[32] He goes on to say that these goods are self-evident; that is, 'these truths are known (*nota*) without any middle term (*per se*), by understanding what is signified by their terms.'[33] Thus, for Grisez, knowledge of the basic goods that give substantive content to the principles of practical reason is underived and therefore self-evident (although this is not to say they are innate, in the sense of being known prior to all experience). As Robert George summarizes it: '*Qua* basic, such goods, and reason for acting they provide, cannot be deduced from still more fundamental practical principles or from theoretical truths. ... They are, rather, underived, and, in that sense, "self-evident".'[34]

The distinction between theoretical and practical reason At this point it is important to make a clear distinction between theoretical and practical reason. *Theoretical reason* is used to pursue knowledge about reality. It seeks to establish the truth of a proposition by testing the conformity of the content of that proposition with some prior reality, actual or possible.[35] Operating using both deductive and inductive forms of reasoning, it produces theoretical or speculative knowledge. Examples of such knowledge include history, biology and theology. Such knowledge is distinguished from practical knowledge by being founded on prior realities. Grisez states: 'In coming to know theoretically, one comes into accord with prior reality. But in coming to know practically, one becomes able to bring something into reality. It follows that practical knowledge cannot have its truth by conformity to what is known.'[36] Hence, *practical reason* is concerned with bringing realities into being. In using practical reason to make a decision, a person seeks to act on the basis of a possible future reality rather than an existent prior reality. Thus, practical reasoning is used when concerned with moral questions, for example, 'Should I have an abortion or not?' The answers to such questions will be knowledge that was not and cannot have been known prior to asking them. Therefore, the function of practical reason is to enable people to make intelligent choices about how to pursue human fulfilment. Thus, it is through practical reason that Grisez comes to the first principle of morality. The first principle of morality might best be formulated as follows: in voluntarily acting for human goods and avoiding what is opposed to them, one ought to choose and otherwise will those and only those possibilities whose willing is compatible with a will towards integral human fulfilment.[37] Note that this conceives human goods not simply as diverse fields for possible action, but as comprising the totality of integral human fulfilment. This avoids subordinating moral reflection to specific objectives; instead, the upright person is to remain open to goods that go beyond his or her present capacity for realizing them in action.

The self-evidence of the principles of practical knowledge does not preclude their being rationally defended. Grisez sees such a defence as dialectical and necessarily theoretical. He notes that: 'Theoretical reflection deepens understanding of the basic goods.'[38] He gives the example of the need for knowledge of biology in order to promote health. Grisez goes on to outline three dialectical arguments that can be used to defend practical principles. These are: first, insights won from empirical studies, the data of which supports the list of basic goods as basic; second, the very possibility of anthropology which would be inexplicable unless there were common starting points of cultural development; and third, that rejecting the first principles of practical reason is theoretically indefensible.[39] However, none of these compromises the separation between theoretical and practical reason. Nor do they suggest any need for an account of how traditions with different theoretical knowledge might have incommensurable conceptions of ethics. Rather, we can conclude from this discussion of Grisez's account of first principles, practical rationality and basic goods, that the implication of Grisez's moral theory is that, ethical disputes are to be resolved not through some dialectic of traditions, as MacIntyre contends, but via a general ethics grounded on a universal practical rationality.

Grisez's conception of practical truth Grisez summarizes his conception of practical truth thus:

> What human persons *can be* through their freedom and action depends on practical knowledge rather than vice versa, and so the adequation which is the truth of practical knowledge is not conformity to some already existing order. The adequation of practical knowing is not that of theoretical knowing, namely, conformity of knowledge to known. But neither is it a merely formal truth involving a 'conformity to its own structures' or something of that sort. The *truth* (that is, the adequation) of practical knowledge is the *conformity of what is to be* through knowing *to* the *knowledge* which will help to bring it about.[40]

Therefore, moral truth for Grisez is a kind of practical truth. As he phrases it: 'The truth of practical knowledge with respect to its first principles is their adequation to possible human fulfilment considered precisely insofar as that fulfilment can be realized through human action.'[41] That which is practically true seeks that which leads to integral human fulfilment, whereas that which is false is specified by its incompleteness; that is, it lacks adequacy to possible human fulfilment.[42] For example, the statement 'One must look after number one' is false because it lacks adequacy to the necessity of community in human fulfilment. In short, practical knowledge, which is universal and self-evident, is the means of discerning moral truth.

The basic goods The self-evidence of practical knowledge as the foundation for moral action is established by it being based on non-inferential acts of understanding in which we grasp possible ends or purposes as worthwhile for their own sake. It is basic goods, known by way of practical reason, rather than theoretical observation, that form the reasons for acting. In acting on the first principle of practical reason we can identify the eight basic goods that enable us to seek integral human fulfilment. As noted above, Grisez divides these basic goods into two groups. The first is *substantive* goods that provide independent grounds for our choices, but which are not themselves defined or made intelligible by our choices. These substantive goods are life, knowledge and the appreciation of beauty, and excellence in work or play.[43] *Reflexive* or 'existential' or 'moral' goods are both reasons for choosing and are in part defined in terms of choosing. These goods are: self-integration (or harmony between all the parts of a person which can be engaged in freely chosen action), practical reasonableness or authenticity, justice and friendship or interpersonal harmony, and religion or harmony with God or the gods, or some non-theistic but more-than-human-source of meaning and value.[44] And in *Living a Christian Life* Grisez adds marriage to this list of reflexive basic goods.[45] These two kinds of basic goods are intrinsically related. Grisez conceives of the substantive goods as 'the "stuff" of a morally good life'[46]; that is, substantive goods are the vehicles for reflexive goods.

These basic goods are that which define the nature and parameters of human flourishing or fulfilment. It is in this sense that they are part of human nature. For as Grisez understands it, the basic goods are neither a mere contingent fact about psychology nor an accident of history. Rather, 'being aspects of the fulfilment of persons, these goods correspond to the inherent complexities of human nature.'[47] It is thus on the strength of his account of basic goods that Grisez claims to be giving a natural law account of morality.

The natural law Grisez's conception of natural law is summarized by Joseph Boyle. Boyle states that natural law refers to 'a set of universal prescriptions whose prescriptive force is a function of the rationality which all human beings share in virtue of their common humanity.' He goes on to say that:

> The basic principles and norms of the natural law, as *natural*, are addressed to all human beings, and they are held to be accessible to all who are capable of forming the concepts which comprise them. Furthermore, the foundations of moral life and judgment are in the moral *law*, and moral laws are propositional realities, 'dictates of reason'.[48]

This concurs with the view Grisez sets out in *Beyond the New Theism* where he argues for a form of rationality that believers and non-believers share, which is independent of religious belief and which can be used to judge whether religious beliefs are rationally defensible.[49] In other words, Grisez is committed to an idea of a shared, common, neutral philosophical rationality to which appeal can be made on disputes about morality that is independent of faith commitments for its authority.

As noted earlier, while Grisez does have a Christian ethic, he maintains that this ethic has no distinctive content. Black argues that Grisez should abandon the claim that Christian faith brings no new moral principles.[50] Black contends that all the modes of responsibility, when they arise from a Christian understanding of reality, will be new moral principles. They will be new moral principles because the acceptance of Christian faith radically changes the nature of one's understanding to such an extent as to bring radical changes to what is thought to be practically reasonable.[51] Black states: 'Correspondingly, it also appears that all the modes of Christian response *insofar as they arise from a Christian understanding of reality* will likewise be "new" moral principles.'[52] However, Black's argument, making the case for the possibility of new moral principles within Grisez's framework, is questionable. While Grisez's framework may well be strengthened by changing it along the lines Black sets out, Grisez's existing position is that there is no materially distinct Christian moral knowledge. Black himself notes that more often than not in Grisez's work, Christian modes become peripheral rather than central.[53] Black highlights Grisez's discussion of abortion and just war to point out how Grisez recognizes distinctly Christian insights about these issues, yet never includes them in his discussion.[54] He thus calls for Grisez to recognize explicitly the epistemological distinctness of a Christian ethic so that analysis of issues like abortion might take account of specifically Christian insights.[55] However, what Black does not account for is that Grisez's own method rules out such an approach. Grisez is logically committed to the view that the ethical judgements of Christians cannot be distinct epistemologically from judgements that never consider Christian revelation.

The conclusion to draw from this analysis of Grisez's account of ethics is that he denies any significant incommensurability of moral judgement between Christians and non-Christians. I shall now assess how this diverges from MacIntyre's position. This assessment is achieved through comparing and contrasting the two writers' respective conceptions of coming to know moral truth: first, in relation to the role tradition and community play in this; and second, in relation to the role of practices and virtues in moral decision making.

Grisez and MacIntyre's different conceptions of the role of tradition

While Grisez does accept a limited role for tradition in acquiring knowledge of morality, unlike MacIntyre he does not accept that tradition in any way authorizes moral knowledge. There are various kinds of tradition-dependence that Grisez's natural law theory accepts. Joseph Boyle points to two. The first is that all intellectual effort depends on cultural contingencies and particularities: for example, language. Any body of knowledge is dependent, in a variety of ways, upon its cultural inheritance. Boyle recognizes that while natural law theorists have not developed an account of this, they need not deny it. He states: 'The apparently undeniable dependence of all enquiry on language and on other cultural features is consistent with what natural law theorists are required by their own views to believe about their own theorizing.'[56] However, a universal prescription cannot be impugned just because an individual moralist in a particular culture formulates it. Contingency of enquiry and language does not necessarily prohibit universal applicability.[57] This allows there to be some overlap with MacIntyre's insistence on rationality involving a degree of historicity and communal practice. However, as will be demonstrated below, MacIntyre possesses a fuller, more in-depth account of the problem of translatability and the inherent incommensurability of different moral traditions.

There is a second form of tradition-dependence that Boyle accepts applies to new natural law theory. He states that new natural law theorists recognize themselves 'to be developing a body of thought which prior thinkers have originated and developed but left incomplete, at least as far as its application to the problems and challenges, both internal and external, which the theory must deal with at any given time [is concerned].'[58] Boyle again admits that there is currently a lack of self-consciousness about this aspect of natural law that tends to stifle the development of its internal resources in order to address external challenges.[59] Again, there is overlap with MacIntyre's conception of tradition as a form of open-ended enquiry that must be developed through dialectical engagement with internal and external problems. One can thus see two ways in which Grisez would accept that tradition plays a part in reasoning rightly about morality.

There is a third form of tradition dependence which Grisez rejects. It is the view that ethical enquiry must be rooted in the lived experience of people who share a common way of life and its goods and live them out within a community which embodies these shared values as part of an on-going moral tradition.[60] While Grisez does envisage a positive role for community, it is a very limited one. He follows Aristotle in understanding humans to be naturally social animals. We become self-conscious and establish our individuality only within interpersonal relationships so that integral human fulfilment requires community. Grisez asserts: 'This natural vocation to community belongs to human persons as made in God's image, it foreshadows the revelation of their likeness in communion to the Trinity, and is the natural foundation for their calling to enter into communion with the divine family.'[61] Hence Grisez is far from being atomistic in his understanding of sociality. Like MacIntyre, he conceives of the moral life as a quest that requires help and advice from others.[62] The issue for Grisez is that making moral decisions is neither dependent upon nor sanctioned by community and its fruit – character, practices and virtue. He states:

> No culture [or community] has standards of morality superior to the principles and norms human beings naturally know – principles and norms reaffirmed and further specified by God's revelation, which is handed on by the Church's belief and teaching.[63]

So community and tradition do have a role but knowing what one ought to do is not dependent on them. Grisez's criticism of MacIntyre is that the latter has no way of countering a phenomenon like slavery, because there is nothing extrinsic to a particular tradition by which to evaluate its practice. He states: 'I do not think [MacIntyre's] proposed shift in priorities will help much. Character and community are simply the fleshed-out living wholes whose form comes from principles and whose existence comes from choice.'[64] Grisez goes on to criticize MacIntyre for introducing a more subtle form of legalism by confusing given social requirements with the moral truth.[65] One sees here a critical difference made explicit. As Boyle puts it:

> The [new] natural law account of moral life and thinking includes a set of views according to which much of moral thought is not essentially dependent upon the lived values of a moral community. … For a key [new] natural law claim is that these principles are known or at least knowable by anyone independent of whether one is part of a vital moral community.[66]

Therefore, while tradition might condition specific moral norms, these norms are intelligible naturally, and do not of necessity require either community or tradition.[67] By contrast, coming to think truthfully about morality for MacIntyre *is* dependent upon participating in a particular tradition and community that is ordered to a particular conception of the common good. Furthermore, MacIntyre sees as a central weakness in the new natural law theory its inability to account for why, in a modern context, the precepts of natural law are ignored or flouted. He locates this inability in the way in which Grisez and Finnis underplay the role of family and community in coming to know and act on the precepts of the natural law.[68]

This discussion of the place of tradition in Grisez's work demonstrates again that Grisez does not see that there is a problem of incommensurability between rival traditions which have different conception of the ultimate good. Indeed, for Grisez, Christianity and other traditions share a self-evident practical rationality that enables them to share common moral frameworks. This difference between MacIntyre and Grisez comes to the fore in their different conceptions of virtue.

Grisez and MacIntyre's different conceptions of the role of practices and virtues

For MacIntyre there is an intrinsic relation between the ability to make right moral choices and one's virtue. In MacIntyre's view one must become a particular kind of person in order to make particular kinds of decisions that are counted as moral by one's community. Furthermore, 'it is only through the acquisition and exercise of the virtues that individuals and communities can flourish in a specifically human mode.'[69] By contrast, while Grisez counts virtues as an essential part of the moral life their cognitive function is strictly limited and subordinated to the modes of responsibility and the prior exercise of choice.

For Grisez the exercise of choice lies prior to the cultivation of virtue. This is not, however, immediately apparent. Griscz states that: 'Virtues are character traits, which organise the various aspects of the complex human personality. The ordering of these aspects establishes some form of harmony among feeling, judgment, choice, performance.'[70] As Black notes, virtue in Grisez's account can be described as a disposition which 'orders an aspect of a person's choosing so that all the elements which are involved in that choosing – intentions, emotions, beliefs and actions – are consistently in harmony with one another and with a person's prior moral commitments'.[71] The issue then is, what is the relationship between virtue and prior moral commitments? Do one's prior commitments and choices determine what counts as a virtue or is virtue intrinsic to what constitutes good choice? For Grisez commitments establish an individual's identity:

> Human persons are historical beings who day by day build themselves up by their free choices. One shapes one's own life, one determines one's self, by one's free choices. To be responsible ultimately means to be a self one cannot blame on heredity, environment, or anything other than one's own free choices.[72]

He then relates virtue and choice: 'A personality is formed by choices which are in accord with the first principle of morality and the modes of responsibility, the virtues embody the modes.'[73] Virtues embody the modes that pre-exist them, with these modes of responsibility predetermining what will count as a virtue. Thus virtues are known through choices, with the modes of responsibility directing people towards a virtuous character. Black, who significantly extends and develops Grisez's account of the relationship between choice and virtue, surmises that in Grisez's approach, virtue is cultivated 'by consistently choosing to pursue the good and then, where necessary, integrating the appropriate emotions into the process of choosing and pursuing the good.'[74] Through such a process the individual arrives at the virtuous life by way of distinct choices.

Grisez's view is the reverse of the position held by MacIntyre, for whom the cultivation of certain virtues enables good choices to be made and not vice versa. As MacIntyre puts it:

> Without developing some range of intellectual and moral virtues we cannot first achieve and then continue in the exercise of practical reasoning; and without having developed some range of those same virtues we cannot adequately care for and educate others so that they first achieve and are then sustained in the exercise of practical reasoning.[75]

As noted previously, MacIntyre's criteria for being moral, or acting well, are defined by the kind of practice in which we are engaged, not by the decision or preference of the individual. This conception of morality gives a central place to the virtues (which are the goods internal to the practice) rather than to general rules or abstract principles. MacIntyre insists that morality should be construed primarily in terms of a life embodying the virtues (as opposed to the virtues embodying a set of moral norms as in Grisez); and our understanding of what the virtues are, and why they are virtues, is crucially dependent on coming to recognize their place in the practices (not the principles or modes of responsibility) which define them. Unlike Grisez,

MacIntyre understands there to be a necessary connection between virtue and seeking the good life. Furthermore, in contrast to Grisez, the virtues for MacIntyre are central to the formation of personal identity and the very pattern and shape of life together in society.

The difference between Grisez and MacIntyre in relation to virtue raises the question, for Grisez, of how the basic goods relate to the practices of a community. As noted above, Grisez conceives of the basic goods as being self-evident and existing prior to and independent of any given tradition. This essentially disembodied view of goods contrasts with MacIntyre, for whom the goods are internal to practices, and practices constitute the embodied goods of a given tradition. For MacIntyre, goods such as marriage and health may be universal, but they are not universally accessible. They can only be acquired through being practised within a particular tradition's conception and embodiment of what marriage or health in fact consists of.

This comparison of how Grisez and MacIntyre treat the role of tradition, virtue and goods in moral decision making emphasizes that their accounts of ethics are fundamentally divergent. While they both agree that ethical disputes between Christians and non-Christians are capable of resolution, MacIntyre considers such resolution to be hard won, whereas Grisez considers it to be relatively unproblematic given that both Christians and non-Christians share a practical rationality. No synthesis is possible. The choice is between following Grisez or MacIntyre's account of what might be an appropriate response to resolving ethical disputes between Christians and non-Christians. If Grisez is right, the problem of incommensurabilty highlighted by MacIntyre is not so great; for Grisez, there is sufficient common ground between Christians and non-Christians for them to resolve ethical disputes by recourse to evaluations grounded on practical reason. Indeed, the differences between Grisez and MacIntyre suggests two challenges that Grisez presents to MacIntyre's work. First, Grisez's account of ethics represents a fundamental challenge to MacIntyre's claim that ethical disputes are the result of incommensurability between rival moral traditions. Second, Grisez's account challenges MacIntyre's claim that contemporary moral discourse is fundamentally incoherent and that modern moral traditions (for example, liberalism), lack the internal resources to heal themselves.

The challenges Grisez poses to MacIntyre

Grisez's challenge to MacIntyre's account of incommensurability

Grisez's account of ethics represents a fundamental challenge to MacIntyre's claim that interminable ethical disputes are the result of incommensurability between rival moral traditions. This challenge is based on Grisez's account of first principles and practical rationality, and his conception of basic goods as self-evident. Together, these constitute an account of a tradition-free, general ethics through which ethical disputes can be resolved which arise between people of different cultures, languages and traditions.[76] Thus, Grisez's approach dispenses with any need to formulate a process by which different traditions might first understand each other and then resolve disputes. In short, questions of incommensurability between different traditions do not arise for Grisez. The discussion of Grisez's account of ethics given above clarifies why this is the case. Grisez's account of first principles, practical rationality and basic goods suggests that for Grisez, ethical disputes are to be resolved not through some dialectic of traditions, as MacIntyre contends, but via a general ethics grounded on a universal practical rationality.

Grisez challenges MacIntyre's diagnosis of the contemporary context

Grisez is acutely aware that rational thought about morality and 'living a Christian life' is beset by numerous problems in contemporary Western society and that these problems are distinct to the modern era. In addition, he recognizes that Christians live surrounded by a secular culture in which the whole idea of Revelation and a way of life based upon it is dismissed out of hand, and that believers have no 'insulation' against 'the intrusive witness of non-belief'.[77] However, while he recognizes the contemporary context is becoming increasingly inhospitable to rational deliberation about morals, and to Christianity in particular, Grisez does not accept MacIntyre's description of the context as suffering fragmentation and the modern tradition of ethics (initiated by Kant) as inherently flawed. Thus the second challenge Grisez's account of ethics represents is to MacIntyre's claim that contemporary moral discourse is fundamentally incoherent. This challenge is based on Grisez's view that the shift away from teleology was not a disaster for moral reasoning, and his acceptance of the proposition that one cannot derive an 'ought' from an 'is'. Whereas the basis of the first challenge was made clear in the earlier comparison of MacIntyre and Grisez, the basis of this second challenge needs some further explanation.

Unlike MacIntyre, Grisez does not see the modern shift away from teleology as a problem in moral reason. Hence, he would not accept MacIntyre's two parables about the fragmentation of moral reason as it forgot the overarching context that gave its prescriptions meaning. In Grisez's view, we are still capable of reasoning rightly about morality, even if many do not, because right reasoning about morality does not require a comprehensive teleological framework in order to make sense. While Grisez does see proportionalism as the predominant mode of moral reason, and sees it as irrational, he would not ascribe to it the hegemony and actively destructive role that MacIntyre gives to liberalism. Rather, for Grisez, as long as people are prepared to reflect along the lines of the first principle of practical reason, they will reason rightly. As noted above, this process of reasoning is not dependent on some prior theoretical knowledge because it is self-evident and universal. Furthermore, and in contrast to MacIntyre's teleological conception of natural law, Grisez criticizes

Aristotle, Augustine and Aquinas for positing a final (dominant) end, as though there is a determinate and objective hierarchy of human goods prior to choice. It is precisely this notion, he argues, that leads to various species of consequentialism and proportionalism; that is, that human goods can be subordinated, instrumentalized, or acted against for the sake of a 'greater good'.[78]

Grisez's rejection of natural teleology is founded on his acceptance of the dictum that it is logically impossible to derive any conclusions about what is good or what ought to be from premises containing any sort of empirical or metaphysical claims about the way things are. Grisez treats the prohibition of moves to derive a moral 'ought' from a theoretical/factual 'is' as an undeniable tenet of pure logic. He rejects scholastic natural-law theory because: 'It moves by a logically illicit step – from human nature as a given reality, to what ought and ought not to be chosen. Its proponents attempt to reinforce this move from what is to what ought to be, by appealing to God's command.'[79] Instead, Grisez proposes:

> The moral *ought* cannot be reduced to the *is-to-be* of practical truth without eliminating the distinction between the directiveness of a practical judgment that something immoral is to be done and the normativity of the moral truth that it should not be done. The *is-to-be* of practical truth cannot be reduced to the *is* of human nature without eliminating the distinction between, on the one hand, action and fulfilment through it, and, on the other, what persons are by nature, prior to their exercise of free choice.[80]

Grisez does, however, recognize a limited relationship between what is and what ought to be. He goes on to say:

> Still, this twofold irreducibility does not mean that morality is cut off from its roots in human nature. For the normativity of the moral *ought* is nothing but the integral directiveness of the is-to-be of practical knowledge. And any adequate theory of human persons will include among its true propositions: Everyone who does rationally guided actions naturally knows the first principles of practical knowledge and naturally wills (by simple volition) the goods to which they direct. In this sense, the is-to-be of the first principles of practical knowledge is itself an aspect of human nature.[81]

Even given the limited concession made by Grisez, Grisez's view directly contradicts MacIntyre's position. MacIntyre holds that one can derive an 'ought' from an 'is' if one uses functional concepts. For example, a good watch should tell the time accurately because this is what a good watch does. The problem for post-Enlightenment thought is that man, unlike for Aristotle, is conceived of as an individual prior to and apart from all roles, so that 'man' ceases to be a functional concept. For MacIntyre, following Aristotle and Aquinas, to call something good is also to make a factual statement. He states:

> To call a particular action just or right is to say that is what a good man would do in such a situation; hence this type of statement too is factual. Within [the

Aristotelian] tradition moral and evaluative statement can be called true or false in precisely the way in which all other factual statements can be so called. However, once the notion of essential human purposes or functions disappears from morality, it begins to appear implausible to treat moral judgments as factual statements.[82]

So against the division between 'is' and 'ought' made by Hume and Grisez, MacIntyre argues for the intrinsic relation between what is and what ought to be. For MacIntyre, the conception that 'facts' (what is) are independent entities which stand in judgement over mere theories (what ought to be), and to which appeal can be made in solving any and all theoretical disputes is wrong. It is wrong because it is a false dichotomy. Statements about what 'is' presuppose, and can only be made sense of in relation to, statements about what 'ought' to be. In MacIntyre's view, post-Enlightenment thought denied this connection and thereby rendered its own moral statements incoherent. For MacIntyre, moral judgements can be facts in the same way as scientific judgements can be statements of fact, for both depend on *presuppositions* about the world as it is.

In summary, Grisez accepts what MacIntyre rejects: that is, the modern, post-Enlightenment epistemology that attempts to found morality on reason and/or choice independent of metaphysical presuppositions about the way the world is. For MacIntyre, any notion of moral norms or basic goods as existing without the guidance of the theistic and teleological context in which they were originally at home means that moral judgements lose any clear status and their meaning becomes highly debatable. Any project that seeks to provide a rational vindication of morality in such a way has, as far as MacIntyre is concerned, decisively failed. MacIntyre holds that the morality of our predecessor culture – and subsequently of our own – lacks any public, shared rationale or justification.[83] So in MacIntyre's view, Grisez's attempt to make a claim for such a rationality is unfounded and unsustainable.[84] For Grisez, however, MacIntyre's view is irrational and incoherent.

These two challenges outline why, in Grisez's view, MacIntyre's critique of contemporary moral discourse is wrong and his thought constitutes an inappropriate resource for Christians to utilize. According to Grisez, Christians can resolve disputes with their neighbours on the basis of a shared practical rationality and a general, or universal, ethic. The differences of approach between Grisez and MacIntyre to the contemporary context can perhaps be encapsulated in the distinctions between their remedies. While MacIntyre advocates the formation of communities that can nurture and induct into, and teach people about, morality, Grisez emphasizes the need to draw out or clarify what people can already know but either deny, or are mistaken about, or are inured to through sin.

These two challenges to MacIntyre by Grisez raise the question: should MacIntyre be abandoned at this point in order to proceed instead by using Grisez's account of the contemporary context and his understanding of ethics? To address this question further assessment of Grisez is needed.

A critique of Grisez and the new natural law theory

Closer examination of Grisez reveals two sets of problems. The first set relates to inconsistencies within Grisez's own work. The second set of problems relates to foundational issues concerning the relationship between Grisez's approach to ethics and its theological basis.

Problems internal to Grisez's account of ethics

The impact of sin and the self-evidence of the basic goods   Grisez has a very strong account of the impact of sin at an individual and a social level, and how they are interrelated. He states: 'The cultural consequences of sin set up a kind of vicious circle. Distortion at the cultural level returns to, and reinforces, distortion already existing at the individual psychological level.'[85] This vicious circle can result in what recent papal encyclicals have referred to as a 'culture of death':[86] that is, 'whole societies settle for solutions which mutilate human nature'.[87] This recognition of the deep impact of sin leads Grisez to realize that: 'The necessary reasoning does not always occur spontaneously. ... Moreover, because human nature is fallen, redeemed, and called to heavenly glory, the full moral truth needed to guide Christian life can be found only by using the light of the gospel.'[88] And adherence to this light requires checking one's personal faith and insight into God's plan 'against the Church's faith and moral teaching'.[89] There is a clear sense then, that sin severely distorts the human ability to reason rightly and that the morality upheld by the church will not necessarily be accepted by those outside the church.

Grisez's account of sin raises two problems. The first is the problem that if we really do know the truth, and can know it by practical deliberation, then how and why do 'societies settle for solutions which mutilate human nature'? The answer would seem to be, through wrong or sinful choices. However, this brings us to the second problem. To say we *may* know the truth, but no longer know it because of sin, is one thing, but to insist, in the face of the impact of sin, that we *must* know the truth is another. Yet this seems to be Grisez's line of argument. For Grisez, it is not the case that the appeal to conscience and reason *may* work, but rather that it *must* work. However, in the light of his own account of sin, the possibility of healing mutilated societies via the supposedly metaphysics-free realm of conscience and rights appears somewhat remote. Conversely, if it really is the case that appeals to conscience will bring people, inured by sin, to direct their choices to integral human fulfilment, then we must question how significant was the mutilation of the society in the first place. This lack of clarity raises a question about the means available in Grisez's moral theory for Christians to resolve ethical disputes with their neighbours within a sinful world.

The separation between theoretical and practical reason   If it turns out in practice that Grisez does not, or cannot, separate theoretical and practical reason then this will undermine his challenge to MacIntyre's account of incommensurability. This is because, if theological accounts of the way the world is are inseparable from ethical prescriptions for how we are to act then those who do not share a Christian account of the world will have difficulty in understanding and sharing the ethical prescriptions derived from such an account. Leaving aside MacIntyre's account of how moral terms can be factual one can see that Grisez himself violates the rigid separation he advocates.

Russell Hittinger gives a critique of Grisez's separation of practical and theoretical knowledge. He analyses in detail how, in relation to the basic good of religion, Grisez fails to keep a separation between theoretical and practical reason. Grisez wants to claim that it is self-evident and not in need of theoretical specification, but according to Hittinger, this is plainly not the case. As Hittinger argues, to have any purchase as a good, 'religion' must be specified by a particular form of religion; that is, there is no such thing as a 'religion', there are only particular 'religions'.[90] By implication the good of religion must be tied to a particular account of a religion in order to bear any significance when it comes to making a choice. If the good of religion floats free of a particular religious tradition then it lacks any motivational weight in determining choice: that is to say, without specification the good of religion is too vague and empty a notion to constitute a real choice. To paraphrase MacIntyre, to choose religion as a good we must first answer the question: whose God ought we to obey and why?

Hittinger charts how Grisez in practice makes exactly this move. He notes that in Grisez's writing, the good of religion gradually becomes defined in more and more particular terms, and thus becomes less and less self-evident. In *Contraception and the Natural Law* (1964) Grisez defines the good of religion as 'the tendency to try to establish a good relationship with unknown higher powers'. By 1970, in the book *Abortion*, Grisez defines religion as: 'worship and holiness – the reconciliation of mankind to God'. This is a highly specific statement involving the substantive theological terms: 'holiness', and 'reconciliation'. By 1980 in *Beyond the New Morality* the effort to define religion as a good becomes even more complicated. In the book Grisez struggles to pin down the precise nature of religion as a value. Hittinger outlines the problem at the heart of this struggle:

> There is the problem of how to keep ethics and the religious sphere distinct, and yet coherently related. This is further complicated by the question of *which* religion we are intending to interrelate with ethics: the immanent good of religion, or the good of religion once seen in the light of [Christian] faith.[91]

Hittinger points out that for Grisez, moral norms govern the manner by which goods are chosen. By implication, any difference in the formal way in which religion is grasped as a good will become crucial. For example, if religion is one good, but is grasped differently depending upon the presence or absence of faith, one runs the risk of saying that there are two different, and morally significant, attitudes towards the same value. Conversely, if there are two different goods – religion as immanent good, and religion as a share in the supernatural life – then Grisez must either change his axiology accordingly (and make the supernatural life the overarching good) or run the risk of promoting the same moral attitude towards things that are different and incommensurable in value. In short, Hittinger is saying that the good of religion is inconsistent with Grisez's account of the first principles of practical reason: what is attractive about the good of religion as it is viewed first in the light of Grisez's pre-moral natural law theory, is incompatible with why it is attractive in the light of faith. As Hittinger puts it:

> When [Grisez] goes on ... to say that 'there would be no genuine religious community to which any person could belong apart from God's redemptive work,' it is exceedingly difficult to see not only how we are referring to the same value of religion, but how the value can be upheld as a good that satisfies moral requirements in *any* respect without an explicit faith in Christianity.[92]

Pauline Westermann provides an even stronger critique of Grisez's attempt to separate theoretical and practical reason. She argues that Grisez's inconsistency is inherent in his approach to natural law. Against the claim that the 'new natural lawyers' do not have a teleological and theoretical vision of the good she states:

> The selection of the basic goods is clearly informed by their belief that these seven basic goods are truly 'perfective' of man's nature. Because they are perfective of man's nature, they are regarded as intrinsic values. It is no good pretending that the basic goods are first selected on the basis of their 'self-evidence', and only afterwards 'happen' to be perfective of human nature.[93]

She goes on to say: 'The conclusion seems to be justified that the modern formulation of natural law rests on a hidden assumption of teleology, coupled with the belief in God.'[94] Nigel Biggar, in his comparison of Barth and Grisez, identifies the same problem. Biggar notes that Grisez fails to take sufficient account of how the basic goods are necessarily situated within a particular 'theological context'. He states:

> Where Grisez is wrong is to suppose, as he sometimes does, that there is a coherent body of knowledge about the human good, its components and its moral implications, which is sound per se, and to which reason can in fact attain 'naturally' – that is, without illumination by revelation. The theory of the good and the moral law that Grisez presents as attainable 'naturally' is actually formed by specifically Christian presuppositions. It is in fact a Christian theory, formally abstracted from the theological context in which alone it makes sense.[95]

The criticisms of Grisez made by Hittinger, Westermann and Biggar raise again the problem of incommensurability between traditions. If Grisez's ethical prescriptions are situated in, and grounded on, a particular teleology, and cosmology, then resolving ethical disputes with traditions with a different vision of the good and an alternative conception of God cannot be as straightforward as Grisez's moral theory seems to suppose. For the purportedly self-evident basic goods only seem self-evident to someone situated within a particular, overarching vision of that in which the human good consists.

These questions about the consistency of Grisez's account of ethics, especially in relation to its universality, become even more pressing in the light of a theological assessment of his work.

The relationship between Grisez's approach to ethics and theology

The primary issue at stake in analysing how Grisez's ethics relates to wider theological questions is the following: given that Grisez's proposal for how Christians and non-Christians are to resolve ethical disputes rests on a self-evident, general ethics, is there anything substantially and identifiably 'Christian' in his proposal for how Christians are to resolve their disputes with non-Christians? The short answer to this is: no, there is not. The reason for this answer is twofold. First, Grisez fails to take full account of the implications of the resurrection and eschatology for ethics; and second, Grisez subsumes the Word of God to a general ethics.

The implications of the resurrection and eschatology for Grisez's ethics   As discussed earlier, Grisez thinks that while there can be a distinct Christian moral knowledge, this knowledge is not substantively different from moral knowledge derived from right reason alone. In effect, Grisez is saying that Christ simply republishes the moral law. While recognizing that knowledge of the moral law can be severely impaired, true and full knowledge of what it means to enjoy integral human fulfilment is available outside of relationship to Jesus Christ. Hittinger notes that for Grisez 'faith makes up for a certain deficiency in the motivation that ought to be at work without faith'.[96] As Grisez himself puts it: 'Even though people *can* naturally know a great deal about right and wrong, in the fallen human condition they often have trouble doing so. Thus, God generously reveals a number of moral truths which in principle could be known without revelation.'[97] However, Grisez fails to take seriously enough the implications of the resurrection and eschatology for ethics.

Revelation does not merely enable enhanced intelligibility of an already existent morality. While it does do this, it does more than this as well. Revelation furnishes the Christian with a materially new content that entails distinct moral demands. By contrast, creation for Grisez represents the limits of the possibility of 'fulfilment in Christ' and there is nothing substantially different or new into which we may now move in and through Jesus' resurrection.[98] Grisez fails to account for how humankind, even if it remained sinless, could not have known or fulfilled all the goods. This is to say, that even without the Fall we would still not enjoy integral human fulfilment, nor, more importantly, could we know what this fulfilment in fact consisted of. This is because the true horizon by which to evaluate what integral human fulfilment consisted of is only revealed fully in Jesus Christ. Through the resurrection, humankind is both redeemed (from sin and death) and can now enter a new order of being. Christ's resurrection constitutes both humanity's redemption *and* its transformation and perfection.[99] Therefore, however long and hard one studies creation, one can never discern its full meaning. O'Donovan clarifies the implications of this when he states:

> Eschatological transformation resolves the unanswered question of creation, the question of what its temporal extension means. This question would be unanswered even in an unfallen world and to an unfallen mind; the sealed scroll of history is painfully inscrutable even to one who has gazed devoutly and joyfully on the order of creation in all its wholeness.[100]

Hence, Christian ethics is materially, not just formally, dependent on Jesus Christ. There is a distinct 'Christian' knowledge about what is good and right which is in addition to that knowable apart from Revelation.[101]

Grisez partially addresses this issue by stating that 'in history' integral human fulfilment is an 'ideal' and thence unrealizable.[102] This view, however, misses the implications of one of the central teachings of the doctrine of eschatology: that is, that in Christ our fulfilment is already realized and this fulfilment can now, through the Holy Spirit, break into the present age. By implication, our participation in Christ, through the Holy Spirit, brings new insight, and calls (and enables) new kinds of responses to old problems. Furthermore, this knowledge, given in Revelation, must at times call into question and correct both fallen and shortsighted knowledge founded on practical reason alone. Thus the logical prohibition against such a transaction collapses in the face of tighter analyses of ethics in relation to eschatology.

The implication of Christians having a distinct knowledge is that when they are engaged in ethical disputes there are specifically Christian insights into moral issues which non-Christians may accept (for a variety of reasons) but cannot access by reason alone. Therefore, contrary to Grisez's position, the problem of incommensurability between Christian and non-Christian moral judgements cannot be overcome by recourse to a universal ethic based on practical reason.

Subsuming the Word of God to a general ethics Following on from the problem of whether Christianity brings new moral insight is the question of how Grisez relates his general ethics to his Christian ethics. In contrast to Grisez, I contend that a properly Christian ethic cannot hold to the notion of a general ethics and remain Christian. To advocate this is to demand that Christians who are subject to the Word of God share that allegiance with something which is autonomous from God's Word. For Christians to resort to an autonomous general ethics, as a means of arbitrating their disputes with non-Christians, constitutes a denial of the authority Christians have as creatures of the Word of God. To resort to a general ethic to justify Christian moral claims demonstrates a lack of faith in Christ. It lacks faith in Christ because it is a failure to believe that Christ really does reveal the nature of reality and holds that there might be another source of knowledge about what is good and right apart from Christ.

The theological problem at the heart of this issue is that Grisez allows a parallel lordship to God's by allowing a validity and autonomy to general moral enquiry. As Banner argues, to advocate an autonomous general ethics is to cast doubt on the authority of Christian ethics by supposing, in effect, that Christian ethics and general ethics rule jointly over the same sphere.[103] The impact of this in relation to resolving ethical disputes is that Christian approaches to ethical issues, even within Grisez's framework in which Christian ethics is a further specification of general ethics, must always be ready and able to prove itself to be consistent with, and authorized by, general moral enquiry. However, as Banner contends, a thoroughly Christian ethic must in no way be constrained or conditioned by the extraneous demands of a prior epistemological commitment to a general ethics.[104] Christians are authorized to understand, interpret and make judgements solely on the basis of what is revealed in Jesus Christ. For Christians to do otherwise is to call into question the validity of this revelation.[105]

O'Donovan further draws out the problematic nature of the relationship between Christian ethics and general ethics in the new natural law in his discussion of Finnis's defence of exceptionless moral norms. O'Donovan notes that in the attempt to safeguard the exceptionless character of moral norms and emphasize the distinction between practical and theoretical reason, Finnis insists on the autonomy of the norms even from revelation. O'Donovan notes that even when revelation does disclose authoritative norms, these are distinct from evangelical affirmations. The result is a tight distinction between Law and Gospel.[106] Such a distinction is very far from an evangelical morality in which obedience is authenticated not because the norm is good in and of itself according to the process of practical reason, but because it is an intrinsic part of the joyful proclamation of the redemptive goodness of God. In effect, Grisez and Finnis's insistence on a division between theoretical and practical reason, and the autonomy of a general ethic, constitutes a refusal to allow the reality of what God achieves in Christ to influence or change morality.

Summary

This chapter analysed the following proposition: that Grisez calls into question Alasdair MacIntyre's diagnosis of the contemporary context and his conception of the incommensurability between Christian and non-Christian ethical action. The analysis revealed that Grisez is mistaken at a number of crucial points and that his moral theory cannot furnish us with what is necessary in order to fully address the question of how to resolve ethical disputes between Christians and non-Christians. In the light of this assessment of Grisez's approach to ethics I concluded that Grisez's challenges to MacIntyre does not succeed. The problem of incommensurability between Christians' and non-Christians' moral judgements remains a problem. Thus,

MacIntyre's analysis of the problem of incommensurability needs further consideration. This conclusion is based on the following arguments: that there is a tension between Grisez's insistence on the deep impact of sin and his contention that the basic goods are self-evident; that there is an inconsistency between Grisez's advocacy of a separation between theoretical and practical reason and his actual ethical arguments in practice; that Grisez fails to take full account of the implications of the resurrection and eschatology for Christian ethics; and that he subsumes the Word of God to a general ethics. Therefore, while Grisez does seem to pose a real challenge to MacIntyre, further analysis reveals that the differences between Christians and non-Christians really are substantive and they do not share a general ethics; thus disputes between them cannot be resolved on the basis of such an ethics. Christian ethics is necessarily *Christian*: that is, it is distinct and particular. The response to this proposition is that it is necessary to analyse the nature of the differences between Christian and non-Christian moral judgement further to discern how significant are these differences, and thus whether resolution between Christians and non-Christians regarding ethical disputes is possible. To this end I shall now compare and contrast the work of Oliver O'Donovan and MacIntyre.

Notes

1 See Grisez's critique of proportionalism: Germain Grisez, *The Way of the Lord Jesus: Christian Moral Principles*, 3 vols (Chicago: Franciscan Herald Press, 1983), I, pp. 141–71; hereafter referred to as CMP.

2 James Hanink, 'A Theory of Basic Goods: Structure and Hierarchy', *The Thomist*, 52 (1988), p. 222. For a full account of his arguments see Germain Grisez, *Abortion: The Myths, the Realities, and the Arguments* (New York: Corpus Books, 1970).

3 The same concerns underlie Grisez's critique of nuclear deterrence which seeks to preserve political community by instrumentalizing human life and putting at risk the wider community of the innocent throughout the world. See John Finnis, Joseph Boyle and Germain Grisez, *Nuclear Deterrence, Morality and Realism* (Oxford: Clarendon Press, 1987).

4 Germain Grisez, *The Way of the Lord Jesus: Living a Christian Life*, 3 vols (Quincy, IL: Franciscan Press, 1993), II, p. 348. Hereafter this work will be referred to as LCL.

5 Nigel Biggar, 'Review of The Way of the Lord Jesus, vol. 2', *Studies in Christian Ethics*, 8.1 (1995), 105–18 (p. 113). *Studies in Christian Ethics* will hereafter be referred to as SCE.

6 Germain Grisez, *Beyond the New Theism: A Philosophy of Religion* (Notre Dame: University of Notre Dame Press, 1975); and Germain Grisez, Joseph Boyle and Olaf Tollefsen, *Free Choice: A Self-Referential Argument* (Notre Dame: University of Notre Dame Press, 1976).

7 See especially: Finnis *et al.*, *Nuclear Deterrence*; and Germain Grisez, Joseph Boyle and John Finnis, 'Practical Principles, Moral Truth, and Ultimate Ends', *American Journal of Jurisprudence*, 32 (1987), 99–151. Although Grisez has collaborated with a number of other writers, including his wife, Jeannette Grisez, it is Finnis and Boyle with whom he has worked the most.

8 Pauline Westerman, *The Disintegration of Natural Law Theory: Aquinas to Finnis* (Leiden: Brill, 1998), p. 3.

9 Ibid.

10 TRV, pp. 133–35.

11 Keith Pavlischek, 'Questioning the New Natural Law Theory: The Case of Religious Liberty as Defended by Robert P. George in *Making Men Moral*', SCE, 12.2 (1999), p. 29.

12 For the fullest expression of MacIntyre's critique of Grisez and Finnis along these lines see Alasdair MacIntyre, 'Theories of Natural Law in the Culture of Advanced Modernity', in *Common Truths: New Perspectives on Natural Law*, ed. Edward McLean (Wilmington, DE: ISI Books, 2000), pp. 91–115.

13 TRV, pp. 133–34

14 Porter, *Recovery of Virtue*, p. 47. See also Ralph McInerny, 'Ethics', in *The Cambridge Companion to Aquinas*, eds N. Kretzmann and E. Stump (Cambridge: Cambridge University Press, 1993), pp. 200–202.

15 Porter, *Recovery of Virtue*, p. 48.

16 TRV, p. 134.

17 Germain Grisez, 'First Principle of Practical Reason: A Commentary on the Summa Theologiae 1–2, Question 94, Article 2', *Natural Law Forum*, 10 (1965), pp. 194–95. For a direct comparison between Grisez and Aquinas on this point see Jean Porter, *Natural and Divine Law: Reclaiming the Tradition for Christian Ethics* (Grand Rapids, MI: Eerdmans, 1999), p. 93.

18 John Haldane, 'MacIntyre's Thomist Revival: What Next?', in *After MacIntyre*, pp. 91–107.

19 CMP, p. 124.

20 Ibid., p. 184.

21 For a pithy summary of Grisez's position see James Hanink, 'On Germain Grisez: Can Christian Ethics Give Answers?,' in *Theological Voices in Medical Ethics*, eds Allen Verhey and Stephen Lammers (Grand Rapids, MI: Eerdmans, 1993), pp. 157–77. Cf., Rufus Black, 'Introduction: The New Natural Law Theory', in *The Revival of Natural Law: Philosophical, Theological and Ethical Responses to the Finnis-Grisez School*, eds Nigel Biggar and Rufus Black (Aldershot: Ashgate, 2000), pp. 1–25.

22 For an extensive discussion of this in relation to marriage see Germain Grisez, 'The Christian Family as Fulfilment of Sacramental Marriage', SCE, 9.1 (1996), 23–33.

23 Germain Grisez and Russell Shaw, *Fulfillment in Christ: A Summary of Christian Moral Principles* (Notre Dame: Notre Dame University Press, 1991), pp. 304–305.

24 CMP, p. 607.

25 Ibid., p. 608.

26 Oliver O'Donovan, *Resurrection and Moral Order: An Outline for Evangelical Ethics* (Grand Rapids, MI: Eerdmans, 1986), p. xi. Hereafter this work will be referred to as RMO.

27 CMP, p. 178.

28 Ibid.; emphasis in original (note that where italics is used for emphasis in extracts throughout this book, this is an original source).

29 Ibid., pp. 178–79.

30 Ibid., p. 180.

31 These basic goods do differ between different 'new natural law theorists'. For example, cf., John Finnis, *Natural Law and Natural Rights* (Oxford: Clarendon Press, 1980), pp. 85–92.

32 Grisez *et al.*, 'Practical Principles, Moral Truth, and Ultimate Ends', p. 106.

33 Ibid.

34 Robert George, 'Natural Law and International Order', in *Catholicism, Liberalism and Communitarianism: The Catholic Intellectual Tradition and the Moral Foundations of Democracy*, eds Kenneth Grasso, Gerard Bradley and Robert Hunt (London: Rowman & Littlefield, 1995), p. 136.

35 Grisez *et al.*, 'Practical Principles, Moral Truth, and Ultimate Ends', p. 115.

36 Ibid., pp. 115–16.

37 CMP, p. 194.

38 Grisez *et al.*, 'Practical Principles, Moral Truth, and Ultimate Ends', p. 111.

39 Ibid., p. 113.

40 Ibid., p. 117.

41 Ibid., p. 125.

42 CMP, p. 117.

43 Griscz *et al.*, 'Practical Principles, Moral Truth, and Ultimate Ends', p. 107; and CMP, p. 124.

44 CMP, p. 124.

45 LCL, pp. 567–69.
46 CMP, p. 130.
47 Grisez *et al.*, 'Practical Principles, Moral Truth, and Ultimate Ends', p. 107.
48 Joseph Boyle, 'Natural Law and the Ethics of Traditions', in *Natural Law Theory: Contemporary Essays*, ed. Robert P. George (Oxford: Clarendon Press, 1992), p. 4.
49 For a full discussion of Grisez's arguments about the proof of the existence of God and his epistemological methodology see John Ross Berkman, 'The Politics of Moral Theology: Historicizing Neo-Thomist Moral Theology, With Special Reference to the Work of Germain Grisez' (unpublished doctoral dissertation, Duke University, 1994), pp. 194–209.
50 Rufus Black, 'Is the New Natural Law Theory Christian?', in Biggar and Black, *The Revival of Natural Law*, p. 157.
51 Ibid., pp. 152–53.
52 Ibid., p. 156.
53 Rufus Black, *Christian Moral Realism: Natural Law, Narrative, Virtue, and the Gospel* (Oxford: Clarendon Press, 2000), p. 167.
54 Ibid., p. 168. See also, Black, 'Is the New Natural Law Theory Christian?', p. 157.
55 Ibid.
56 Boyle, 'Natural Law and the Ethics of Traditions', p. 7.
57 Ibid., p. 6.
58 Ibid., p. 7.
59 Ibid., p. 8.
60 Ibid., p. 9.
61 LCL, p. 333.
62 Ibid., p. 249. This is implicit in the whole *raison d'être* behind his three-volume opus.
63 Ibid., p. 258.
64 Germain Grisez, 'Review of "Revisions: Changing Perspectives in Moral Philosophy", eds Stanley Hauerwas and Alasdair MacIntyre', *Theological Studies*, 45 (1984), p. 580. Whether this is a valid criticism of MacIntyre's current position is another matter.
65 Ibid., pp. 580–81.
66 Boyle, 'Natural Law and the Ethics of Traditions', p. 11.
67 See Black, 'Introduction: The New Natural Law Theory', p. 10.
68 MacIntyre, 'Theories of Natural Law in the Culture of Advanced Modernity', pp. 104–14.
69 DRA, p. 112.
70 Grisez *et al.*, 'Practical Principles, Moral Truth, and Ultimate Ends', p. 129.
71 Black, *Christian Moral Realism*, p. 298.
72 CMP, p. 42.
73 Ibid., p. 192.
74 Black, *Christian Moral Realism*, p. 306.
75 DRA, p. 97.
76 An example of how Grisez's account of ethics might resolve conflicts arising from cross-cultural interaction is developed in: Sabina Alkire and Rufus Black, 'A Practical Reasoning Theory of Development Ethics: Furthering the Capabilities Approach', *Journal of International Development*, 9.2 (1997), 263–79.
77 Russell Shaw, 'Pioneering the Renewal in Moral Theology', in *Natural Law and Moral Inquiry: Ethics, Metaphysics and Politics in the Work of Germain Grisez*, ed. Robert P. George (Washington DC: Georgetown University Press, 1998), p. 242.
78 It should be noted that MacIntyre is also very critical of utilitarianism. For a discussion of MacIntyre's critique of utilitarianism in relation to a defence of it see Paul Kelly, 'MacIntyre's Critique of Utilitarianism', in Horton and Mendus, *After MacIntyre*, pp. 127–45.
79 CMP, p. 105.
80 Grisez *et al.*, 'Practical Principles, Moral Truth, and Ultimate Ends', p. 127.

81 Ibid.
82 AV, p. 59
83 Ibid., p. 50
84 MacIntyre, 'Theories of Natural Law in the Culture of Advanced Modernity', pp. 104–14.
85 Grisez and Shaw, *Fulfillment in Christ*, pp. 167–68.
86 See John Paul II, *Evangelium Vitae* (London, Catholic Truth Society, 1995).
87 CMP, p. 182.
88 LCL, p. 246.
89 Ibid., p. 261.

90 For a more general critique of the genealogy of the term 'religion' see Talal Asad, 'The Construction of Religion as an Anthropological Category', in *Genealogies of Religion: Discipline and Reasons of Power in Christianity and Islam* (Baltimore: Johns Hopkins University Press, 1993), pp. 27–54; and William Cavanaugh, '"A Fire Strong Enough to Consume the House:" The Wars of Religion and the Rise of the State', *Modern Theology*, 11.4 (1995), 397–420.

91 Russell Hittinger, *A Critique of the New Natural Law Theory* (Notre Dame: University of Notre Dame Press, 1987), p. 120.

92 Ibid., p. 122.
93 Westerman, *Disintegration of Natural Law Theory*, p. 254.
94 Ibid., p. 256.

95 Nigel Biggar, 'Karl Barth and Germain Grisez on the Human Good: An Ecumenical Rapprochement', in Biggar and Black, *The Revival of Natural Law*, p. 179.

96 Hittinger, *A Critique of the New Natural Law Theory*, p. 143.
97 Grisez and Shaw, *Fulfillment in Christ*, p. 76.

98 This is not to say that Grisez does not have a strong emphasis on the bodily resurrection; he does. Cf., Grisez and Shaw, *Fulfillment in Christ*, pp. 390–97.

99 RMO, p. 57. Black contends that while Grisez does not entertain the possibility that Christians' moral principles are new, Grisez does describe Christians' moral principles as the 'transformation' of 'apparently parallel secular moral principles'. However, as we shall see, the transformation envisaged by Grisez is not truly eschatological in character. Rufus Black, 'Is the New Natural Law Theory Christian?', in Biggar and Black, *The Revival of Natural Law*, p. 152.

100 RMO, p. 55.

101 This point is drawn from the criticism Banner makes of the same problem in *Evangelium Vitae*. See Michael Banner, 'Catholics and Anglicans and Contemporary Bioethics: Divided or United?', in *Issues for a Catholic Bioethic*, ed., Luke Gormally (London: Linacre Centre, 1999), pp. 34–57.

102 Grisez and Shaw, *Fulfillment in Christ*, p. 80.
103 Banner, 'Catholics and Anglicans and Contemporary Bioethics', pp. 41–42.
104 Ibid., p. 42.

105 For a theological defence of natural law and a general ethic against this kind of criticism see Porter, *Natural and Divine Law*, pp. 169–77. However, her conception of natural law is very different from that of Grisez.

106 Oliver O'Donovan, 'John Finnis on Moral Absolutes', SCE, 6.2 (1993), p. 66.

CHAPTER 3

Oliver O'Donovan and the distinctiveness of Christian ethics

What this book is trying to develop is a coherently theological account of whether Christians can resolve ethical disputes with their non-Christian neighbours in the contemporary context. To do this I have been assessing whether MacIntyre can provide such an account or even a generic framework within which such an account can be developed. A central issue of contention is the depth of difference between Christians' and non-Christians' ethical thought and action. This chapter aims to assess whether a theologically grounded account of ethics, as given by Oliver O'Donovan, calls into question the adequacy of MacIntyre's proposals for overcoming the incommensurability between Christians and non-Christian moral judgements.

Modernity: the apostate child of Christianity

It is important to establish how the contemporary context affects and shapes relations between Christians and non-Christians. Therefore, before proceeding to assess the challenge O'Donovan poses to MacIntyre's account of how to resolve ethical disputes, I analyse whether MacIntyre's critique of contemporary moral discourse is concurrent with O'Donovan's theologically grounded critique. If O'Donovan's critique is concurrent with MacIntyre's, then even if there is no agreement between them about how to resolve ethical disputes, there can at least be agreement about the context in which Christians and non-Christians engage with one another.

Unlike Grisez, O'Donovan offers a similar critique of modernity to that given by MacIntyre: that is, modern moral discourse is without the internal resources to heal itself and modern approaches to ethics are fundamentally incoherent. In *The Desire of the Nations* O'Donovan reviews different critics of modernity, among whom is MacIntyre.[1] O'Donovan understands their primary criticisms of modernity to be threefold: that modernity postulates a primacy of the will which creates itself out of nothing; it replaces practical reason with technique; and it holds to the possibility of having a view from nowhere. O'Donovan then sets out his own parallel critique. The major difference between his critique and the others' is that he seeks to understand how modernity is rooted in Christianity. O'Donovan considers this important for: 'This helps us understand at once how modernity is the child of Christianity, and at the same time how it has left its father's house and followed the way of the prodigal.'[2]

O'Donovan concurs with MacIntyre's view that the loss of teleology in moral reasoning is central to understanding the incoherence of most contemporary moral discourse. For O'Donovan, this loss expresses itself most clearly in voluntarist notions of freedom wherein freedom is conceived as the assertion of the human will by an autonomous, self-sufficient agent. Like MacIntyre, O'Donovan understands this vision of freedom to emerge out of the matrix of the attempt by medieval scientific enquiry to rid itself of teleological philosophy and the objection by thinkers of the Enlightenment to the idea that the moral will can be determined by a teleological order discerned within nature. This dual thrust led to a division between will and nature. O'Donovan states: 'On the one hand scientific thought is anxious to free nature from immanent purposiveness; on the other, moral philosophy wishes to free the will from any purposiveness in nature. It suits both of them to assign purposiveness exclusively to the human will, and to dissociate it from nature.'[3] Like MacIntyre, O'Donovan sees both Hume and Kant as key figures in bringing about the rejection of natural teleology that results in the false understanding of freedom as an unbounded assertion of the will.[4]

In addition to this critique of modernity's denigration of teleology, O'Donovan shares MacIntyre's critique of technology and technical rationality. O'Donovan believes that critics who make 'technology' the centre of their account of modernity (often following Heidegger's famous essay *Die Frage nach der Technik*) mean not technical achievements, but the mutation of practical reasoning into 'technique'. It is in this sense that MacIntyre can be understood to be a critic of technology. According to MacIntyre, practical reason has been usurped by 'technique'.[5] Using a parallel argument, O'Donovan states: 'Set free from obedience to comprehensible ends of action, confronting all reality as disposable material, [reason's] primary imperative is manipulation.'[6] For example, politics is understood to be about 'making a better world' through the efficient and effective management of resources, instead of about determining the common good through reflection and deliberation. O'Donovan states: 'The fate of a society which sees, wherever it looks, nothing but the products of the human will, is that it fails, when it does see some aspect of human activity which is not a matter of construction, to recognise the significance of what it sees and to think about it appropriately.'[7] He gives numerous examples, especially in the realm of medicine. For example, cloning and certain forms of artificial reproduction render the child a project – a subject of human making – so that the child ceases to be an irreplaceable gift of equal dignity to other humans, and becomes a product at the disposal of other humans.[8]

Further to his critique of technology and the loss of teleology, O'Donovan's critique of individualism and the privatization of morality is parallel to that given by MacIntyre. In O'Donovan's view, individualism and the privatization of morality are two additional consequences of the modern emphasis on the individual will. O'Donovan recognizes that there is a right and proper freedom from society (which is, for O'Donovan, inaugurated by Jesus Christ). The new social reality created by Christ relativizes all other forms of society and lordship. According to O'Donovan, the one who follows Christ is no longer subject to her family, tribe and nation. She takes responsibility for decisions she alone can take and on grounds that are not given her from within the old forms of society. This provides a model of the individual as one fully engaged in and for society; so that society itself becomes free by being upheld by the free self-giving of each member.[9] There is thus no dialectic between the individual and the collective, but a dialectic of two freedoms, in which both community and believer are authorized to be free agents.[10] However, the individualism of modernity is not about free self-giving but the assertion of individuality, whether that be freedom from control or freedom for self-realization. Within this modern conception, freedom is not creative, but is essentially passive. As O'Donovan contends: 'It is the freedom of consumers, rather than participants.'[11] It is the freedom to exist in a private realm in which no one may interfere with one's family arrangements, religion, sexual practice, eating habits and so on; however, the inverse of this freedom is that judgements about the 'private life' of others are prohibited because to make a judgement would be to infringe on another's freedom. As O'Donovan puts it: 'To presume to exercise freedom of conscience in one's *public* dealings is, as we say, "thrusting your private convictions down other people's throats", that is to say, bringing them out of the private realm into the public forum where they might challenge community policy.'[12] Thus morality is privatized and decisions in the public realm are judged in terms of good administration and effective management and not in terms of how wise or virtuous they are. In practice, this leads to a fundamentally incoherent, and highly conflictual, public discourse about morality.

We have seen above that like MacIntyre, O'Donovan understands there to be extensive and deep-rooted problems in contemporary moral discourse. He shares MacIntyre's pivotal concerns in two ways. A central theme of O'Donovan's work, like MacIntyre's, is the attempt to recover an understanding of what constitutes appropriate authority. Furthermore, O'Donovan, like MacIntyre, perceives that the roots of the current confusion about legitimate authority, and the resultant oppressive, incoherent and fragmented discourses about morality, lie in the historical development of the primary, contemporary philosophical framework – liberal individualism – and that to understand and so address the problem we must trace the history of liberalism. However, O'Donovan diverges from MacIntyre in that his focus is more concrete and his premises are theological.

O'Donovan agrees with MacIntyre that modern liberalism does not have the resources to heal itself and can find no rational justification for its project.[13] However, O'Donovan understands the primary cause of this problem to be that liberalism lost its roots as a theological venture. Therefore, it is not just that liberalism tried to deny the importance of history, tradition and context, but more importantly, it denied the Christ-event as its very foundation. MacIntyre believes that the primary resource for recovering the rationality of moral discourse is for liberalism to take on the moral frameworks of Christianity (as instantiated in Thomism); however, his concern is with the form of Christianity's moral discourse, rather than the content. By contrast, while he is concerned about the form of contemporary moral discourse, O'Donovan's primary concern is the content of that discourse. For O'Donovan, it is a re-engagement with the person of Jesus Christ, and not just the recovery of modes of moral discourse, that will enable liberalism, both philosophically and politically, to recover its sanity. In short, liberalism must reconnect to political theology, and thus take seriously again the Gospel's claim to be public truth. The implications of this difference between MacIntyre and O'Donovan will become apparent when their accounts of how Christians should engage with non-Christians are compared.

O'Donovan's narration of history runs parallel to MacIntyre's in that he does see a disjunction after the development of the early modern liberal state. In *The Desire of the Nations* O'Donovan gives an account of the rise of the limited state and the development of the rule of law from the Christ-event up to the sixteenth century. After this point, O'Donovan recounts a story of decline wherein the liberal polity, mirrored in liberal philosophy, becomes an instance of the anti-Christ: that is, it is a 'parodic and corrupt development of Christian social order'.[14] It is important to note that, according to O'Donovan, the canker at the heart of this decline was the existence of problems within theological discourse and the corruption of particular Christian social practices.

O'Donovan's evangelical ethics

While MacIntyre and O'Donovan agree about the context and state of contemporary moral discourse, O'Donovan's conception of ethics is theologically grounded, as distinct from MacIntyre's philosophically grounded account. The rest of this chapter contains extensive exegesis of O'Donovan's theologically grounded conception of ethics. This exegesis is important in order that the differences between O'Donovan's theologically derived account of ethics and MacIntyre's account of ethics may be made transparent. With the differences made clear it is possible to evaluate whether MacIntyre's account of ethics can be appropriated by Christians as a lens by which to analyse and approach ethical disputes with non-Christians.

Natural and evangelical knowledge

For O'Donovan, a person's ability to know the order of creation, and so participate in it, will depend on her knowledge. This is because, in O'Donovan's conception, knowledge is the particular way humans participate in creation.[15] Hence, right participation depends on right knowledge. However, such knowledge is difficult to win. In this lies a critical distinction for O'Donovan. He distinguishes between an ontology of creation – there really is a proper or natural order to which we can conform – and the epistemological issues of how we know that order. This clarification of the ontological and epistemological issues in ethics underpins one of the central thrusts of O'Donovan's work; its attempt to restore the concept of 'the natural' and the doctrine of creation within Christian ethics.[16] By separating the ontological from the epistemological issues O'Donovan can affirm that nature/creation is good, although fallen, while allowing that discernment of that order is problematic.

The distinction between the ontological and epistemological issues in ethics leads O'Donovan to ask the question: 'What kind of knowledge can this be that has the order of creation as its object?'[17] This knowledge is the knowledge of things in their relation to the totality of things. O'Donovan does not imply that humans must know the totality of things; that is the prerogative of God. Rather, humans know what they do know as part of a meaningful totality. This overall picture allows us to give meaning to the particular. However, there can be no Archimedean point from which the subject can stand over and above creation, evaluating from the 'outside'. Following MacIntyre's critique of the modern conception of the neutrality of rationality, O'Donovan holds that we are all actors upon the same stage. The knowledge that we can have is 'existential': that is, it occurs only as the subject participates in what she knows. O'Donovan states:

> Knowledge of the universe never takes shape at an observer's distance; it is not knowledge-by-transcendence. We may, of course, know particular objects in this way, from a relative distance; that is what makes the natural sciences possible. But the more encompassing the object of observation is, the more difficult it is to isolate and transcend.[18]

Thus the knowledge we may possess, even though it is knowledge of the totality of things, always has both an incomplete character, and is subject to continual refinement in the light of new particulars. An analogy to illustrate O'Donovan's conception of knowledge is that of a picture. One sees a picture in its totality, with all its parts in relation to one another. As the picture is contemplated, so the differing elements come to be understood with an ever-increasing degree of nuance and subtlety. One also views a picture from a particular angle or position in relation to it. Likewise, humans can only view the order of creation from a particular position; however, unlike the viewer of the picture, humans are situated within that which they contemplate.

For O'Donovan, as distinct from MacIntyre, all knowledge is contingent in two other ways. First, it is subject to the Creator; and second, it is subject to judgement and transformation (not abolition) at the *eschaton*. This knowledge, however, is unitary: whether knowledge is true or false, in accord with reality or not, there is only one reality to know. This is in contrast to Gnostic or Manichean conceptions of reality as dualistic: that is, split, and forever in a battle between good and evil, or ethereal and material. We can have assurance that the order of things will not be suddenly overthrown by a different one.

O'Donovan summarizes his understanding of knowledge in stating:

> It must be apprehensive knowledge of the whole of things, yet which does not pretend to transcendence over the universe, but reaches out to understand the whole from a central point within it. It must be a human knowledge that is co-ordinated with the true performance of the human task in worship of God and obedience to the moral law. It must be a knowledge that is vindicated by God's revelatory word that the created good and man's knowledge of it is not to be overthrown in history. Such knowledge, according to the Christian gospel, is given to us as we participate in the life of Jesus Christ. ... True knowledge of the moral order is knowledge 'in Christ'.[19]

This conception of true knowledge being 'in Christ' makes clear that knowledge is grounded in being, and human knowledge specifically in Christ's human being.

The cornerstone of O'Donovan's ethics, and what makes it different in substance from MacIntyre's, is that for O'Donovan we have access to the shape of the order of things through the resurrection of Jesus Christ. This is a universal claim 'because the good news that we *may* live in [creation] is addressed to all mankind'.[20] This foundational claim leads O'Donovan to state, in contrast to MacIntyre, that the resurrection is the only sure basis on which moral decisions might be made. While the order of creation is good, it can do nothing to reconcile rebellious man to itself, nor can it interpret itself to humankind's disordered reason: 'Hence [nature] is tyrannous, arbitrary and sometimes frankly misleading in character.'[21] Only when humans participate in God's life (which is to say in God's ways) can they be sure to apprehend the proper order of creation and so act in accordance with it.

The difference between MacIntyre and O'Donovan in relation to how revelation relates to natural knowledge is highlighted in how they envisage non-Christian thought being utilized. For MacIntyre, Thomas represents a systematic synthesis of classical thought, Aristotle in particular. As Thomas Hibbs notes, for MacIntyre: 'The theological engagement of the philosophic tradition on its own terms involves the correction and fulfilment of the *telos* of ancient philosophy by means inaccessible to unaided reason.'[22] In short, for MacIntyre grace complements and fulfils what is naturally knowable. By contrast, for O'Donovan, the true 'nature' of man was not properly apprehended by classical thought, so it is not the case that nature, as they understood it, can be perfected by theological insight. Rather, the disparate jigsaw pieces of fallen natural knowledge about justice or human nature, which are strewn around classical thought, are sifted and brought together by understanding them in the light of who Jesus Christ is. This places such knowledge in a proper order and so a true picture begins to emerge. Further pieces of the jigsaw can then be added to the sketchy outline of human nature as more reflection on human nature is undertaken in response to what has been revealed. Christian morality is humankind's glad response to the deed of God 'which has restored, proved and fulfilled that order, making man free to conform to it'.[23]

An example of the different approaches to classical thought in MacIntyre and O'Donovan is provided by Augustine's treatment of slavery. Augustine drew on classical thought about human nature yet redefined it in reference to the revelation of

God in Jesus Christ. Thus, in contrast to Aristotle and Plato, for whom slavery was natural, Augustine understood slavery to result from the Fall and not to be part of nature. He states: '[God] did not wish the rational being, made in his image, to have dominion over any but irrational creatures, not man over man, but man over beasts. Hence the first just men were set up as shepherds of flocks, rather than as kings of men.'[24] Augustine's treatment of whether men are 'naturally' slaves or not exemplifies O'Donovan's conception of the relationship between grace and nature. For O'Donovan, the fragmentary knowledge in classical thought about human nature is properly grounded in the revelation of Jesus Christ and the proper order of creation is thus able to be apprehended. By contrast, for MacIntyre, the problem is not that Plato and Aristotle fundamentally misunderstood human nature, but that their account of that nature was basically right but lacking in certain respects.

Within O'Donovan's conception of 'evangelical' moral knowledge, Christian ethics becomes a fruit of the Spirit, for it is the Spirit which 'forms and brings to expression the appropriate pattern of free response to objective reality':[25] that is, it is the Spirit which enables humans to respond subjectively to the objective, created order of things which was restored and vindicated by Jesus Christ in his resurrection. The proper form this pattern takes is love, which is itself ordered and shaped in accordance with the order it discovers in its object. It is the task of Christian ethics, guided by the Spirit, to trace, participate in and so bear witness to this ordering of love.

O'Donovan's conception of natural and evangelical knowledge raises serious questions about MacIntyre's conception of the incommensurability between Christians and non-Christians and his account of how to resolve ethical disputes between them. However, before addressing the question of whether MacIntyre takes sufficient account of the incommensurability between Christians and non-Christians, it is necessary first to consider MacIntyre and O'Donovan's respective accounts of sin.

Sin and the inherent disarray of moral discourse

Having understood O'Donovan's conception of knowledge, further consideration must be given to why he thinks knowledge of creation is problematic. For O'Donovan, Christ's life is one of conflict between true human life and misshapen human life, a conflict which continues in the present age when the false continues to exclude the true. This exclusion of true human life by its parody may happen through structures of domination or injustice, or it may occur at a more personal level through temptation to compromise, for example, seeking sexual satisfaction outside of its true place. However, the resurrection declares this exclusion of true human life temporary. The implications of the exclusion of true human life is that, in this age, there will be goods that cannot be fully enjoyed given the present alienation between humankind and the created order that we see played out in Christ's crucifixion. For example, sexual desire and satisfaction is a good of creation, but given its present distortion, humans are unlikely to enjoy it fully in its proper form.

At the root of the exclusion of true human life by misshapen human life is the Fall. The Fall distorts the human capacity to know and will the good. In the Fall we lost our place in the universe (which is intimately bound up with ordering our lives towards the love of God), and so we lost our understanding of the proper relationship between Creator and creation which is the ground of the intelligibility of the created order. Despite this, the universe, though fractured and broken, displays the fact that its brokenness is the brokenness of order and not merely disordered chaos.[26] Man in his own strength either tries to participate in the created order of God; or through his fallen knowledge completely misconstrues or misinterprets this order. This results in both idolatry (primarily in the form of self-love) and abuse of creation. In contrast, Christian morality, which entails proper participation in the created order, involves both a re-ordering of the will and new moral knowledge. This re-ordered will and true sight of the created order results from participation in the life of God, empowered by the Spirit, through the life, death and resurrection of Jesus Christ.

It is important to note that O'Donovan is not saying that revelation in Christ completely replaces our fragmentary knowledge. The Christian moral thinker has no need to deny or destroy what she finds valued in any culture, including her own, neither does she have to prove that anything of worth in them arises out of Christian influence. But she cannot simply embrace the perspectives of any culture, be it liberal, Hindu, or otherwise. As O'Donovan argues, the Christian can only approach other cultures and traditions critically

> evaluating them and interpreting their significance from the place where true knowledge of the moral order is given, under the authority of the gospel. From that position alone can be discerned what there is to be found in these various moral traditions that may be of interest or of value.[27]

While MacIntyre does allow for the impact of sin (it is incorporated into his account of Thomistic Aristotelianism via Augustine), O'Donovan's account, as stated above, is fuller and more systematic. O'Donovan's account of sin gives rise to a stronger sense of the inherent disarray of all moral discourse in every period of history.

For O'Donovan, the only way to have a secure and coherent understanding of morality is to reflect and deliberate on morality in the light of who Jesus Christ is. There is no ground in fallen history on which to gain access to reality, for what is arbitrary cannot provide security. O'Donovan states: 'To repudiate arbitrariness, we must regain contact with that which is not arbitrary.'[28] Neither reason, nor will, nor any human action can enable humans to regain contact with that which is not arbitrary. Rather, true cognition of reality depends on the re-orientation of the will and reason to their object. This is what is meant by 'conversion'. As O'Donovan puts it:

> Conversion, then, is not something in which either the will or the reason has a leverage upon the other, by virtue of a residual connection which either can claim with objective good. It is an event in which reason and will together are

turned from arbitrariness to reality, an event which is 'miraculous' in that there are no sufficient grounds for it, whether rational or voluntative, within the subject himself.[29]

Or we might add, within any given tradition. Between fallen human history and the new creation, there is a radical discontinuity between the old will and the new one, and between the old knowledge and the new one. MacIntyre's notion of 'epistemological crises' allows for the need for conversion.[30] Furthermore, following his reading of Augustine, MacIntyre accepts that the human will 'is systematically misdirected and misdirected in such a way that it is not within its own power to redirect itself.'[31] But a question remains as to whether MacIntyre has a sufficient grasp of how deeply human knowledge is affected by sin.

As stated before, O'Donovan's tradition-specific account raises questions about MacIntyre's generic account of the differences between Christians and non-Christians. The primary question is: does MacIntyre allow for greater commensurability between Christians and non-Christians than O'Donovan's tradition-specific account actually allows for? As will be seen, the answer is both 'yes' and 'no'.

O'Donovan and MacIntyre compared

I have argued that O'Donovan's explicitly theological account of ethics leads to a somewhat different conception of moral knowledge to that of MacIntyre. By comparing their respective accounts of the ground on which knowledge of morality is based, and how they understand knowledge of morality to be mediated, the differences between O'Donovan and MacIntyre will be clarified in relation to their respective accounts of the incommensurability between Christianity and other moral traditions. If it is the case that O'Donovan's account of incommensurability is substantively different from, and raises questions about, MacIntyre's, then MacIntyre's account of how, in practice, Christians might resolve ethical disputes with non-Christians must be analysed further. If, on further analysis, MacIntyre's account is rejected, then another approach needs to be formulated for thinking about relations between Christians and non-Christians with regard to ethical disputes.

O'Donovan and MacIntyre's different conceptions of what authorizes moral knowledge

Both MacIntyre and O'Donovan hold that 'natural' knowledge is, to a greater or lesser degree, only known via a particular tradition. In relation to morality, MacIntyre emphasizes how knowledge is relative due to its contextual character, while O'Donovan gives greater weight to sin as the cause of its relativity. This does not imply that morality itself is relative. Both MacIntyre and O'Donovan agree that there really is a moral order humans can conform to. However, while there is a definitive shape to nature which presses in upon and limits human action, there is no way to determine which of the regularities we encounter in nature should be counted as normative for determining moral action. It is at this point that differences between MacIntyre and O'Donovan emerge. Both understand the natural order to be opaque in its meaning, but while MacIntyre seeks to determine what is normative via a dialectic of tradition-guided rationalities, O'Donovan understands nature to have an unmediated authority and Divine authority to be the only secure means by which to determine normative moral thought and action. It is their respective accounts of the role of nature and tradition in authorizing moral action to which I now turn.

First, it is important to distinguish between 'morality' and 'moral action'. The term 'morality' refers to the moral order as a totality. By 'moral action' is meant particular attempts to correspond to this overarching order. Morality of itself is grounded in the creation or natural order. Moral action is not. This is because it is part of the human endeavour to conform to the overarching order of things, and as such, it is subject to the finitude, contingency and fallenness of human knowledge of that order. Therefore, the question to ask in relation to moral action is: how can one determine whether moral action is in conformity with morality?

The authority of nature and tradition

Like MacIntyre, O'Donovan has a correspondence theory of truth. As noted above, tradition does not provide a rational foundation for knowledge, but it is vital for the transmission of morality and for enabling moral action. However, in O'Donovan's view, to ground knowledge of morality on tradition alone would be to mistake communication of knowledge (which has its own particular kind of authority) for knowledge itself.[32] The truth or falsity of this knowledge can only rest on whether it corresponds to reality, whatever a tradition decrees. For example, a tradition may hold that the earth is flat, but reality will intrude upon this doctrine. This is not to say that for O'Donovan the authority of tradition is not a legitimate form of authority.

There is a close affinity between O'Donovan and MacIntyre in their conception of the role of tradition in relation to determining moral action. For O'Donovan all common knowledge, in that it is possessed by a society (as distinct from being possessed by a group within society) is possessed through the medium of tradition. In specific relation to the Christian tradition, O'Donovan identifies four *loci* of moral authority.[33] First, he includes in tradition not only the formulated moral wisdom of the past but the whole record of the way the Christian life was lived by former generations in the history of the Church: the ensemble of story and memory as well as of thought. The second locus is moral norms. Within a tradition there is a special place for moral norms (the identification of generic principles or policies), which communicate the intelligible structure of the community's life. O'Donovan states: 'Such norms are valid only insofar as they succeed in giving faithful expression to the tradition, just as the tradition is valid only insofar as it succeeds in giving faithful expression of what has been disclosed to us in Christ.'[34] Norms, like tradition, require the disciplines of critique and engagement. Without norms though, obedience to Christ's call would be over-laborious and impractical. Third, there is the *didache* or teaching ministry. This keeps the commands and teaching of Christ and the story of his life, death and resurrection, vitally present to the mind of the church so that they distinctively shape the thought and action of its members. Fourth, there is the conscience of the Christian agent. The individual has a particular authority to speak what the law of Christ demands of her in any situation.

Again, like MacIntyre, O'Donovan believes that the recognition that moral knowledge is tradition-situated does not necessitate scepticism or relativism. It does, however, make such knowledge problematic, because a spurious appearance of self-evidence may attach itself to opinions simply because they are widely or historically held within a tradition. However, O'Donovan, like MacIntyre, makes allowance for the problematic nature of moral knowledge by requiring that we engage in the disciplines of tradition-situated rationality. These are the disciplines of reasoning and engagement (exposing our ideas to argument from other traditions).[35] These disciplines ensure that a tradition remains open to greater discernment of the moral order. A central part of the practice of these disciplines is dialogue with the past. For O'Donovan ethics cannot be studied seriously unless it is studied with a historical dimension. In his view, without a dialogue between the ages there can be no serious critical questions about the prejudgements with which our society approaches practical reasoning.[36] The disciplines of reasoning and engagement – which includes dialogue with the past – belong to the process of tradition formation, and for O'Donovan, the above ways of testing claims are built into the activity of social communication embodied in a tradition.

Beyond this point, O'Donovan and MacIntyre part company in their conception of the relationship between morality and tradition. O'Donovan circumscribes severely the role of tradition. For O'Donovan, tradition is but one of a number of natural authorities. He identifies four forms of natural authority: beauty, age, community and strength (which includes the range of natural virtues from might to wisdom). For him tradition is merely part of the natural authority of *age*. This hints at the more substantive point that nature itself is not an inert, meaningless thing waiting to be assigned meaning. Rather, it has its own inherent meaning and authority. O'Donovan states: 'The created order carries its authority for action in itself, because agents, too, are a part of the created order and respond to it without being told to.'[37] This natural authority is given/created by God and so has a created independence and order that can evoke a proper response, undetermined by tradition. Hence, far from being something we choose or construct or which is solely dependent upon tradition, moral reasoning must treat morality as a claim upon humans. For O'Donovan what we recognize when we recognize a *moral* claim is the claim of certain generic categories of relation that can be grasped as transhistorical, transcultural realities. In the concrete moral demands that are placed upon us we discern the call, albeit faintly, of a moral order that is part of reality.[38] While knowledge of this objective moral order can be common knowledge through being the possession of a community via tradition, the authority of the moral order is independent of tradition.

There is still the problem of determining how we can say that the regularities in nature with which we are confronted are normative. To this problem MacIntyre and O'Donovan present different responses: MacIntyre relies solely on tradition-guided rationality, whereas O'Donovan secures moral knowledge in Divine authority. I will now analyse O'Donovan's conception of Divine authority, especially how Christ and the Spirit serve to make this authority present to humans. This analysis is important because it is O'Donovan's conception of Divine authority, and the role of Christ and the Spirit in relation to morality, that most sharply distinguishes O'Donovan's theologically derived account of ethics from MacIntyre's account. It is on the basis of O'Donovan's account, especially his account of the role of Christ and the Spirit, that I will assess the adequacy of MacIntyre's account of the incommensurability between Christianity and other moral traditions.

Divine authority in relation to tradition

In O'Donovan's work, the Divine authority is absolute authority since it commands us as absolute reality. O'Donovan states: 'Authority presupposes a foundation in being, and, just as truth prevails over the natural authority because it is the truth of reality as a whole, so divine authority will prevail only because it belongs to that first reality in which truth is grounded.'[39] O'Donovan argues that the only appropriate response to Divine authority is trusting obedience since this is the only appropriate self-critical reaction on man's part. This in turn renders any other form of natural authority, including the authority of tradition, contingent.

Divine authority is not oppressive or destructive, because it is rooted, through Christ, in the created order. O'Donovan states:

> Since the Word became flesh and dwelt among us, transcendent divine authority has presented itself as worldly moral authority. It comes to us not as a *mysterium tremendum* which simply destroys all worldly order, but as creation restored and renewed, to which God is immediately present in the person of the son of man. The teaching and life of Jesus must be *morally* authoritative if we are not to be thrown back upon the gnostic gospel of a visitor from heaven who summons us out of the world.[40]

This reaffirms that the kingdom of God is not in opposition to creation; rather, the incarnation and resurrection, the divine 'yes' to creation, is the foundation of ethics. Therefore, we look to Christ to determine true moral action because Christ is Divine authority made present to and in the creation order. In looking to Christ we can see the totality of things and thus we can situate our particular actions in relation to their place in the whole.

O'Donovan points out that the content of Christ's teaching is not unique (the content of his teaching is replicated by others with no relation to Christ or

Christianity). Rather, its uniqueness is founded on the fact that the moral teacher is also saviour and redeemer who in some manner re-creates the hearer of his teaching. Thus to say the content is unique would be to confuse what Christ said with the foundation on which he said it. Any number of people can say: 'Forgive your enemies'. The point at which Christ becomes irreplaceable is as the ground of the moral order, for in his resurrection God publicly and cosmically vindicated the moral order.[41] This is not to say that his moral teaching is irrelevant: the reverse is true. The moral teaching of Christ *is* good news: it is evangelical because it speaks of Christ's redemption of all things. Jesus Christ is ultimately authoritative for morality because he constitutes the ontological ground of morality. Thus, the uniqueness of Christian morality does not lie in the teachings of Christ *per se*, but in the nature of the teacher.

Christ's authority is also historical. For God confers meaning on a particular event giving it unique significance within the flow of other similar events. Thus it is Christ, the Word of God, who confers upon the totality of events their shape and point as 'history'. This leads O'Donovan to contrast Christ's historical authority (which can reconcile) with his moral authority (which can only judge). If Christ is the ultimate authority in relation to morality, then anything that does not conform to Christ must be judged as not moral. However, the passing of history enables that which is not moral to be reconciled with, and so conformed to, Christ. Within history it seems as if there are contradictory actions in God's relationship to the world. However, while there may be moral conflicts in the 'story', these are reconciled through seeing the whole picture at the summing up of history. Christ's life, death and resurrection are the revelation of this 'summing up'.

The authority of the Holy Spirit in relation to tradition

If Christ re-establishes the ground of creation, it is the Holy Spirit who makes this present to us and enables us to participate in it. The role of the Spirit in relation to morality is crucial to understanding a properly Christian account of ethics and how Christian ethics differs from and converges with the morality of non-Christians.

O'Donovan states that it is the Holy Spirit who makes the authority of Christ's eschatological triumph subjectively present and immediate to us.[42] O'Donovan says of the work of the Spirit, first, 'that the Spirit makes the reality of redemption, distant from us in time both *present* and *authoritative*', and second, that the Spirit 'evokes our *free* response to this reality as moral agents.'[43] The events of Jesus' life, death, resurrection and ascension shape our present reality through the actions of the Spirit who makes this history present: 'The work of the Holy Spirit defines an age – the age in which all times are immediately present to that time, the time of Christ.'[44] Indeed, it is the Spirit who makes the eschaton present to us, bringing the reality Christ establishes to bear upon our fallen reality:

> The effect of this is twofold: our world is judged, and it is recreated. ... The Holy Spirit brings God's act in Christ into critical opposition to the falsely structured

reality in which we live. At the same time and through the same act he calls into existence a new and truer structure for existence.[45]

Thus the Spirit gives substance to the renewed creation in Christ, giving it historical embodiment in present human decisions and actions. We can already begin to see that the role MacIntyre gives to tradition in transmitting moral knowledge is severely curtailed in the light of O'Donovan's account of the role of the Spirit.

Ultimately, it is the Spirit who enables true judgement and action. Character or virtue may well be enabled by the Spirit, but, on O'Donovan's account of the role of the Spirit, and in contrast to MacIntyre's position, character and virtue in isolation cannot be relied upon to enable true judgement and action. It is the Spirit who enables authentic agency, both by the individual and the community through time, by enabling them to participate in the order of creation by true knowledge and action. Such knowledge and action is the basis of freedom. There is thus an intrinsic relationship between true freedom, which is the ability to know and act truly within an ordered reality, and the action of the Spirit in enabling this on the basis of the actions of Christ. Hence, ethics for O'Donovan is Trinitarian in nature. To be moral is to be judged and re-created by Christ and so free to direct oneself, through knowledge and actions, to one's eschatological transformation; which is being accomplished now through the priestly actions of Christ with the Father, in which we can participate through the actions of the Spirit.

As demonstrated in the first chapter, MacIntyre offers an account of how morality is ultimately secured by or grounded on Divine authority. Crucially, what is distinct about O'Donovan's approach is that this authority is immediately available and present through the actions of Christ and the Spirit. Furthermore, this comparison between MacIntyre and O'Donovan draws out the ambiguity of whether MacIntyre takes sufficient account of the incommensurability between Christian and non-Christian moral knowledge. O'Donovan's account of the 'evangelical' nature of Christian morality suggests that MacIntyre fails to appreciate the depth of the differences. However, O'Donovan's insistence on the authority of other natural authorities, and the circumscribing of the role of tradition via the unmediated action of Christ and the Spirit, indicates that Christians and non-Christians can share moral knowledge independent of their respective traditions. I now analyse this ambiguity in more detail.

Ad hoc commensurability or a clash of traditions?

On the basis of O'Donovan's account of Christ and the Spirit in relation to tradition an important criticism can be derived of MacIntyre's approach: that is, theologically, MacIntyre overemphasizes the role of tradition. This in turn leads him to misconstrue the nature of the incommensurability between Christians and non-Christians. In contrast to MacIntyre, O'Donovan wants to avoid what he calls an 'angel-ecclesiology': that is, after Christ, there is no longer any need for mediating structures (or angels) between God and His people (as there was for the Israelites) because, through Christ, all may now have direct access to God. O'Donovan argues that after Christ tradition may not be the sole means by which Christ's moral law is mediated to individual Christians.[46] When tradition is understood to be the sole means then the church becomes the only route to the formation of Christian thought and action. Yet to say the church and tradition are the only route to the formation of Christian thought and action ignores the possibility of direct action by Christ through the Spirit. For O'Donovan, MacIntyre overemphasizes the role of tradition and in so doing denies the possibility that individuals may encounter the moral authority of Christ by means other than the tradition of church law and discipline.

Ethics as tradition-situated and not tradition-guided

Central to understanding the relativity of tradition in relation to Christian thought and action is the role of the Holy Spirit, who re-directs us, on the basis of what Christ has achieved, to our redeemed, and reconciled, life in God. If Christ is the one in whom all things hold together, the Spirit is the one who maintains the particularity, distinctiveness, and uniqueness through the Son, of each within this unity.[47] In doing so, the Spirit sustains our humanity by enabling us to participate in the renewed creation, and its moral order, in a truly human way. The consequence of this is that the Spirit breaks down the need for a particular tradition to mediate participation in the moral order and enables direct communication with God. O'Donovan clarifies this when he states:

> It is the Holy Spirit who bears witness with our spirit, addressing us at the seat of our individual agency and teaching us to pray the Abba prayer with Jesus (Rom. 8:15–16). And it is the Holy Spirit who breaks down the Mosaic mediatorial community-structure, which concealed God as much as it revealed him, and who creates a different relationship of freedom and openness within the Christian community.[48]

An overemphasis on tradition is, for O'Donovan, a denial of the work of the Spirit. It masks the possibility of direct relationship with God, mediated through Christ in the power of the Spirit, and not through tradition.[49] The reliance on tradition in the formation of moral judgements in MacIntyre's conception of ethics seems to fall prey to precisely O'Donovan's criticism of 'angel-ecclesiology'.

O'Donovan understands Christian ethics not to be tradition-guided but Spirit-guided. It is the Spirit who guides us into all truth. Tradition is a means of mediation, which, while it might be a condition of, is not sufficient for, guiding us into truth. Some might argue that there is no need for tradition if it is the Spirit who guides Christians into truth. However, even though the risen and ascended Jesus Christ exists as a present reality, he cannot be known apart from the Jesus of scriptural description. This in turn is mediated through the tradition of interpretation (which is theology) and of embodied practices. Christians measure the shape and authenticity of their interpretative and embodied response to Christ through dialogue with scripture that is the primary and authoritative testimony to human responses to Jesus, empowered by the Spirit. As Colin Gunton frames it:

> Tradition is necessary because the present Jesus is the one who at a particular time in our past lived a certain life, died upon the cross and was raised from the dead for our justification, and as the Lord both absent and present is mediated in different ways by scripture and its tradition of interpreters. Tradition in the church, then, is a process of gift and reception in which the deposit of faith – the teaching and ethics of the Christian community – is received, interpreted and handed on through time.[50]

O'Donovan affirms the above in conceiving tradition in terms of a legacy, or an inheritance, we living receive from the dead. However, this legacy is not mere diachronic transmission; rather, it must involve a synchronous sharing, for it is 'a passing round of goods among contemporaries rather than a handing-on'.[51] O'Donovan comments further: 'The monstrous inequity of generational succession is that all our possession becomes a kind of robbery, something we have taken from those who shared it with us but with whom we cannot share in return.'[52] It is only through the Spirit that such a synchronous sharing is possible, and it is then only really possible at the *parousia* when this age is fulfilled and the resurrection of the dead makes equal and reciprocal sharing among generations a dynamic reality. Those who have responded to the Spirit's prompting now (and in the future) inherit from, and look forward to, the day when they will share with those who have gone before. The Christian tradition is thus a fruit of human responses to Christ, empowered by the Spirit.

In an attempt to formulate a definition of tradition in the light of O'Donovan's theology we can say the following: our knowledge and moral practice is tradition-situated, but the Spirit validates it as true knowledge, and Christ is the ground and object of this knowledge. In this age, our knowledge is partial and necessarily tradition-situated, and we accept the revelation of the truth in faith, via the actions of Christ and the Spirit. Therefore, the Christian tradition provides the resources for, and the means of transmission of, human knowledge of Jesus Christ and human responses to acts of the Spirit. *In short, the Christian tradition constitutes the concrete accretion in Scripture, social practices and doctrine of redeemed humanity's response to Christ, empowered by the Spirit, within the rightly ordered creation and through history.* As such, to paraphrase Jaroslav Pelikan, tradition is the living faith of the dead. Tradition-situated ethics helps shape human responses to Christ, led and empowered by the Spirit, in harmony with previous faithful responses. Indeed, the living faith and faithful testimony of the dead, encountered in their concrete accretion in Scripture, social practices and doctrine, furnish faithful living in the present with the necessary resources, such as moral norms, for truthful responses to Christ.

On the basis of this definition of the Christian tradition the differences between MacIntyre and O'Donovan in relation to the role of tradition in Christian thought and action comes into sharp focus. In summary, where O'Donovan sees Christ and the Spirit as the determining authority for making moral judgements, MacIntyre sees tradition as having the determining authority for moral action (as distinct from morality *per se* which is grounded on Divine authority). In the light of O'Donovan's theological account of the role of tradition in relation to Christian thought and action it seems that MacIntyre overemphasizes the role of tradition in relation to ethics. However, MacIntyre himself is not unaware of this problem. Nor does it imply that MacIntyre's moral theory is not open to further theological development.

Beyond relativism: Christ or dialectics?

There appears to be an ambiguity at the heart of MacIntyre's ethics. The ambiguity centres on whether MacIntyre's account of the role of tradition in guiding moral thought and action is consistent with his account of how different moral traditions resolve ethical disputes. This ambiguity provokes a number of responses by commentators on MacIntyre's work.

Some commentators see MacIntyre avoiding the problem of an over-reliance on tradition as the ground of moral thought and action by resorting to an exterior process of rationality: namely, dialectics. As noted previously, many criticized *After Virtue* as slipping into relativism.[53] However, as already stated, in his later work, MacIntyre has developed a conception of natural law. This move results in MacIntyre placing much greater emphasis on human rationality *per se*. To some commentators MacIntyre goes too far in this direction. For example, John Milbank argues that:

> MacIntyre's realism conflicts with his historicism, and ... he actually downplays the potentially more relativizing, rhetorical aspects of Aristotle. This means that MacIntyre is more firmly bound within Aristotle's ethical categories than Aristotle himself, by making them more emphatically a matter of universal reason and natural law.[54]

Michael Banner is another such commentator. Banner notes how MacIntyre seeks to offer an account of moral reasoning and justification as highly tradition-specific, while at the same time offering an account of how traditions may lay claim to, and indeed contest alternative claims to, rational justification. Banner considers MacIntyre's position to 'represent a continuing affinity with the so-called "enlightenment project" of which MacIntyre has been such a stern and penetrating critic.'[55] This 'continuing affinity' is witnessed in MacIntyre's 'presentation of the resolution of the dispute between moral realism and moral relativism as one which depends crucially on the willingness of advocates of a realist viewpoint to maintain, *inter alia*, that any moral tradition they support be capable of exhibiting its argumentative superiority to its rivals.'[56] John Milbank makes a similar criticism when he states that: 'MacIntyre totally subordinates the telling and acting out of different stories [or narrative traditions] to the dialectical process of question and answer which gradually opens up for us 'reality'.[57] In other words, MacIntyre is criticized for responding to the charge of relativism by resorting to a schema whereby the rationality of one tradition must be proved to be philosophically better than that of a rival tradition. Milbank and Banner are suggesting that for MacIntyre rationality is not tradition-guided, as we originally suggested, but is grounded on a prior, universal rationality. While this circumvents the problem of his 'angel-ecclesiology' it does introduce the same problem highlighted in relation to Grisez's work: that is, it introduces a reliance on an autonomous, universal rationality that takes insufficient account of Divine authority and the particularity of 'evangelical' moral knowledge.

Another commentator on MacIntyre, David Fergusson, also argues that MacIntyre is not a relativist. However, against those, like Banner and Milbank, who say MacIntyre resorts to a quasi-foundationalism, Fergusson contends that MacIntyre does not believe in a rationality antecedent to, or independent of, any tradition by reference to which one tradition can prove itself superior to others. For Fergusson, MacIntyre's position is that there is an *ad hoc* commensurability, which allows for gradual absorption from one tradition to another and for common ground to be established.[58] If this were the case, then the accusation that MacIntyre posits an autonomous, universal rationality would be forestalled.[59]

If Fergusson is correct in his analysis of MacIntyre, then MacIntyre's account could still provide an adequate account of how Christians can engage with non-Christians in relation to ethical disputes. The reason for its potential adequacy as an account of how Christians are to relate to non-Christians are as follows: given the previously argued point that Christ and Spirit are not limited to the Christian tradition, resolving disputes between Christians and non-Christians cannot simply be a question of one tradition being philosophically vindicated over another. There will of necessity be an *ad hoc* commensurability because Christ and the Spirit are at work in other traditions and therefore Christians should expect to find convergence with other traditions. Furthermore, all traditions are subject to the natural authorities and so Christians should expect to discover parallels between their approach to certain moral problems and the approaches established in other traditions. However, it is on the issue of the means of evaluation that Christians come into conflict with non-Christians. It is at this level that the question of incommensurability is raised. Christ is the sole measure of truth and thus it is only on the basis of what accords with Christ that Christians can fully resolve disputes with their neighbours. Therefore, any account of relations between Christians and non-Christians with regard to ethical disputes must account for a degree of both continuity and discontinuity between Christians and non-Christians. Fergusson's interpretation of MacIntyre suggests MacIntyre can take account of this simultaneous continuity and discontinuity.

The theological ground of the necessity of continuity and discontinuity between Christianity and other traditions is set out in the doctrine of eschatology. Within an eschatological framework the Spirit is understood to make present the restored and fulfilled creation now, to all people everywhere; however, the restored and fulfilled creation will not be fully present until Christ returns. The theological premise that the ascended and absent Christ is made present by the Spirit to humans, while we await the full disclosure of Christ's kingdom, emphasizes how Christians exist between two ages. The result of Christians self-consciously living between this age and the next is that they are marked off from non-Christians, not by race, or culture, or even by religion, but by their union with Christ whose ascension marks a relativization of this age and the inauguration of the new age. Christians must accept this situation of continuity and radical discontinuity with those around them. O'Donovan's ethics represents a self-conscious attempt to spell out the ethical life amid this tension. I shall now analyse whether MacIntyre is open to such an account. The analysis will re-visit the issue of whether the account MacIntyre gives of the role of tradition in guiding moral thought and action is consistent with his account of how different moral traditions resolve ethical disputes.

It is my contention that what Fergusson suggests is the right direction, but he is wrong to describe it as the direction MacIntyre takes. MacIntyre gives too much significance to the internal coherence of traditions to be proposing we should look for *ad hoc* commensurability. Likewise, the break up of coherent traditions appears to MacIntyre to be a tragic loss. In MacIntyre's view, currently we all stand 'betwixt and between' a variety of traditions from which we draw our resources.[60] Miroslav Volf notes that for MacIntyre: 'Being "betwixt and between" presents an inconsistent and unstable state. The person living "betwixt and between" is neither a "citizen of nowhere", as a good liberal should be, nor "at home" in a tradition, which is where any wise person would want to be.'[61] Volf's account of MacIntyre is at odds with Fergusson's reading of MacIntyre. In Volf's view, far from positing an *ad hoc* model of relations between traditions, MacIntyre demands traditions engage one another in a coherent and unified manner. This leads to a highly conflictual model of relations between traditions. Volf comments: 'The more integrated traditions are, the more their relations will be agonistic. One tradition struggles against another, its justice against the justice of another tradition, until one defeats the other by proving itself rationally superior.'[62] By contrast, Volf suggests that traditions themselves are never 'pure' but, through their history of interaction and encounter, they themselves depend and draw on other traditions. He proposes, as Fergusson does, that we do not seek overall victory but look for piecemeal convergence and agreement. For this 'more modest' endeavour, Volf believes that MacIntyre's tradition-based conception of justice and rationality is helpful. It is helpful because MacIntyre is right to argue that we need some means of determining how traditions might relate as 'thick' moral discourses. However, success or failure in determining how traditions can relate as 'thick' moral discourses does not preclude, prior to any conclusions about the ability of traditions to relate as 'thick' moral discourses, there being an *ad hoc* commensurability between the moral and social practices of Christians and non-Christians. It does, however, demand retaining theological presuppositions as the criteria for evaluating what is morally right. A question remains as to whether

MacIntyre gives an adequate account of how the Christian tradition can relate to other traditions as a 'thick' moral discourse in such a way that it does not preclude there being *ad hoc* commensurability between Christians and non-Christian moral and social practices.

Fergusson thinks a theologically specific approach can be accommodated within MacIntyre's framework. He holds that MacIntyre, following Thomas, conceives of grace as converting partial understanding. He states: 'MacIntyre approaches Aquinas primarily as a resource to complement and correct an Aristotelian moral philosophy.'[63] This would seem to draw MacIntyre closer to O'Donovan's theologically specified position. However, as Fergusson himself says: 'If the Christian life is viewed merely as the correction of the moral life, the radical nature of God's grace ... is threatened.'[64] For Fergusson this is a lacuna in MacIntyre's work rather than a fatal flaw. He is confident that theology can fill this lacuna and still retain MacIntyre's framework. However, we must assess whether Fergusson is right to suggest MacIntyre's account of how to resolve ethical disputes between Christians and non-Christians is open to a more theologically specific approach to the same issue; that is, do the omissions in MacIntyre's account represent a lacuna (and thus is MacIntyre open to theological specification) or do these omissions represent a fundamental flaw in MacIntyre's thesis?

The rest of this chapter assesses whether MacIntyre is open to theological specification. In the next chapter, there is further analysis of the nature and shape of *ad hoc* commensurability between the moral and social practices of Christians and non-Christians. This assessment will be carried out in the light of an analysis of MacIntyre's concrete suggestions for how Christians are to engage the contemporary context.

MacIntyre's openness to theological specification

MacIntyre cannot be blamed for not giving an account of the role of Christ and the Spirit in relation to the nature, authority and mediation of moral knowledge. He is after all a philosopher and not a theologian. However, the critical question that must be addressed is this: is MacIntyre's generic account open to further specification in the light of O'Donovan's 'thicker' Christian account of the nature and basis of ethics? The answer is ambivalent. As we have seen there is much that can be taken up, as the convergence and continuities analysed above between MacIntyre and O'Donovan's accounts demonstrate. However, there is a fundamental difference between the shape of MacIntyre's ethics and that of O'Donovan's explicitly Christocentric ethics. The differences between MacIntyre and O'Donovan in relation to how tradition is relativized and how Christ and the Spirit make moral knowledge available point to a very different overall shape to their ethics, and thus to their conception of the relationship between Christians and non-Christians with regard to ethical disputes.

Stanley Hauerwas, whose own work can be seen as the most consistent attempt to make use of MacIntyre's work, brings into sharp focus the underlying issue we have been hinting at.[65] Hauerwas questions whether MacIntyre's teleology is compatible with Christian eschatology. Hauerwas states: 'It is an important and largely unexplored question as to what the relation may be between Paul's eschatology and the teleology insisted upon by MacIntyre.'[66] Elsewhere he comments: 'I worry that the kind of grand narrative MacIntyre develops, particularly a grand narrative that is a narrative of declension, entails assumptions about history that betray the eschatological character of the gospel.'[67] Hauerwas does not directly address the questions he raises about the compatibility between MacIntyre's work and Christian eschatology; however, their combatibility forms one of the key questions of this book, for central to this question is how we understand tradition in relation to eschatology and, consequently, what is the nature of the relationship between Christians and non-Christians with regard to ethical disputes. The primary point of disagreement that needs investigating is MacIntyre's metaphysics and whether it is sufficiently open to theological considerations or whether he is insufficiently attentive to the very tradition from which he claims to derive his substantive theory.

The need for an eschatological horizon

From the emphasis on the work of Christ and the Spirit in O'Donovan there emerges a very different conception of time and history to that at work in MacIntyre. O'Donovan understands there to be a single reality which itself is under transformation by the eschatological kingdom of God: hence God already determines the 'future'. We can encounter history and novelty without terror because God reveals the overall shape of things and their destiny in the life, death, and resurrection of Jesus Christ. This contrasts sharply with MacIntyre for whom the shape of reality is opaque and the future undetermined.

Perhaps unsurprisingly for someone primarily concerned with moral philosophy, MacIntyre lacks an eschatological perspective. However, there is a shape to his conception of time. It is my contention that the implications of his conception drive his ethics in a distinctly unchristian direction. For MacIntyre, the true meaning of history is immanent within history and so is something to be established through human endeavour rather than received from God. O'Donovan disagrees fundamentally with this view.

Both O'Donovan and MacIntyre want to see a proper conception of teleology re-established as a central feature of moral discourse. Furthermore, both see all things as created with inherent possibilities or ends. However, MacIntyre's teleology is wrong in the eyes of O'Donovan. O'Donovan's eschatological teleology affirms the created independence of nature and the ordering of nature to certain ends. At the same time, O'Donovan holds that these ends find their resolution and perfection in the eschaton and not in creation. The fulfilment of these ends is only possible insofar as they participate, through the Spirit, in the new creation inaugurated by Christ's resurrection and ascension. After the Fall, the true direction of creation's teleology is re-established in Christ. That which does not participate in Christ has a 'misdirected progress' and can in no way fulfil itself out of its own resources.[68] The notion of 'misdirected progress' can be helpfully elucidated by reference to Irenaeus. For Irenaeus creation is imperfect, that is to say, it does not arrive *ex nihilo* in full bloom but must grow up and mature in order that it might then receive its perfection in Christ. The Fall constitutes a turn away from maturity and results in humans walking backwards into chaos and nothingness. As Douglas Farrow puts it: 'In the fall man is 'turned backwards.' He does not grow up in the love of God as he is intended to. The course of his time, his so-called progress, is set in the wrong direction.'[69] In direct contrast to MacIntyre's position, perfection within an eschatological teleology denotes radical transformation, so that the perfection of nature is not immanent within itself but is given by God.

MacIntyre's latent historicism comes to the fore at this point. For him the meaning of history and its direction is implicit in its own possibilities. In this respect, he is similar to Grisez in that there can be nothing truly 'new': creation, and human action within creation, are conceived of as the limit of possibilities. For O'Donovan, history does not contain all possibility immanent within itself. Just as creation is distinct from history, so is the fulfilment of history – the *eschaton* – distinct from the historical process. It is Jesus Christ alone who confers destiny and purpose to history; history cannot achieve this for itself nor can it justify itself. Only Christ is 'worthy to open the scroll' and reveal the meaning of history.[70]

At the heart of this difference is the distinction between MacIntyre's historicist, protological teleology and O'Donovan's Christian eschatological teleology. For O'Donovan, the transformations by man within history are entirely different in kind from the transformation God is bringing about. For unlike man, God is not just responding to the necessities intrinsic to creation, but is doing something new. As O'Donovan puts it:

> The transformation is in keeping with the creation, but in no way dictated by it. This is what is meant by describing the Christian view of history as 'eschatological' and not merely as 'teleological'. The destined end is not immanently present in the beginning or in the course of the movement through time.[71]

John Zizioulas clarifies this when he says:

> In the eschatological approach … the Spirit is the one who brings the eschata into history. He confronts the process of history with its consummation, with its transformation and transfiguration. By bringing the eschata into history, the Spirit does not vivify a pre-existing structure; He *creates* one; He changes linear historicity into a *presence*. It is no longer possible to understand history simply as 'past', i.e. to apply to it the psychological and experiential notion of *anamnesis* in the sense of the retrospective faculty of the human soul. When the eschata visits us, the Church's *anamnesis* acquires the eucharistic paradox which no historical consciousness can ever comprehend, i.e. the *memory of the future*.[72]

Christ's resurrection has the double aspect of being resurrection from sin and death (thus healing and restoring creation) and glorification at God's right hand (thus looking forward to the eschatological transformation and perfection of creation as a new creation, as distinct from a revolutionary or teleological transformation of the existing creation). By contrast, MacIntyre's ethics appears closed to the possibility of this kind of newness or transformation.

An eschatological conception of history and teleology allows for radical newness and continuity as well as openness to genuinely new development rather than fulfilment of what is already present. A truly 'Christian' ethic must be open or have space for this kind of eschatological transformation. Through an assessment of O'Donovan's eschatology, it can be seen why this is the case, and by implication, why MacIntyre's lack of openness to eschatology is not merely a 'lacuna', as Fergusson believes it is, but a major problem, especially in relation to MacIntyre's account of how the Christian tradition can relate to non-Christian traditions.

The key to understanding this emphasis on eschatological teleology for O'Donovan is his doctrine of justification and predestination. Thus, his concern for eschatological teleology in ethics springs from some of the fundamental building blocks of Christian life and thought. For O'Donovan, justification is a total relation to Christ whereby we are never independent in any of our actions from Christ, each action being justified by Christ's prior action. When we speak of justification as finished and accomplished this does not apply to our individual lives. Rather it is finished and accomplished in world-history. O'Donovan states: 'The individual biography moves, not in an upward curve away from the resurrection of Christ as a starting point, but in a circle around it, always in the same relation to it.'[73] This does not deny individual progress and development in Christ, but it does deny a biographical relation whereby justification is a starting point. We are always justified in Christ, from beginning to end: our indebtedness is 'coextensive with life itself'.[74] God created humans to be a certain way: being more or less human does not merit favour with God.

Directly related to O'Donovan's account of justification is his conception of the doctrine of predestination. O'Donovan describes this doctrine as follows:

> Predestination, like justification, is salvation in Christ; but where justification associates us with the righteousness of Christ made manifest in his human life, predestination associates us with the eternal relation between Son and the Father before all time. ... The phrase 'chosen in Christ' is not to be understood as though *we* were chosen and *he* was merely the instrument by which our choosing was given effect. We are chosen in him, because *he* is the chosen one, the eternal object of the Father's good pleasure. Just as our justification means our participation in his righteousness, so our predestination, our 'election', means our participation in his position as the object of the Father's favour from eternity.[75]

Predestination, or the doctrine of election, is a formal way of expressing our participation, in Christ, in the communion of the Trinity.

This understanding of justification and predestination underpins O'Donovan's conception of the moral life as 'good news'. For the moral life bears witness to the possibility of true life: the life of the Trinity. Hence, the structure of the good life is not that of a protological teleology wherein true life is born out of the substance of nature. Rather, true life lies in greater conformity to the freedom that already exists in the Trinitarian communion of God. Thus, human fulfilment is not constituted by the resolution of inherent possibilities but its assumption into a previously defined reality and an already achieved set of relations. For as Kathryn Tanner points out: 'There is nothing yet to achieve beyond what God's own Trinitarian perfection already instantiates. In giving rise to the creature and elevating it to God's own level, God is always bringing about something less rather than something more than what the triune God already is in itself.'[76] In saying this, I am not setting up a false dichotomy between the potential of creation and its fulfilment in the eschaton; rather, the issue is whether one views creation as the limit of possibility or whether Christ can introduce something new into creation (albeit something that already exists in what the triune God already is). In short, if Christ's fulfilment of creation does involve something new to creation, then human fulfilment is not dependent on anything immanent within creation; instead, we can seek, by faith, and empowered by the Spirit, to anticipate and participate in the new future already established by Christ – the ground and pattern of which already exists in the Triune God. By contrast, MacIntyre's ethics postulates precisely the kind of protological movement that is challenged by this eschatological approach.

A further criticism that transpires from O'Donovan's eschatological teleology is that MacIntyre fails to see that tradition is a child of time which has an end: this end being the *eschaton*. For without eschatology there is no ultimate horizon to, and transformation of, the present, only an endless dialectic of traditions. Thus there is no stable vision of the good life. It could be argued that MacIntyre anticipates the time when one tradition – Thomist Aristotelianism – vindicates itself against all other traditions. Then its vision of the good life would predominate. However, there is a false messianism here whereby MacIntyre hopes one particular tradition will be vindicated above all others by its own rational superiority. For O'Donovan, it is not rational superiority that will be vindicated as the means of resolution, but the true Messiah, the good and faithful servant. Neither can a single tradition provide us with the definitive vision of the good life, only Jesus Christ can.

MacIntyre's lack of an ultimate horizon, due to his protological teleology, means he is unable to specify how ethical disputes can finally be resolved. Insecurity is inherent in his framework: despite one tradition vindicating itself over another, there is always the possibility that another tradition might arise which can usurp the former victor. There is no room for slipping into such insecurity in Christianity: the gospel is good news precisely because the future is already achieved in Christ and we can now trust that goodness and justice will prevail against all that oppose their establishment. Despite our present problems in resolving ethical disputes, we know now that all disputes are ultimately resolved in Christ. It must be asked, therefore, whether

MacIntyre's meta-theory of how to resolve disputes is an appropriate model for Christians to use.

In addition, there is a need to question MacIntyre's essentially pessimistic outlook on history, an outlook that arises from his lack of eschatology. At the end of *After Virtue* MacIntyre concludes that we have entered a 'new dark ages' of 'barbarism and darkness'. His ground for hope is the possibility of constructing 'local forms of community within which civility and the intellectual and moral life can be sustained'.[77] This is a slender hope. Without Christ and the Spirit, these local forms of community will have no light to bring to the 'new dark ages'. In contrast, O'Donovan understands the 'future' as determined by the eschaton that is constantly breaking into the present. Therefore, the future is secure and provides light, however dark the present age.

This lack of a secure future directly impacts MacIntyre's central concern that justice should not be what the strong make it. MacIntyre, through his substantive thesis about tradition-guided rationality, wants to suggest that justice can be found in a particular tradition and at a local level. By his own admission, the justice found in these places is flawed and constantly in need of improvement. Furthermore, precisely at the point at which he seeks concrete guidance to shape present resistance to the incursions of advanced capitalism and the bureaucratic nation-state he resorts to invoking Utopia. He states in relation to his concrete suggestions about how to shape local politics: 'These are of course Utopian standards, not too often realized outside Utopia, and only then, as I have already suggested, in flawed ways.'[78] It seems that for MacIntyre true justice is firmly established nowhere and can be seen only in Faustian dreams of Utopia, which, time and again, are more oppressive than that which they seek to rectify.[79] This resort to Utopia makes MacIntyre guilty of precisely the charge which he levels at Aristotle: that is, the justice he seeks can neither be found nor established.

One positive response to the above charge might be to say that such hesitancy about the possibility of justice is entirely consonant with the theological, Augustinian view that the justice of the earthly city is always flawed. However, MacIntyre, unlike Augustine, lacks the eschatological vision of Christianity and it is this lack that gives rise to MacIntyre's essentially pessimistic view. By contrast, for O'Donovan justice is found and firmly grounded in the ascended Christ. O'Donovan does not look to this world for justice, but looks to the in-breaking kingdom of God, established by Jesus Christ, in whom the nations are to put their hope (Mt. 12:21) and whose justice rolls like a river from heaven (Amos 5:24). This is not a utopian, protological vision, but an eschatological one. Its form is neither oppressive nor unrealizable. Rather, it is present by the Spirit who enables true freedom and 'just generosity' both in the church and in a limited form in the state when political authority acts in accord with its subjection to Christ's rule.[80] It is on the basis of this eschatological vision, in contrast to MacIntyre's Utopian dreams, that I formulate a constructive proposal for how Christians and non-Christians can relate in the contemporary context.

A perpetual dialectic as against an eternal peace

This comparison between MacIntyre's and O'Donovan's conception of time and history reveals that the shape and trajectory of MacIntyre's work is very different from one borne out of attention to distinctively theological presuppositions. The heart of the problem seems to be MacIntyre's realism which owes more to the metaphysics of Aristotle than a distinctively Christian, Trinitarian ontology. MacIntyre needs an ontology properly attentive both to creation and to eschatology. Hence, if it is to be sufficiently open to theological development, MacIntyre's conception of tradition should be shaped by an eschatological teleology rather than a protological one. O'Donovan's theologically specified account of the end of the moral life as a gift from God provides precisely what is lacking in MacIntyre's account.

The importance of the need for an eschatological teleology in MacIntyre's work can be illustrated by how such an eschatology would answer a major criticism of MacIntyre by Milbank and Hauerwas. Milbank and Hauerwas argue that MacIntyre's basic vision of relations is one of violence in which there is no real place for the peace achieved by Christ on the cross and through the resurrection. Milbank argues that MacIntyre's second order theory of how different traditions relate seems to ontologize violence as basic to reality. He notes that MacIntyre never avows a heroic conception of virtue and the overcoming of difference through competitive conquest.[81] This is pressing because the pagan account of virtues is founded on a politics of violence and exclusion, which is radically different from the account of the virtues given in Christianity. Milbank identifies the key difference in the respective accounts of virtue as being between Greek *arete* and Christian *caritas*. Hauerwas, who shares Milbank's concerns, states:

> *Arete* has meaning in relation to a fundamentally heroic image that has no telos other than conflict. The hero vanquishes his foes, and the virtues are his wherewithal, as well as those traits for which he is accorded honor in the polis he violently defends. By contrast, *caritas*, the very form of the virtues for Aquinas, sees the person of virtue as essentially standing in mutuality with God and with her fellow human being.[82]

This difference leads to a contrast that MacIntyre never identifies: that is, the contrast between the Greek *polis* and the church. Following Augustine, Milbank and Hauerwas see the church, insofar as it is based on *caritas* and not *arete*, as bringing to the *polis* the possibility of true peace. Hauerwas states:

> In effect, the ancient world knew no peace, it knew only the absence of conflict in an exclusive *polis* where the virtuous life always took meaning and direction from heroism in war. ... Unlike *arete*, Christian charity ... transcends a model of the person whose telos involves the practice and perfection of the virtues in conflict, and it offers the new political possibilities of mutuality and community that previously were inconceivable.[83]

Thus in the church it is peace (defined by Jesus Christ) and not violence which is ontologically basic. MacIntyre, however, admits his revival of virtue leads to conflict, but he thinks this conflict can be managed via dialectics. However, Milbank argues that dialectics is no more than Greek conceptions of the normative character of violence writ large. *Three Rival Versions of Moral Enquiry* can be read as an example of Milbank's criticism: each tradition is placed in competition against its rivals for the prize of dialectical superiority. Of particular focus is the last chapter wherein MacIntyre uses this competition as the basis for a new vision of the university as a place of 'constrained disagreement'. Hauerwas notes that 'MacIntyre has no means, and perhaps no desire, to stop the war, nor to confine it to discussions occurring among academics in the university.'[84] This charge is unwarranted. However, what the critique offered by Milbank and Hauerwas does highlight is the need, in MacIntyre's work, for an eschatological horizon that takes account of the future already achieved in Christ and thereby posits an end to the agonistic rivalry between traditions and opens up the possibility of a peaceful communion present now in human relations.

Incommensurability and the resolution of moral disputes revisited

In the light of this comparison between MacIntyre and O'Donovan, the validity of MacIntyre's meta-theory of how different traditions relate is called into question as an appropriate model for Christians to follow. From the above comparison we can draw two conclusions: first, MacIntyre underestimates the discontinuities between Christians and non-Christians; and second, MacIntyre overemphasizes the role of tradition in guiding moral action. Hence, the problem of whether Christians can ever really resolve disputes with their neighbours is raised once more.

MacIntyre underestimates the discontinuities between Christians and non-Christians

I have argued that for the Christian tradition Jesus Christ is the only secure way of knowing the good. Those who do not evaluate moral issues in the light of who Jesus Christ is will not share the same evaluative criteria as Christians. MacIntyre's proposal that Christians might prove their tradition to be of greater philosophical sufficiency than rival traditions allows for this. However, it does not take adequate account of how the Spirit guides all moral action, including that of non-Christians. The central difference between O'Donovan and MacIntyre is founded on their respective accounts of the teleology of the moral life. O'Donovan takes account of eschatology, while MacIntyre does not. Within his eschatological framework, O'Donovan is able to account for the continuity and radical discontinuity between this age and the age to come. O'Donovan is thus able to account for the continuity and discontinuity between Christian and non-Christian approaches to morality.

MacIntyre, by contrast, is ambiguous in relation to the continuity and discontinuity between Christians and non-Christians. On the one hand MacIntyre emphasizes the role of tradition in determining moral judgement, but on the other, the basis of this judgement is secured through a dialectical process independent of any tradition.

MacIntyre overemphasizes the role of tradition in resolving moral disputes

The distinctively Christian cosmology, which I set out above, leads to a relativization of MacIntyre's conception of resolving ethical disputes. Tradition possesses a proper, created, authority, but it is only one of a number of such created authorities. Like all created authorities, the authority of tradition is subject to the Fall and contingent upon Divine authority. In Christ, and through the Holy Spirit, created authorities may now be re-directed to their true fulfilment. Furthermore, we may now encounter Divine authority directly. Thus, the work of Christ and the actions of the Spirit both reveal the limits tradition can play, and relativizes its importance in enabling moral action. The eschatological horizon of true action relativizes the significance of tradition-situated ethics: we look forward to a time when no mediation, via tradition, between God and humans is necessary, nor between one generation and the next, for we shall participate fully in the presence of God and will share equally and reciprocally with everyone, including past generations. Therefore, MacIntyre's conception of the problem in terms of how the Christian tradition (or in his case the Thomist Aristotelian tradition) relates to other traditions is insufficient. In turn, his lack of a distinctively Christian cosmology leads him to rest too much weight on the coherence and integrity of a tradition. Instead, greater attention needs to be given to the *ad hoc* nature of commensurability between Christian and non-Christian approaches to moral problems and the way in which Christians live 'betwixt and between' different traditions.

Notes

1 Oliver O'Donovan, *The Desire of the Nations: Rediscovering the Roots of Political Theory* (Cambridge: Cambridge University Press, 1996), p. 18. Hereafter this work will be refered to as *Desire*. Cf., RMO, p. 18.
   2 *Desire*, p. 275.
   3 RMO, p. 46.
   4 O'Donovan notes how Hume's advocacy of conscientious conviction as central to moral judgement and Kant's 'rational will' both attempt to vindicate freedom as autonomy, that is, freedom of action belongs entirely to the moral agent herself and can in no way be derived from external reality (RMO, pp. 118–19).
   5 AV, pp. 30–31.
   6 *Desire*, p. 274.
   7 Oliver O'Donovan, *Begotten or Made?* (Oxford: Clarendon Press, 1984), p. 2.
   8 This is one of the central points of *Begotten or Made?*
   9 O'Donovan, *Desire,* p. 254. One of the key assumptions here is that we can talk about social realities and societies as being entities or objects or facts independent of the wills of their members. This is an alien

idea to much modern political thought, which, after Hobbes, and the emphasis on society being the result of a 'social contract', tends to see society and any social entity as dependent for its existence on the will of its members.

10 RMO, p. 164.

11 O'Donovan, *Begotten or Made?*, p. 9.

12 Ibid., p. 10.

13 AV, p. 241.

14 *Desire*, p. 275.

15 RMO, p. 76.

16 This concern was first expressed in an early article that amounts to a manifesto for his later work: Oliver O'Donovan, 'The Natural Ethic', in *Essays in Evangelical Social Ethics*, ed., D. Wright (Exeter: Paternoster Press, 1978), pp. 19–35.

17 RMO, p. 76

18 Ibid., p. 79.

19 Ibid., p. 85.

20 Ibid., p. 17

21 Ibid., p. 22

22 Thomas Hibbs, 'MacIntyre, Tradition and the Christian Philosopher', *The Modern Schoolman*, 68 (1991), 211–23 (p. 218). Cf., WJ, pp. 150–54.

23 RMO, p. 76

24 Augustine, *City of God*, XIX, trans. Henry Bettenson (London: Penguin, 1972), p. 15.

25 RMO, p. 25

26 Ibid., p. 88

27 Ibid., p. 90.

28 Ibid., p.113

29 Ibid. As we shall see later, O'Donovan's account of conversion is commensurate with his account of justification and election. Conversion constitutes the re-directing of the human will and knowledge to their ontological justification and fulfilment in Christ.

30 For a positive assessment of MacIntyre's notion of 'epistemological crises' in relation to resolving disputes between Christians and non-Christians see Stanley Hauerwas, 'The Non-Violent Terrorist: In Defence of Christian Fanaticism', in *Sanctify Them in the Truth* (Edinburgh: T&T Clark, 1998), pp. 183–87.

31 WJ, p. 157.

32 Oliver O'Donovan, 'What Can Ethics Know About God?', *The Doctrine of God and Theological Ethics*, eds Alan Torrance and Michael Banner (Edinburgh: T&T Clark, forthcoming).

33 Oliver O'Donovan, 'Moral Disagreement as an Ecumenical Issue', SCE, 1.1 (1988), 5–19.

34 Ibid., p. 16.

35 For O'Donovan's systematic account of moral reason see Oliver O'Donovan, 'Christian Moral Reasoning', in *New Dictionary of Christian Ethics and Pastoral Theology*, eds David Atkinson and David Field (Leicester: Inter-Varsity Press, 1995), pp. 122–27.

36 O'Donovan, 'What Can Ethics Know About God?', p. 6. Cf. Oliver O'Donovan, *On the 39 Articles: A Conversation with Tudor Christianity* (Carlisle: Paternoster Press, 1986), p. 8 and p. 14. In this book there is an inherent respect for tradition as a proper and worthy conversation partner in the discernment of truth in relation to the presuppositions of a particular community. The necessity of engaging with the past is explicitly seen in O'Donovan's political theology, a central feature of which is the recovery and retrieval of the history and tradition of Christian political theology so that the Church can faithfully address the contemporary context fully armed with the wisdom of millennia of experience and reflection.

37 RMO, p. 127

38 O'Donovan, 'What Can Ethics Know About God?'.

39 RMO, p. 132

40 Ibid., p. 143.

41 Kathryn Tanner clarifies this point in relation to doctrine when she states: 'What is unusual about Jesus – what sets him off from other people – is his relationship to God (his relationship to the Word who assumes his humanity as its own), the shape of his way of life (as the exhibition of the triune life on a human level), and his effects on others (his saving significance). Jesus is not then distinct from others in any way that would jeopardize his human nature. His human nature is simply human; what is different is its source – Jesus lives in so far as he is God's own – and its concrete shape or mode.' Kathryn Tanner, *Jesus, Humanity and the Trinity* (Edinburgh: T&T Clark, 2001), p. 20.

42 RMO, p. 163
43 Ibid., p. 102
44 Ibid., p. 103
45 Ibid., p. 104.
46 Ibid., p. 165
47 Ibid., p. 199. Cf., Colin Gunton, *The One, The Three and The Many: God, Creation and the Culture of Modernity, The 1992 Bampton Lectures* (Cambridge: Cambridge University Press, 1993), pp. 206–209.
48 RMO, p. 156.
49 Ibid., p. 168
50 Colin Gunton, *A Brief Theology of Revelation* (Edinburgh: T&T Clark, 1995), p. 103.
51 *Desire*, p. 287.
52 Ibid., p. 288.
53 Cf., RMO, p. 222.
54 John Milbank, *Theology and Social Theory: Beyond Secular Reason* (Oxford: Basil Blackwell, 1990), p. 339.
55 Michael Banner, 'Turning the World Upside Down – and Some Other Tasks for Dogmatic Christian Ethics', in *Christian Ethics and Contemporary Moral Problems* (Cambridge: Cambridge University Press, 1999), pp. 42–43.
56 Ibid., p. 43. For the clearest statement of this position in MacIntyre's work see Alasdair MacIntyre, 'Moral Relativism, Truth and Justification', in Knight, *The MacIntyre Reader*. See also Mark Kingwell, *A Civil Tongue: Justice, Dialogue and the Politics of Pluralism* (Pennsylvania: Pennsylvania State University Press, 1995), p. 131.
57 Milbank, *Theology and Social Theory*, p. 344.
58 David Fergusson, *Community, Liberalism and Christian Ethics* (Cambridge: Cambridge University Press, 1998), pp. 109–37.
59 Ibid., pp. 131–37
60 WJ, p. 397
61 Miroslav Volf, *Exclusion and Embrace: A Theological Exploration of Identity, Otherness, and Reconciliation* (Nashville: Abingdon Press, 1996), p. 209.
62 Ibid., p. 207. Stout makes a similar observation: cf., Jeffrey Stout, 'Homeward Bound: MacIntyre on Liberal Society and the History of Ethics', *Journal of Religion*, 69 (1989), pp. 230–31.
63 Fergusson, *Community, Liberalism and Christian Ethics*, p. 135. This is contrary to Milbank's view as stated above. Milbank sees MacIntyre as closer to Aristotle than Aquinas in method and content.
64 Ibid.
65 For references to the direct influence of MacIntyre on Hauerwas see: Stanley Hauerwas, *The Peaceable Kingdom: A Primer in Christian Ethics* (Notre Dame: University of Notre Dame Press, 1983), p. xxv, p. xiii; p. xix; and there are a further seven strategic references to MacIntyre's work in this book. He admits his debt to MacIntyre in Stanley Hauerwas and Charles Pinches, *Christians Among the Virtues: Theological Conversations with Ancient and Modern Ethics* (Notre Dame: University of Notre Dame Press, 1997), p. 60, and makes substantive use of MacIntyre's work elsewhere in the book. See also Stanley Hauerwas, 'Medicine as Tragic Profession', in *Truthfulness and Tragedy: Further Investigations into Christian Ethics* (Notre Dame: University of Notre Dame Press, 1977) where Hauerwas makes use of MacIntyre's earlier work. More recently Hauerwas discusses the influence of MacIntyre on his own thought in *Performing the Faith: Bonhoeffer and the Practices of Nonviolence* (London: SPCK, 2004),

pp. 215–40. The connection between Huaerwas and MacIntyre is made by numerous commentators on Hauerwas's work. See, for example, Joseph Woodill, *The Fellowship of Life: Virtue Ethics and Orthodox Christianity* (Washington DC: Georgetown University Press, 1998), pp. 5–6. Hauerwas gives an account of how they differ, especially in their respective accounts of the relationship between philosophy and theology, in Stanley Hauerwas, *With the Grain of the Universe* (London: SCM Press, 2002), pp. 18–26.

66 Hauerwas and Pinches, *Christians Among the Virtues*, p. 118.
67 Hauerwas, *Performing the Faith*, p. 233.
68 *Desire*, p. 251.
69 Douglas Farrow, 'St Irenaeus of Lyons. The Church and the World', *Pro Ecclesia* 4 (1995), p. 348.
70 RMO, p. 85.

71 Ibid., p. 64. From a Jewish perspective, Michael Wyschogrod, draws the same kind of contrast, noting the transformation of nature God brings about is not evolutionary but apocalyptic. He states: 'It is a transformation that is discontinuous with nature as it has been. It envisages a break with the autonomy of nature brought about by God's intervention and not by working itself out of the *telos* of nature.' Michael Wyschogrod, *The Body of Faith: God in the People of Israel* (San Francisco: Harper and Row, 1983), p. 226.

72 John Zizioulas, *Being as Communion: Studies in Personhood and the Church* (New York: St Vladimir's Seminary Press, 1985), p. 180.

73 O'Donovan, *On the 39 Articles,* p. 80.
74 Ibid., p. 81.
75 Ibid., p. 83.
76 Tanner, *Jesus, Humanity and the Trinity*, p. 68.
77 AV, p. 263
78 DRA, p. 145.

79 See Marshall Berman, *All That is Solid Melts into Air: The Experience of Modernity* (London: Verso, 1983), pp. 72–74; and David Harvey, *The Condition of Post-Modernity: An Enquiry into the Origins of Cultural Change.* (Oxford: Blackwell, 1993), pp. 14–15.

80 *Desire*, pp. 233–34; and for his critique of utopianism see: *Desire*, pp. 228–29.
81 Milbank, *Theology and Social Theory*, pp. 352-3.
82 Hauerwas and Pinches, *Christians Among the Virtues*, p. 63.
83 Ibid., p. 65.
84 Ibid., p. 67.

PART II
THE NATURE AND SHAPE OF CHRISTIAN HOSPITALITY

CHAPTER 4

Local politics, ecclesiology and resisting modernity

The central question that has surfaced is, how can a 'thick' account of Christian ethics resolve disputes with similarly thick accounts in other traditions while retaining its own distinctively Christian criteria for evaluating moral claims? On the basis of the comparison between MacIntyre and O'Donovan we have seen that a theologically specified account of ethics cannot vindicate itself against its rivals on the basis of its philosophical cogency alone. However, what began to emerge, and what I will analyse more closely in this chapter, is how Christians and non-Christians may share an *ad hoc* commensurability in relation to their social practices.

The differences between O'Donovan and MacIntyre lead to very different conceptions of how, in practice, Christians are to relate to non-Christians. MacIntyre proposes both a way for the Christian tradition to relate to other traditions, and a response to the contemporary context. Earlier we noted that MacIntyre has a first order theory of traditions and a meta-theory of how different traditions relate. In addition to determining his conception of how Christians can relate to non-Christians, they form the basis of MacIntyre's suggested response to the contemporary context. MacIntyre proposes that particular traditions should form communities of resistance in which the practices and rationality of that particular tradition can be lived out and the dominant, incoherent patterns of moral discourse in the contemporary context can be resisted. These communities of resistance can then engage in forms of 'local politics' that are just and rational. This form of 'local politics' allows for the kind of conversation and convergence between traditions that MacIntyre sees as crucial to resolving disputes between different traditions. In the light of MacIntyre's conception of Christianity as a tradition in relation to other traditions and his suggested response to the contemporary context, a model of Christian and non-Christian relations can be constructed.

As attention is focused on MacIntyre's practical suggestions for how Christians might respond to the contemporary context and structure relations with their non-Christian neighbours, a number of problems that were touched on in the last chapter are clarified. These problems centre on giving an account of how Christianity can retain its distinctive criteria of evaluation yet at the same time have an *ad hoc* commensurability at the level of its social practices. The tension between the incommensurability of criteria of evaluation and the inherent overlap of social practices between Christians and non-Christians establishes a paradox. MacIntyre argues for the possibility of philosophical convergence of tradition yet the model of practice he suggests is characterised by conflict and rivalry. The reverse is true for

O'Donovan. For O'Donovan there can be no ultimate theoretical convergence. However, at the level of social practice and 'penultimate goods'[1] there can be a great deal of convergence between Christians and non-Christians.

I analyse this paradox by comparing MacIntyre's conception of local politics with O'Donovan's account of relations between Christians and non-Christians. It is ecclesiology that frames O'Donovan's account of relations between Christians and non-Christians. It is framed in these terms because, while acknowledging the role tradition plays in enabling people to know revelation, O'Donovan understands there to be more involved than just tradition. Christians do not structure their relations with non-Christians simply in terms of how the Christian tradition relates to other traditions. The primary category for thinking about relations between Christians and non-Christians is 'the church'. O'Donovan helps us determine the relationship between Christian ethics and ecclesiology, for his ecclesiology relates directly to his conception of Christian ethical thought and action and how it is distinct from non-Christian thought and action. An analysis can then be given of how, within a theological framework, Christians relate to non-Christians, and thus how MacIntyre's model of such relations is contrary to this.

Local politics and resisting modernity

In the light of his critique of post-Enlightenment thought and its embodiment in capitalist, liberal democratic states, MacIntyre proposes some strategies of resistance. In effect, he proposes a politics of the local community. He sees the renewal of contemporary social, economic and political structures as emerging from local reflection and local political structures. This is in accord with the initial emergence of political thought via local traditions of practice and MacIntyre's substantive theory that all rational thought and justice must be rooted in a particular tradition. It makes sense, therefore, to seek to build up a conception of the common good from particular, local social and political embodiments of such a conception. Furthermore, MacIntyre has little invested in the continuation of the modern nation-state, which can never, by its very nature, constitute the context for shared deliberative rationality about the common good. Indeed, 'insofar as the rhetoric of the nation-state presents itself as the provider of something that is indeed ... a common good, that rhetoric is a purveyor of dangerous fictions.'[2] It is only in the context of local communities that a common good can be rationally deliberated upon, an approximation of justice secured, and that the requisite virtues of acknowledged dependence and independent practical reason might be nurtured.

Contrary to what some critics have asserted, MacIntyre's emphasis on the politics of the local community does not constitute a withdrawal into 'sectarian' ghettos and an abdicating of engagement with and responsibility for wider society.[3] Rather, such local embodiments of conceptions of the good seek, and are the source of, universal conceptions of the common good that can then be generalized as visions for the wider society. Furthermore, through maintaining or developing such local embodiments, one is sustaining models of what justice should consist of and what rational debate about the common good involves. Even prior to the adoption of a particular conception of the common good by the wider society, particular policies can be advocated more generally as true and good policies, since they have been tested and lived out within the politics of the local community.

There will inevitably be dealings between local communities and both the state and the wider market economy. Any local community will have to concern itself with, and secure resources from, the nation-state and national and international markets. The question is whether this can be done at a price acceptable to the local community.[4] There will also come times when such communities must align themselves with a particular party in order to defeat such politically destructive forces as those of imperialism, or Nazism, or Stalinist communism.[5] However, the primary relations between the politics of the local community and contemporary wider society, structured as it is to support the state and capitalism, will be one of conflict, for 'the state and the market economy are so structured as to subvert and undermine the politics of local community'.[6]

The basis of this conflict is clarified by MacIntyre's critique and response to the economic order of advanced capitalism. It should be noted that MacIntyre is not against a market economy *per se*. Rather, as he puts it:

> Market relationships can only be sustained by being embedded in certain types of local nonmarket relationships, relationships of uncalculating giving and receiving, if they are to contribute to overall flourishing, rather than, as they so often in fact do, undermine and corrupt communal ties.[7]

In effect, MacIntyre is against any economic order that is structured to pursue the goods of effectiveness to the exclusion and detriment of the goods of excellence. He is thus as opposed to the centrally planned economies of Communist states as he is to capitalism. However, the issue MacIntyre does draw from Marx is the question of the relationship between so-called free markets and the atomization of society and thus the eroding of local communities and ties of reciprocity. MacIntyre seeks an economic order that is not inherently individualistic and unjust, but one that enables reciprocal patterns of sociality characterized by justice (that is, people being treated as they deserve according to their contribution) and generosity (that is, more than justice requires is given).[8] While recognizing that justice will always be imperfect, he states:

> Between independent practical reasoners the norms [of a just society] will have to satisfy Marx's formula for justice in a socialist society, according to which what each receives is proportionate to what each contributes. Between those capable of giving and those who are most dependent and in most need of receiving – children, the old, the disabled – the norms will have to satisfy a revised version of Marx's formula for justice in a communist society, 'From each according to her or his ability, to each, so far as is possible, according to her or his needs.'[9]

MacIntyre envisages – and at this point many would accuse him of being a Luddite – an economic order based around small-scale producers. He states: 'Genuinely free markets are always local and small-scale markets in whose exchanges producers can choose to participate or not.'[10] He recognizes that such a society probably could not achieve the levels of economic and technological sophistication of advanced modernity. However, to refuse this is not irrational; it is to opt in favour of a different conception of the common good. He states: 'The conflict between the kinds of local community that I have been characterizing and the international and national economic order is at the level of practice, as well as that of theory, a conflict between rival conceptions of the common good.'[11]

MacIntyre's call for a politics of the local community is not a call, as some have supposed, for establishing communities that exclude dissent and are inherently oppressive.[12] Nothing MacIntyre envisages precludes the existence of individuals and groups who hold radically different conceptions of the common good and who are different from others in the community. Rather, MacIntyre thinks:

> What will be important to such a society, if it holds the kind of view of the human good and the common good that I have outlined, will be to ask what can be learned from such dissenters. It will therefore be crucial not only to tolerate dissent, but also to enter into rational conversation with it and to cultivate as a political virtue not merely passive tolerance, but an active and enquiring attitude towards dissenting views, a virtue notably absent from the dominant politics of the present.[13]

MacIntyre substantiates this argument in *Dependent Rational Animals* where he grounds toleration on the relationship between justice, practical rationality and the virtues necessary for both. He makes the case that while the practices of giving and receiving are exercised primarily in relation to members of one's own community and social networks, justice requires extending this to those who are 'other' for two reasons. First, we owe hospitality to the stranger in our midst, and second, we must practise the virtue of *misericordia*: that is, the regard for the urgent and extreme need of those outside one's immediate community.[14] The practice of hospitality and what is in effect love of neighbour is learnt by due care of the disabled and dependent within one's own community. It is through encounters with them that we discover errors both in our own practical reason and in the norms of our community.[15] Therefore, it is through encountering difference – not the difference of some abstract 'Other' but the particular differences of concrete persons – that errors in the shared deliberative reasoning of any given community are discovered. And thus the community is better able to transform its reasoning and practices so as to enable all its members to flourish and all its relations, both within and with those outside the community, to be characterized by just generosity. Conversely, MacIntyre recognizes that the politics of local community is not good *per se*. He states: 'Local communities are always open to corruption by narrowness, by complacency, by prejudice against outsiders and by a whole range of other deformities.'[16] These arise when the virtues of just generosity and of shared deliberation are absent.

The politics of the local community seems to involve a threefold dynamic. There is, first, a partial withdrawal from public debates as currently conducted; second, a simultaneous renewal of emphasis on demonstrations of particular conceptions of the common good in practice, and third, an engagement with the politics of local community wherein the reform of practices; and institutions can take place through rational debate between rival communities of resistance. Within the societies of advanced modernity this politics of the local community will take many forms. Embodiments of particular conceptions of the common good can be anything from a church, to household farms, to schools, and businesses which do not subsume the goods of excellence to the goods of effectiveness.[17] MacIntyre states: 'We need to *show* as well as to say what an adequate conception of justice amounts to, by constructing the types of institutionalised social relationships within which it becomes visible.'[18] However, to construct such embodiments requires engaging in co-operative enterprises with those whose point of view is very different. Thus, disagreements will be formulated in concrete terms as we make and remake schools, clinics, workplaces, and other institutions. MacIntyre notes:

> At this level, such disagreements will be local and specific, concerned with the ends and thus the goods of particular types of policy, practice, and institution.... Thus, it is in the actualities and complexities of practice that we shall be able to find opportunities of a kind generally denied to us in the larger arenas of public debate.[19]

Hence the politics of local community involves an active engagement with concrete practices and institutions in a particular area with a constituent element of such engagement involving embodying in a church, or some other association, the particular conception of the common good we advocate.[20]

Many theologians, for example, Stanley Hauerwas, follow something like MacIntyre's model of local politics. This is because it recovers the importance of the Christian community by placing it at the centre of distinctive Christian witness and engagement with the contemporary context. I shall now develop MacIntyre's implicit, normative model of relations between Christians and non-Christians within the contemporary context. An assessment can then be given as to whether this attention to MacIntyre's work by a number of theologians is indeed justified.

MacIntyre's conception of relations between Christians and non-Christians

I have discussed how MacIntyre envisages different traditions to be incommensurable, and how, given the right conditions this incommensurability might be overcome. An example of this is a dialogue between Confucianism and Thomism.[21] However, within the context of late modernity such conditions are unlikely to prevail anywhere except at a local level and in a small scale way. Hence, in the contemporary context it is necessary to establish communities of resistance which together can engage in a rational form of local politics. For MacIntyre, the Christian community can be just such a community of resistance.

There are three ways in which MacIntyre envisages relations between Christian and non-Christians to be structured. At a fundamental level, both Christians and non-Christians operate within a 'teleologically ordered ... theistic universe'. Within this universe natural law is the basic condition of rational deliberation and just relations. Whether people adhere to natural law or not, it is natural law which sets the context of relations between traditions. However, and this brings us to the second aspect of relations between Christians and non-Christians within MacIntyre's framework, natural law and beyond that, the understanding of the universe as theistic, can only be arrived at from within a particular tradition. Thus MacIntyre rejects natural theology or any notion of a universal rationality (although, as we have seen, there is some ambiguity about this). The Christian tradition, and its institutional embodiments, will encounter other traditions, each with its own conception of the ultimate good. While Christianity will be incommensurable with these other traditions, rational adjudication between them is possible along the lines set out in MacIntyre's meta-theory. MacIntyre himself provides a model of this adjudication process in his discussion of how Aquinas synthesized Christianity with Aristotelianism. Relations between Christians and non-Christians will be dialectical and agonistic as Christianity seeks to vindicate itself as more rational and just than its rivals. Its relations will thus be inherently conflictual: that is, they will be characterized by rivalry, even if they are not relations of enmity.

This clash of traditions is only possible at a local level within the contemporary context because liberalism dominates public discourse and suppresses all other rivals, including Christianity. Furthermore, the bureaucratic nation-state, and the dominant economic order, actively militates against the faithful practice of Christianity, and thus Christians *qua* Christians will find themselves in hostile relations with these wider structures. This necessitates Christians forming an alternative *polis* within the context of modern, liberal, capitalist nation-state, and local Christian communities constituting communities of resistance. However, as communities of resistance they will not seek their own welfare, but the 'welfare of the city' (that is the common good), by (in the long term) enabling public debate to be more rational and the practice of politics and economics to be truly just. While open to national and international politics and economics, such a quest will of necessity operate at the local level where just and rational deliberation between different conceptions of the common good is still possible. As communities of resistance Christian communities will preserve a form of life where degrees of justice and rational debate may be known. This activity is akin to how the monasteries preserved the same during the last 'dark ages'.

Ecclesiology and resolving ethical disputes

The question arises as to whether this model of how Christians relate to non-Christians is true to the presuppositions of Christianity. In other words, given O'Donovan's critique of the epistemological basis of MacIntyre's conception of Christian thought and action, it must be asked of MacIntyre's model whether it properly takes into account the ground on which Christian ethical thought and action stand: that is, does he pay sufficient heed to the self-revelation of God given in Jesus Christ? It is my contention that while the model MacIntyre establishes of local politics is very compelling, it requires significant modification in the light of a theological account of how Christians and non-Christians should relate when ethical disputes arise.

The church is more than just a tradition

As we saw in the last chapter, O'Donovan, while largely agreeing with MacIntyre's diagnosis of the contemporary context, has a conception of Christian thought and action and how it relates to non-Christian thought and action that is explicitly formulated in response to the revelation of God given in Jesus Christ. While acknowledging the role tradition plays in enabling people to know revelation, O'Donovan understands there to be more involved than just tradition. It is at this point that questions about ecclesiology arise.

Up until now the question of how Christians resolve ethical disputes with non-Christians in the contemporary context has been addressed in terms of how the Christian tradition relates to other traditions. However, by moving towards the point at which we must describe relations between Christians and non-Christians in practical and explicitly theological terms, we must take account of ecclesiology. Christians do not structure their relations with non-Christians simply in terms of how the Christian tradition relates to other traditions. The primary category for thinking about relations between Christians and non-Christians is 'the church', and the church is more than a tradition. Furthermore, the terms 'the Christian tradition' and 'the church' cannot be used as synonyms for each other. 'The church', of which Christians are a part, makes a claim to be a way of being, it is an ontological category, whereas the term 'tradition' is an epistemological term. As John Zizioulas puts it:

> The Church is not simply an institution. She is a 'mode of existence,' *a way of being*. The mystery of the Church, even in its institutional dimension, is deeply bound to the being of man, to the being of the world and to the very being of God. In virtue of this bond ... ecclesiology assumes a marked importance, not only for all aspects of theology, but also for the existential needs of man in every age.[22]

A properly theological account of how Christians relate to non-Christians with regard to ethical disputes must take account of the role the church plays in such a process.

O'Donovan helps us determine the relationship between ecclesiology and how Christians handle disputes with their neighbours. His ecclesiology relates directly to his conception of Christian ethical thought and action and how it is distinct from non-Christian action. On the basis of O'Donovan's work, I will analyse how, within a theological framework, Christians relate to non-Christians, and the role of the church in determining these relations, and thus how this contrasts with MacIntyre's model of such relations. However, in order to analyse the relationship between ecclesiology and how Christians manage disputes with their neighbours it is necessary to establish a definition of what O'Donovan means by the term 'the church'.

O'Donovan's ecclesiology

O'Donovan has a threefold definition of the church. It is first, the invisible, universal body of Christ, including all the elect, past and present. Second, it is the pre-structural, visible, catholic church, made up of all those who profess the Christian faith and order their lives towards God. O'Donovan states: 'The shape of the pre-structured church, then, is the shape of the Christ-event become the dynamics of a social identity'.[23] Third, it is the particular congregations and institutional arrangements and orders that are expressions of this pre-structural, visible reality.[24] Any particular 'form' of the church has as its 'substance' the pre-structural catholic church. Thus, we should expect these particular and multifarious orders to bear generic 'marks' or 'badges' so they can be recognized as authentic signs: that is, as having a genuinely 'catholic shape'.[25] The first two dimensions of the Church are creations of, and authorized by, the Holy Spirit. The third dimension is inspired by and participates in the Holy Spirit, but is a fallen creation of humans as they seek, drawn together by the work of the Spirit, to participate in God's life in a restored and fulfilled creation, through the life, death, resurrection and ascension of Jesus Christ. Contingent and human churches (and their particular orders) are attempts to serve as witnesses to, and recapitulations of, the self-revelation of God in Jesus Christ. In short, the Church is the community of those redeemed and reconciled to God in which everything is done for the sake of God (and in this lies its unity), through the death and resurrection of Jesus Christ (its only head and authority) and in the power of the Holy Spirit (its strength and guide).

The Church is not to be equated with the Kingdom of God: to do so would be to espouse an over-realized eschatology. However, it is through the actions of the church that human life and culture participate in their transformation or transfiguration. This transfiguration is not a linear development through time in some historicist fashion, but is a 'battle' between redeemed creation directed towards and anticipating its perfection and rebellious and fallen creation. Neither is this transfiguration a supplanting of what already exists; rather, it is a radical transformation of it. The pattern for this transfiguration is given at the Last Supper: Christ did not provide some alien token to remember and anticipate him by, nor did he take pristine grain and grapes; instead, he took bread and wine, the products of human labour and creativity and transformed them into an anticipation of their eschatological fulfilment.[26]

Ecclesiology as a fundamental category in Christian ethics

Given this definition of the church the question arises as to how the church structures the life together and moral thought and action of Christians. This question is vital because the life together of Christians as the church is central to truthful witness; it is thus a central element of how Christians relate to their neighbours. As discussed in relation to MacIntyre, social practices are constitutive of any traditioned ethics. They are thus one of the primary means by which Christians encounter and engage their context. For example, while many social practices – such as keeping the Lord's Day – are particular to Christianity, they constitute a testimony to non-Christians of the actions of the Spirit.[27] As the church – a new and specific community – encounters the world in a myriad of different ways, social practices can point to how God has reconfigured and can yet reconfigure, disordered human relations into anticipations of their eschatological fulfilment. However, as will be argued later, we should beware over-freighting social practices with significance.

The life together of Christians will take on a myriad of forms given that each culture and period of history will provide different material for Christ through the Spirit to transfigure. As noted above, no one shape, form or order can thus claim finality or permanence. Rather, the church is always following after or echoing the initiating action of the Spirit. O'Donovan states:

> The ordering of the church's life *follows* its authorisation as a 'catholic' social reality by the Holy Spirit. The catholic identity of the church derives from the progress of the Spirit's own mission. It is therefore always larger than its ordered structures, taking its shape from the new ground that the Spirit is possessing. It remains for the church's structures to catch up with this mission, to discern what the Spirit has done, and to construct such ordered links of community as will safeguard brotherly love.[28]

One may question the use of the term 'catch up' to describe the nature of the relationship between the Spirit and the Church. However, the point at issue is that the structures and practices of the church are both distinct from the work of the Spirit and validated only in relation to how they bear witness to the prior action of God.

Tentativeness about speaking of any specific marks or order for the church must be balanced with the need to describe the basic and generic shape of the Christian community if it is to be recognized as bearing truthful witness to Christ. For O'Donovan, the generic shape is modelled on the Christ-event which he conceives as the structuring principle for all ecclesiology. He states that the church 'recapitulates the Christ-event in itself, and so proclaims the Christ-event to the world.'[29] O'Donovan summarizes this dynamic thus:

> Through the Spirit the church recapitulates the whole saving event, Advent, Passion, Restoration and Exaltation. In Christ it is represented in the event; in the Spirit it participates in it. These two aspects of the one relation to the representative act confer the church's political identity upon it. Represented, it is authorised to represent Israel, the people of the Kingdom … . Participating, it is authorised to be the gathering nations, finding the new world order in the rule of Israel's God.[30]

Given that the life together of Christians as the church is central to truthful witness, the recapitulation of the Christ-event constitutes the basic shape of Christian moral thought and action. Since such thought and action necessarily involves the life together and social practices of Christians, Christian ethics necessarily involves the church.

O'Donovan identifies three basic moments to the form of the church, each of which recapitulates a moment of the Christ-event. Each of these moments has a corresponding social practice, which is in turn expressed in a sacramental way. (It is important to note that O'Donovan is not fixed on any particular number of sacraments. He identifies four sacraments – baptism, eucharist, keeping the Lord's Day, and the laying on of hands – however, this is a heuristic four, 'which helps us trace the correspondence of the church's formal acts and observances to the shape of the Christ-event'.[31]) First, in response to the Advent of Christ, the church is a gathered community, exercising particular practices of community formation as evidenced in the sacrament of baptism. Second, 'in response to the Passion of Christ the church is a suffering community engaged in conflict with the principalities and powers that Christ has overcome.'[32] This is experienced in the social practices of trial and martyrdom and is expressed in the sacrament of the eucharist. Third, the response to Christ's Exaltation is the gladness or rejoicing of the community as it celebrates the recovery of the creation order. O'Donovan speaks of practices of Christian morality as belonging to this aspect of the church's life together because it springs directly from the vindication of God's rule.[33] Keeping the Lord's Day is a sign of the church's resurrection gladness.[34] There is one further response to Christ's Exaltation, that of the community empowered by the Spirit at Pentecost. The response of the church is to be a community that speaks the words of God through the practices of prophecy and prayer. O'Donovan suggests this is symbolized in the laying on of hands which is a sign of the church's empowerment: 'By this formal means it prays for the gifts of the ascended Christ to be manifest in the service and discipleship of its particular members.'[35]

O'Donovan seems to conflate two distinct moments within his third mark, Christ's Exaltation. In my view, moment three corresponds only to Christ's resurrection. A fourth and distinct moment corresponds to Christ's ascension and the Pentecost event. I will argue later that this fourth moment is embodied in the social practice of hospitality, which has as its corresponding sacramental enactment the fasts and feasts of the church (most notably, Advent and Christmas and Lent and Easter). However, O'Donovan's overall approaches seem to move in the right direction. Each of these moments, and its corresponding social practice and sacramental enactment, structure the life of the Christian community, which is formed in response to God, in a particular way, so that it encounters and engages the world around it in a manner shaped by these moments.[36]

The relationship between the church and its neighbours

Having outlined the marks or the contours of the church and set out how the church patterns and shapes the life together of Christians, an assessment can be given of how the church *qua* church relates to its neighbours and how this pattern of relationship contrasts with an account of such relations derived from MacIntyre.

Many contemporary Christian ethicists have sought to formulate the problem of how Christians relate to and resolve disputes with non-Christians as one which concerns an encounter between distinctive social realities: the meeting of the church with the social realities of the 'nations'.[37] An example of this approach is the work of Stanley Hauerwas. There is not the scope here for a detailed account of Hauerwas's extensive output.[38] Suffice to say that Hauerwas is a good bridge between MacIntyre's approach to the problem of relations between Christians and non-Christians and one that takes account of ecclesiology. The direct influence of MacIntyre on Hauerwas was noted in the last chapter. Hauerwas follows MacIntyre's account of the contemporary context and agrees that 'modern politics is civil war carried on by other means'.[39] More recently, as we have seen, Hauerwas has criticized MacIntyre for maintaining a pagan, Aristotelian conception of the virtues; however, it is clear that MacIntyre shapes several key elements of Hauerwas's thought.[40] Fergusson discerns a distinct shift in Hauerwas's work with the publication of *A Community of Character* in 1981 where the concept of virtue is integrally related to the social concept of a practice in a manner directly equivalent to MacIntyre.[41] William Placher notes the influence of MacIntyre on Hauerwas's conception of how stories shape communities.[42] However, in contrast to MacIntyre, Hauerwas is explicitly theological in his focus and has written extensively on the importance of the church in Christian ethics. For Hauerwas, the church takes up the weapons of the Spirit and engages with the life of its neighbours non-violently, participating in the civil war of modern politics as 'resident aliens'.[43] Thus, Hauerwas states: 'Like [MacIntyre] we believe we cannot and should not avoid conflict. However, as Christians we simply cannot engage in armed conflict because of our understanding of Christian discipleship. That is to say we are Christological pacifists.'[44] For Hauerwas, even though the church can learn from the world,[45] if it is involved in anything less than antagonistic and conflictual relations with non-Christians it has become an instance of civil religion. Hauerwas seeks to recover the basis, and witness of, a critical, confessing church (of which the Anabaptist tradition is his primary model) within a context where the 'Constantinian synthesis' (that is, the co-option of the church by the political order) has broken down.[46] While the church is to be hospitable to the strangers it finds itself amongst, the distance and difference between the church and its neighbours means that its relations with non-Christians will always be, in some measure, conflictual.

An account like Hauerwas's is problematic not because conflict between Christians and non-Christians is always wrong or bad, but because conflict is not the *sine qua non* of relations between Christians and non-Christians. It should not be assumed that conflict is always, in some a priori way, negative and destructive. Conflict can be a necessary and constructive part of both social transformation and the relationship between two groups with incommensurable goals. The point at issue is whether the relationship between Christians and non-Christians is either necessarily or normatively conflictual. Hauerwas, along with many others who emphasize the importance of ecclesiology to ethics, misconceive the nature of the difference between the church and its neighbours and fail to account for how the church is inherently both like and unlike those around it. Its likeness to its neighbours is not only an issue of idolatry and unfaithfulness. While this is sometimes the case, the church can often be like the world in good and generative ways. It can also be unlike the world in negative and degenerative ways.[47] This dynamic must be accounted for theologically. It is my contention that the nature of the difference between the church and its neighbours is only properly understood eschatologically.

Hauerwas himself emphasizes the importance of eschatology for ecclesiology and ethics.[48] However, he never really develops an account of how eschatology relates to the distinctiveness of Christians and how they relate to non-Christians. The roots of this lie in the absence, in Hauerwas's ethics, of any account of the mission and person of the Holy Spirit. This is a criticism he himself has admitted. For instance, he accepts Reinhard Hütter's criticism that he lacks a properly pneumatological eschatology.[49] Hütter argues this lack leads to a deficient ecclesiology in which 'God's presence and activity in the Holy Spirit is of no decisive importance for either [Hauerwas's] ecclesiological construal or [his] ethical reflection.'[50] Samuel Wells (who has given the most systematic account of Hauerwas's work to date) also thinks that Hauerwas requires a fuller doctrine of the Holy Spirit. He argues this would enable Hauerwas to account for how God's purposes are revealed and worked out through people that do not call themselves Christian. Wells states:

> This perception is desperately needed in Hauerwas' writing, lest Christians be paralysed in their membership of other communities besides the Christian one. If the Church genuinely intends to remain committed to communities other than itself, it must be because it believes that there too God lives and reigns, and it wants to be where God is, with the people he has made for his service.[51]

Mindful of this lacunae in Hauerwas's work, I seek to articulate how a 'pneumatological eschatology' shapes the church's distinctiveness and its relations with its non-Christian neighbours.

Hauerwas's highly conflictual model of relations between Christians and non-Christians illustrates the kind of model of relations that is derived from MacIntyre's conception of how Christians and non-Christians are to relate in practice. By contrast, a model derived from O'Donovan's conception of eschatology and ecclesiology can account for both the church's distinctiveness from, and the possibility of the church sharing its life together with, its neighbours. Thus, it is not to MacIntyre but to O'Donovan we should turn for resources to think about how Christians and non-Christians should relate in the contemporary context. This does not mean we need to abandon MacIntyre. Rather, it is to suggest that MacIntyre's account of how different traditions may relate should not constitute the primary architecture for thinking about how the church relates to its neighbours.

Eschatological distinctiveness is wholly different in kind from any difference or similarity that arises as a result of tradition, ethnicity, family, culture, political allegiance or other such human and earthly bonds. There is no clear dividing line between the eschatological social reality constituted by Christ through the Spirit – borne witness to by the church – and the social realities of the church's neighbours. The Spirit is constantly bringing different social realities into relation in new ways so as to enable the possibility that all may respond gratefully to what Christ has done and be directed to the embrace of the Father. Those who have gratefully responded to Christ and live faithful to that response must follow the leading of the Spirit rather than their own arbitrary construction of what constitutes order. However, following the Spirit might well mean mimicking a seemingly non-Christian social reality. For example, Christ commends the faith of the pagan Centurion as against the faithlessness of Israel (Mt. 8:5–13). Furthermore, this reconfiguring work of the Spirit constitutes a rebuttal of any single institution or set of social relations to claim definitive status as the bearer of God's order. As Karl Barth notes, perhaps somewhat surprisingly: 'Between the community and Christians on the one side and the rest of the world on the other, there is a distinct yet not absolute, but only fluid and changing frontier.'[52]

If we cannot map any clear dividing line between Christians and non-Christians then there are a number of implications. One is that charting whether Christians and non-Christians are agreeing or disagreeing with each other (and thus whether they can or should attempt some kind of resolution) necessitates case by case evaluation rather than either establishing a system for resolution as MacIntyre does, or resigning oneself to conflict as Hauerwas does. Another implication is that, at the level of social practice, we should expect to see both convergence and divergence of practice; that is, the social practices of Christians will not, of themselves, always be distinctive from the practices of non-Christians.

While no single institutional form or set of relations can claim finality of truthful expression of God's order, we can say that the church is the place which bears witness to relationship with God through the actions of Christ and the Spirit. It is important to establish this in order to be clear about what makes the church distinctive. Contrary to Hauerwas's position, it is not the social practices of the church in and of themselves that distinguish Christians from non-Christians (although these will often be different).[53] As Nicholas Healy points out, repeated performance of behaviour patterns do not, of themselves, 'issue in the right formation of church members nor the acquisition of Christian virtues.'[54] In other words, identifiably Christian actions may be a necessary component of what makes Christians different from their neighbours, but they are not sufficient in and of themselves. It is the nature of the relationship between the church and God that is decisive in specifying how the church is different from other communities: that is, distinctiveness lies in how God is present to and within the church. Distinctiveness does not *necessarily* lie in what the church looks like or does. This is clarified and affirmed in Paul's epistles. For example, in 1 Corinthians, Paul calls the Corinthians to ensure that their institutional arrangements and social practices bear faithful witness to the actions of Christ and the Spirit. He is concerned in the letter about disunity and disorder in the life together of the community, especially in its public, communal acts of testimony. For Paul, the church is the place where transfigured relations should be experienced.[55] For this body, in Paul's eyes, has taken the place of the Jerusalem Temple as the place where God resides by His Spirit.[56] The church is a 'pneumatic place' where humans are incorporated into the ascended body of Christ and experience and bear witness to the in-breaking new creation.[57] As Gordon Fee puts it in relation to Paul's discussion of how the church is the 'new temple' in Ephesians 2:18–22:

> Here is the ultimate fulfilment of the imagery of God's presence, begun but lost in the Garden, restored in the tabernacle in Exodus 40 and in the temple in 1 Kings 8. It is God's own presence among us that marks us off as the people of God and, in the language of Moses, is 'what distinguishes [us] from all the other people on the face of the earth' (Exod. 33:15). So not only do we have access to the presence of God (v.18), but God himself by the Spirit has chosen to be present in our world in the gathered church.[58]

Hence, the presence of God in the church directly relates to the distinctiveness of the church from its neighbours. In short, it is the ontology of the church (constituted by relations with God) which make the church distinct as a community from other communities. God is at work in all creation, and all may be justified in Christ; however, before the *parousia*, it is given particularly to the church to be the witness to, and the place of, transfigured social relations.[59]

There is a twofold aspect to how the ontology of the church constitutes its specificity. The church is both fashioned out of the world, and hence is like the world, and yet it is fashioned in response to the Word of God, and therefore, is unlike the world. Barth clarifies this twofold dynamic when he states that:

> God's omnipotent Word ... cannot be hindered by the obvious secularity of all human forms of society from creating within these a society which in the first instance is not distinct from them, yet which is still this specific society, the people of God, the Christian community, nor can it be prevented from maintaining, accompanying and ruling this society as such. And, as it can use the secular possibilities of human speech, to establish this particular society it can use the secular possibilities of social structuring, not changing them essentially

nor divesting them of their secularism, but giving to them as they are a new meaning and determination. ... This is what actually takes place in the power of this Word. Intrinsically unholy possibilities in the structuring of man's life in society are sanctified and made serviceable to the gathering and upbuilding of the people of God in the service of its commission and for the purpose of its election and calling.[60]

The reconfiguring of the Spirit enables the 'intrinsically unholy possibilities' of human forms of sociality and language to become generative, proleptic disclosures of eschatological patterns of human sociality. As stated above, there is no definitive or single pattern of sociality that can be the bearer of God's order. Thus, throughout human history, the church will necessarily take many forms and find itself both like and unlike all human cultures. Consequently, unlike (for example) Islam, Christianity does not have a definitive language. Rather, it is free to make use of all languages. And unlike (for example) Parsees, Christianity does not relate to only one particular cultural-linguistic group.[61] Scripture bears witness to how God's action draws a multiplicity of cultures into a single salvation history and elects a particular people whose life together, while specific and particular, is constituted by the transfiguring of other cultures.[62] A paradigmatic example of this transfiguring process at work is David's act of using a city (created by Cain and, as Augustine and others have argued, the paradigmatic embodiment of human alienation from God), and moreover, a pagan city, Jebus, as the basis of Jerusalem, a place where God's glory resided.[63] To use a picture from the New Testament, the water from stone jars becomes the wine at the wedding feast through the transfiguring actions of Jesus Christ empowered by the Spirit. Of course, the use of such biblical analogies is to do no more than point to the basis of the doctrine of the Incarnation: the matter from which the Spirit fashions a body for the Son is the same matter as that which constitutes the persons of other, fallen, human beings, and the perfect life of obedience to the Father that the Spirit enables the Son to live is a life lived within and through the fallen society of a particular social, political and economic context and the sinful relations therein.

The eschatological specificity of the church means that Christians will be both like and unlike non-Christians. The actions of God in transfiguring 'intrinsically unholy possibilities' means that relations between Christians and non-Christians must necessarily involve Christians sharing in and enjoying non-Christian social realities that have been transfigured. If non-Christians are not enjoying the eschatological anticipations of their social realities, the church will need to bear witness to what such anticipations may look like and present the opportunity for non-Christians to participate in them (whether they become Christians or not). It will not always be clear whether any given social reality is or is not 'Christian' *per se*, since its status as an eschatological anticipation is entirely dependent on the actions of what Irenaeus refers to as the 'two hands of God', that is, Jesus Christ and the Holy Spirit. It is, therefore, more helpful to talk of the 'specificity' of the church, rather than its 'distinctiveness'. As Yoder points out: 'To be "specific" is to belong to one's species, to befit one's kind. That will not always involve being different [or distinct], although the cases where it "makes a difference" will be the decisive ones.'[64]

We have already noted how the Christian tradition constitutes the concrete accretion, in Scripture, social practices and doctrine, of redeemed humanity's response to Christ, empowered by the Spirit. However, the church (as distinct from the Christian tradition) is constituted by the living and active presence of God. Therefore, in the light of my analysis of the church, it is insufficient to remain with MacIntyre's conception of the problem of moral plurality in terms of how one tradition relates to another.

Resolving disputes and the place of social practices

It is at this point that something of MacIntyre's own substantive theory, with its focus on practices and virtue, can be recovered. Especially its emphasis on the embodied and participatory nature of moral formation and decision-making. As the previous discussion of ontology suggests, it is only by participation in direct relationship with God and patterns of sociality (that is, social practices) that are faithful responses to, and orientated towards, God, that non-Christians might come to accept the whole response of Christians to moral issues.[65] Conversely, through the participation of non-Christians (who are coming into relationship with God) in Christian practices Christians will have their own approach questioned. This questioning opens up established patterns of Christian sociality to revision, and Christians' responses to moral issues to further specification. The emphasis here is not on philosophical prowess but on the nature of the relationships in which a person is participating.

Christians may share with MacIntyre the conviction that the renewal of contemporary social, economic and political structures will emerge from local reflection and local political structures. It even makes sense for Christians to institute this renewal by building up particular and local political and social embodiments of conceptions of the common good. This is in accord with MacIntyre's statement that: 'We need to *show* as well as to say what an adequate conception of justice amounts to, by constructing the types of institutionalised social relationships within which it becomes visible.'[66] To construct such visible embodiments will require Christians to engage in co-operative enterprises with those whose point of view is very different. However, this co-operation can never be conducted either on the basis of a common philosophy or be seen as an opportunity to prove the philosophical worth of the Christian tradition. Rather, Christians will enter into such shared enterprises on the basis that they are participating in patterns of thought and action directed to the Father, through Christ and in the power of the Spirit.

Eschatology and the nature of Christian distinctiveness

Despite the emphasis on common enterprises, MacIntyre's vision of local politics must, given his meta-theory, necessarily involve something like a jousting tournament of competing communities of resistance. The Christian community cannot participate in such a tournament. As already stated, the church is both fashioned out of the world, and hence is like the world, and yet it is fashioned in response to the Word of God, and hence is unlike the world. Therefore, despite their distinctive criteria of moral evaluation, when it comes to moral actions and social practices Christians will find themselves enjoying an *ad hoc* commensurability with their neighbours. This *ad hoc* commensurability is grounded in the reality not only of Christians sharing the same moral field as their neighbours, but also of the work of the Spirit breaking the eschatological reality in among all people everywhere. On the basis of O'Donovan's eschatology and ecclesiology stated above, I analyse now what the implications of this *ad hoc* commensurability are for relations between Christians and non-Christians.

The nature of the difference between Christians and non-Christians

There is still the remaining problem of how the church can be a distinctive community with its own criteria of evaluation, while, simultaneously, many of its social and moral practices converge with those of its neighbours. It is to this problem that I now turn through an assessment of what eschatological specificity entails.

The life together of Christians is specific in a unique way. Prior to conversion, a Christian might be similar to, or distinct from, their neighbour at any level of identity. After conversion, any similarity or difference is called into question since ethnic, familial, political and all other identities are relativized. A new distance arises between the Christian and non-Christian. Hence the Biblical leitmotif of Christians being 'aliens' and 'sojourners'. The metaphor 'sojourner' or '*perigrinus*' is a powerful one because it sums up central themes from scripture and expresses some fundamental perspectives about the problem of the identity and difference of the People of God from their neighbours.[67] This sense of being a stranger is perhaps best expressed in the term 'pilgrim'.[68] Augustine summarizes the implications of this as follows:

> The Church proceeds, a pilgrim, in these evil days, not merely since the time of the bodily presence of Christ and his apostles, but since Abel himself, the first righteous man, whom his impious brother killed, and from then on until the end of time, among the persecutions of the world, and the consolations of God.[69]

The difference between Christians and non-Christians is at heart an eschatological one. In the midst of the world in which Christians live, they are given a new home that God has established. New birth commences the journey to this new home; however, the journey does not lead away from where they live, it leads them to the epicentre of their former home, for the house of God, although distinct from the world, is bursting the bounds of, and being erected in the midst of, their old home. The church is distinct from its culture, yet it belongs to its culture: it is in the world but not of the world. As at Pentecost, the differences of indigenous cultures are not erased but reconfigured into a unity given of the Spirit.[70] Differentiation and distance from where we 'belong', or what determines our identity, no longer requires an actual geographic move, as it did for Abraham and the Israelites in Egypt, nor a cultural separation either *from* society, as it did for the Essenes, or *within* society as the Pharisees proposed.[71] Neither does it involve building a new home through force of arms and the practice of a politics that is shaped by the 'principalities and powers' as it did for the Zealots, nor the erasing of all existing patterns and traditions of social life in order to start afresh, as various utopians have demanded. And lastly, it does not involve simply performing the right rituals and saying the right words, while settling for the status quo, as it did for the Sadducees. Rather, Genesis is recapitulated so that out of the chaos comes a new creation.[72] It is through the cosmogonic recapitulation of Jesus Christ that we are *born again* out of our existent chaos and disorder: however, this very chaos, that is, our degenerate patterns of sociality, is the very stuff of our new life. It is thus a departure-*in*-the-midst-of and not a departure-*from*-the-midst-of a culture. In other words, being good, pure, holy and moral cannot be secured either by *withdrawal* from our culture, or *assimilation* to it. To withdraw from its cultural context is to deny what the church is reconstituted from, while to be assimilated by its cultural context is to deny what the church is becoming. Hence, we must neither deny our cultural inheritance, nor over-freight it with significance. Neither can we deny the cultural inheritance of others nor over-freight another's culture with significance. The Christian cannot turn against her cultural background in self-hatred, neither can she revel in it as the apogee of civilization. Instead, as someone who has been through the death and new birth of baptism and thus actively participates in the recapitulation of all creation by Jesus Christ, the Christian finds herself in a relation with her neighbours of both distance and belonging. In sum, the thought and action of the church and its members, which proclaims and bears witness to the Gospel, is neither totally alien to any culture (it is not inevitably incommensurable with other traditions) nor is it simply another version of what they already know (it is not self-evident). Therefore, when faced with moral problems, Christians will, depending on the problem, find themselves at times converging with the social practices of their neighbours, and at other times diverging from the practices of their non-Christian neighbours.

The ad hoc *commensurability between the moral and social practices of Christians and non-Christians*

Relations between Christians and non-Christians must account for this eschatological specificity and the patterns of life it entails. As Volf points out:

> Christians do not come into their social world from outside seeking either to accommodate to their new home (like second generation immigrants would), shape it in the image of the one they have left behind (like colonizers would), or establish a little haven in the strange new world reminiscent of the old (as resident aliens would). They are not outsiders who either seek to become insiders

or maintain strenuously the status of outsiders ... Christian difference is therefore not an insertion of something new into the old from outside, but a bursting out of the new *precisely within the proper space of the old*.[73]

The church does not become a self-contained culture; hence, it is not just another culture among many.[74] Instead, the church, and its practices, is the paradigmatic sign of a given culture's redemption through the sacrifice and priesthood of Jesus Christ. The church is to be a people invested with the character of the gospel, which is simultaneously to bear witness to how a given culture may be eschatologically fulfilled.[75] Therefore, Christians cannot stand outside their environment, or against others, but must participate in their wider culture and the enterprises of their neighbours as those transfigured. In this age, no clear dividing lines can be identified between Christians and non-Christians; all such division will only become clear at the *eschaton*. There can be no strongly delineated clash of cultures or civilizations;[76] rather, questions about what to reject and what to retain confront Christians constantly as they participate in God's transfiguration of their context.[77]

An exposition of 1 Peter clarifies, and grounds in scripture, the point I am trying to make about the inherently *ad hoc* nature of the moral and social commensurability between Christians and non-Christians. 1 Peter, in referring to Christians as *paroikoi* and *parepidemoi* (1 Pet. 1:1; 2:11), understands them to be aliens and sojourners.[78] There is a clear difference between those born again and the rest of society. The new birth 'into the living hope through the resurrection of Jesus Christ from the dead' (1 Pet. 1:3), creates a twofold distance: first, it distances one from the old way of life, inherited from one's ancestors (1 Pet. 1:18); second, it is a birth into a living hope, and thus it distances one from the contingency of the present world in which all human efforts ultimately end in death. This new birth does not mean, however, that Christians are to withdraw from civic life.[79] Rather, they are to seek the welfare of the city (1 Pet. 2:11ff.).[80] But in seeking the welfare of what, after their new birth, is a place of exile, they do not encounter a uniformly evil world. Instead, these sojourners meet a complex world that at times opposes, at times resists, at times ignores and at times accepts the reality to which they bear witness through their life together. There is no stark division between good and evil. For example, Satan is not understood to have total control of everything outside the walls of the church. Rather, the devil prowls around, looking for someone to devour (1 Pet. 5:8). This suggests that evil is not uniformly present, but is sporadic. It is a real and present danger, but one is never quite sure where and how one will encounter it. Furthermore, 1 Peter characterizes the reaction of non-Christians in several ways. The church will encounter evil people who persecute Christians and profane what is holy (1 Pet. 4:4; 12); it will meet people who are ignorant and foolish but who will be silenced by Christian behaviour (1 Pet. 2:15); it will meet people who know right and wrong and are used by God (1 Pet. 2:14); and finally it will meet those who see, appreciate and are converted to the Christian faith (1 Pet. 2:12; 3:1). It is thus engaged in a constant series of congruent and incongruent encounters and relations with other traditions and those of no distinct tradition and at a variety of levels from the intimacy of husband and wife (1 Pet. 3:1) to the distance of political authority (1 Pet. 2:13–14).[81] Volf in his exegesis of 1 Peter states:

> The world consists of a plurality of 'worlds'. The values of these worlds do not form tight and comprehensive systems; they are not like balls that touch but do not connect. Rather, each of these worlds consists of a mixture of partly self-consistent and partly disparate practices and thought patterns. In addition, the worlds are in a permanent social interchange which shapes values that are partly common to the interacting social worlds, partly merely compatible, and partly contrary. An essential dimension of the interchange is the struggle for social power. In this struggle, ethical persuasions and various interests collide, not only between various parties, but also within one party or even within a single person.[82]

There can be no simple affirmation or denial of this plural, unstable world. Nor do strongly delineated church–world typologies of the kind set out by H. Richard Niebuhr stand up.[83] Rather, the church encounters a world that has a wide variety of reactions to it and will structure its relations with the world in a myriad of different ways ranging from withdrawal to being an active and public benefactor of the surrounding society.[84] The church will also be confronted with a variety of problems and situations which bring about these encounters, some old (for example, its relationship to political authority) and some new (for example, how it regards having children by means of IVF treatments). We can conclude that there will be *ad hoc* commensurability between the moral and social practices of Christians and non-Christians even while Christians are pilgrims among the patterns of life established by their neighbours.

A further implication of this move beyond tradition to ecclesiology, of the affirmation of the 'evangelical' distinctiveness of Christians, and this theologically grounded conception of *ad hoc* commensurability between Christians and non-Christian social practices is that the church is not a community of resistance. MacIntyre envisages local communities resisting the encroachments of capitalism and bureaucracy. However, his vision is an essentially protological and retroactive one. Essentially, MacIntyre sees local communities engaged in acts of preserving what was. By contrast, the church recapitulates the future already given in Christ. Therefore, the church offers no resistance to the contemporary context; instead, it embodies in its life together the hope for a future already given. Only to resist the encroachments of capitalism and bureaucratic structures would constitute a failure to take who Jesus Christ is seriously enough, because only to resist is to fail to acknowledge the Lordship of Christ, the victory he has won, and the good news that we may now live as those who really are free in Christ. The church must both affirm what is good in the contemporary context, and bear witness to where the Spirit may now redirect what has a 'misdirected progress'.

Summary

The primary problem addressed in this chapter was the critical difference between conceiving relations between Christians and non-Christians in terms of a rivalry between competing traditions and the eschatological shape to a properly Christian understanding of such relations. On the basis of the above analysis it is clear that the line between Christians and non-Christians is fluid and that relations between Christians and non-Christians are not necessarily characterized by rivalry. The assessment of the theological considerations relating to resolving disputes between Christians and non-Christians brought into sharper focus the problem of how the church can be a specific community with its own criteria of moral evaluation, yet have no clear dividing line between its life together and the life of its neighbours. Contrary to Hauerwas's position, I concluded that conflict between Christians and non-Christians over moral issues is not inevitable. But, it must also be said, neither is agreement.

The differences between Christians and non-Christians are eschatological: as distinct from differences based on human social realities such as family or ethnicity. This understanding of eschatological specificity, and how God is present to the church, points to how Christians are involved in relations of simultaneous distance and belonging, with their non-Christian neighbours. This is because the church is to be a people specified by its relationship with Jesus Christ, which is at the same time to display a given culture's own most eschatological truth. Therefore, Christians cannot stand outside their culture, or against it, but must participate in their culture and the enterprises of their neighbours, as those transfigured. No clear dividing lines can be drawn. Indeed, the life together of Christians is fashioned out of the life together of their neighbours. Instead of clearly demarcated lines separating Christians and non-Christians, questions about what to reject and what to retain confront Christians constantly as they participate in God's transfiguration of their context.

Finally, what has emerged in this chapter is the contrast between MacIntyre, who argues for the possibility of resolving ethical disputes between incommensurable traditions, and yet whose account of normative relations between Christians and non-Christians is characterized by rivalry, and O'Donovan, for whom there can be no ultimate theoretical convergence, yet whose account of relations between Christians and non-Christians can allow for a great deal of co-operation and similarity between them at the level of social practices. It is contrary to expectation that MacIntyre, who constantly calls attention to how morality is bound up with social practices, does not give an account of the persuasive capacity of social practices to mediate between incommensurable traditions in and of themselves; instead, MacIntyre endeavours formally to resolve ethical disputes between incommensurable traditions by means of a systematic meta-theory.

Notes

1 Dietrich Bonhoeffer, *Ethics*, trans. Neville Horton Smith (London: SCM Press, 1993), pp. 103–19.

2 DRA, p. 133

3 For example, David Hollenbach states: 'According to MacIntyre's diagnosis, we need a shared vision of the good but lack it. But he has nothing to say about how we might address the problem so defined.' David Hollenbach, *The Common Good and Christian Ethics* (Cambridge: Cambridge University Press, 2002), p. 67. Ironically, Hollenbach echoes many of the concerns that MacIntyre has addressed and sets out a model of engagement that is directly parallel to the one advocated by MacIntyre. Drawing on the texts of Vatican II, Hollenbach argues that the rational basis for a common good is what he calls 'dialogic universalism'. In description, dialogic universalism echoes much of MacIntyre's meta-theory. It is 'universal' in that it presumes human beings are sufficiently alike in that they all share certain characteristics and the need for certain goods. At the same time, pursuit of a common good is necessarily dialogic because cultural differences are so significant 'that a shared vision of the common good can only be attained in a historically incremental way through deep encounter and intellectual exchange across traditions.' Ibid. p. 153. Like MacIntyre, Hollenbach sees Aquinas as the paradigm example of what the process of 'dialogic universalism' involves. The central difference between Hollenbach and MacIntyre lies in their very different approaches to human rights and liberal democracy.

4 DRA, p. 132.

5 Ibid., p. 252.

6 Ibid.

7 Ibid., p. 117.

8 MacIntyre sees 'just generosity' as a central virtue for both oneself and others to flourish in community. Ibid., p. 122.

9 Ibid., pp. 129–30.

10 MacIntyre, 'Politics, Philosophy and the Common Good', p. 249.

11 Ibid., p. 250. Within a broader picture, MacIntyre's argument set out above can be read as a critique of neo-liberalism and what is termed 'globalization' and a defence of the importance of civil society.

12 For a defence of MacIntyre on this point see Keith Breen, 'Alasdair MacIntyre and the Hope for a Politics of Virtuous Acknowledged Dependence', *Contemporary Political Theory*, 1.2 (2002), pp. 188–92. It should be noted that Breen sets his defence of MacIntyre within a critique of MacIntyre's local politics.

13 MacIntyre, 'Politics, Philosophy and the Common Good', p. 251.

14 DRA, pp. 123–28.

15 Ibid., pp. 136–37.

16 Ibid., p. 142.

17 MacIntyre excludes the family because 'the goods of family life are achieved in and with the goods of various types of local community.' Ibid., p. 134. He does not exclude households envisaged as wider than the immediate or nuclear family.

18 MacIntyre, 'Community, Law and the Idiom and Rhetoric of Rights', p. 110.

19 Ibid.

20 For a critique of MacIntyre's account of local politics see Breen, 'Alasdair MacIntyre and the Hope for a Politics of Virtuous Acknowledged Dependence', pp. 192–99. Breen contends that MacIntyre is excessively hostile of liberal political realities, setting up a 'Manichean' opposition between local politics and the politics of the nation-state which leads MacIntyre into an unnecessary 'forlorn resistance'. See also Mark Murphy, 'MacIntyre's Political Philosophy', in *Alasdair MacIntyre*, ed., Mark Murphy (Cambridge: Cambridge University Press, 2003), pp. 170–75.

21 Alasdair MacIntyre, 'Incommensurability, Truth and the Conversation between Confucians and Aristotelians about the Virtues', in *Culture and Modernity: East–West Philosophic Perspectives*, ed., Eliot Deutsch (Honolulu: University of Hawaii Press, 1991), pp. 104–22.

22 Zizioulas, *Being as Communion*, p. 15.

23 *Desire*, p. 171.
24 Cf., O'Donovan, *On the 39 Articles*, pp. 90–96; *Desire*, p. 170.
25 *Desire*, p. 172.
26 Mt. 26:26–29; Mk 14:22–25; Lk. 22:15–20.
27 This is parallel to James McClendon's argument, for which the social practices of worship, evangelism, establishing and maintaining community, and peace-making (forgiveness and reconciliation), conceived explicitly in terms of MacIntyre's framework, drive the church to engage the fundamental power structures of the world and their disordered social practices. James McClendon, *Ethics* (Nashville: Abingdon Press, 1986), pp. 160–86; pp. 209–39.
28 *Desire*, pp. 169–70.
29 Ibid., p. 174. Douglas Farrow, in his extensive survey of ecclesiology affirms this, stating: 'The ecclesial communion as such is the prophetic sign to the world that God has organized all things around the one whom he has enthroned at his right hand. ... It is the community of the *recapitulation*.' Douglas Farrow, *Ascension and Ecclesia: On the Significance of the Doctrine of the Ascension for Ecclesiology and Christian Cosmology* (Edinburgh: T&T Clark, 1999), pp. 32–33.
30 *Desire*, p. 161. Cf., Karl Barth, *Church Dogmatics*, II: 2, trans. A. T. Mackay and others (Edinburgh: T&T Clark, 1957), p. 512.
31 Ibid., p. 173. While it may raise more questions than it answers, I understand a sacrament to be a ritual and symbolic enactment of divine–human relations that draws together the narratives and social practices of Christianity in a particularly dense locus of significance.
32 Ibid., p. 178.
33 Ibid., p. 182.
34 Ibid., p. 186.
35 Ibid., p. 190.
36 Cf., Barth's discussion of the twelve ministries of the church through which the church encounters the world in speech and action as it participates in the mission of God to the world. Karl Barth, *Church Dogmatics*, IV: 3, trans. G. W. Bromiley (Edinburgh: T&T Clark, 1961), pp. 864–901.
37 This does not denote the nation-state, but distinct non-Christian cultural-linguistic groups. For example, Stanley Hauerwas uses the term in this way in the title of the following collection of essays: *Against the Nations: War and Survival in a Liberal Society* (Minneapolis: Winston Press, 1985). Other examples are: John Howard Yoder, *For the Nations: Essays Evangelical and Public* (Grand Rapids: Eerdmans, 1997); and David Yeago, 'Messiah's People: The Culture of the Church in the Midst of the Nations', *Pro Ecclesia*, 6 (1997), 146–71.
38 For an account of the development of Hauerwas's thought see McClendon, *Ethics*, pp. 69–72. For a summary of his position see Fergusson, *Community, Liberalism and Christian Ethics*, pp. 48–79; Robert Jenson, 'The Hauerwas Project', *Modern Theology*, 8 (1992), 285–95; and Richard Hays, *The Moral Vision of the New Testament: A Contemporary Introduction to New Testament Ethics* (Edinburgh: T&T Clark, 1996), pp. 254–66. For a systematic overview of his work see Samuel Wells, *Transforming Fate into Destiny: The Theological Ethics of Stanley Hauerwas* (Carlisle: Paternoster Press, 1998). For a rare systematic overview of his particular vision see Stanley Hauerwas, *The Peaceable Kingdom: A Primer in Christian Ethics* (Notre Dame: University of Notre Dame Press, 1983); and idem, 'On Doctrine and Ethics', in *The Cambridge Companion to Christian Doctrine*, ed. Colin Gunton (Cambridge: Cambridge University. Press, 1997), pp. 21–40.
39 AV, p. 253. For a parallel expression by Hauerwas see: Stanley Hauerwas and William Willimon, *Resident Aliens* (Nashville: Abingdon, 1989), pp. 30–48; and Hauerwas, *The Peaceable Kingdom*, pp. 4–6.
40 For this criticism see Hauerwas and Pinches, *Christians Among the Virtues*, pp. 61–69.
41 Fergusson, *Community, Liberalism and Christian Ethics*, p. 52. For a detailed comparison of AV and *A Community of Character* see John Barbour, 'The Virtues in a Pluralistic Context', *Journal of Religion*, 63 (1983), 175–82.
42 William Placher, 'Postliberal Theology', in *The Modern Theologians: An Introduction to Christian Theology in the Twentieth Century*, ed., David Ford, 2nd edn (Oxford: Blackwell, 1997), p. 349.

43 Ibid.; cf., Hauerwas, *The Peaceable Kingdom*, pp. 14–15; and pp. 114–15; and idem, 'No Enemy, No Christianity: Preaching between "Worlds"', in *Sanctify Them in the Truth* (Edinburgh: T&T Clark, 1998), pp. 191–200.

44 Hauerwas and Pinches, *Christians Among the Virtues*, p. 192.

45 Hauerwas, *Performing the Faith*, p. 231–32.

46 Stanley Hauerwas, *Dispatches from the Front: Theological Engagements with the Secular* (Durham: Duke University Press, 1994), p. 9.

47 It must be said that Hauwerwas does at times argue exactly this point. See for example his essay 'Why Gays (as a Group) Are Morally Superior to Christians (as a Group)', in *Dispatches from the Front*, pp. 153–55.

48 For example, see Stanley Hauerwas with Mark Sherwindt, 'The Reality of the Kingdom: An Ecclesial Space for Peace', in *Against the Nations: War and Survival in a Liberal Society* (Minneapolis: Winston Press, 1985), pp. 107–19.

49 Stanley Hauerwas, 'What Could It Mean for the Church to Be Christ's Body? A Question without a Clear Answer', in *In Good Company: The Church as Polis*, ed., Stanley Hauerwas (Notre Dame: University of Notre Dame Press, 1995), pp. 29–30.

50 Reinhard Hütter, 'Ecclesial Ethics, the Church's Vocations, and Paraclesis', *Pro Ecclesia*, 2 (1993), p. 450. Cf., Colin Gunton, 'The Church as a School of Virtue? Human Formation in Trinitarian Framework', in *Faithfulness & Fortitude: In Conversation with the Theological Ethics of Stanley Hauerwas*, eds, Mark Theissen Nation and Samuel Wells (Edinburgh: T&T Clark, 2000), pp. 211–31.

51 Wells, *Transforming Fate into Destiny*, p. 98.

52 Barth, *Church Dogmatics*, IV: 3, p. 192.

53 See Hauerwas, *Performing the Faith*, p. 231, n. 32.

54 Nicholas Healy, 'Practices and the New Ecclesiology: Misplaced Concreteness?', *International Journal of Systematic Theology*, 5.3 (2003), p. 295.

55 For a study in how Paul is addressing the degenerative relations of the Corinthian church and calling them by a variety of means to a vision of generative sociality see Stephen Barton, 'Christian Community in the Light of 1 Corinthians', SCE, 10.1 (1997), 1–15.

56 See Ibid., p. 34; James Dunn, *Theology of Paul the Apostle* (Edinburgh: T&T Clark, 1998), p. 545; Gordon Fee, *God's Empowering Presence: The Holy Spirit in the Letters of Paul* (Peabody, MA: Hendrickson, 1994), pp. 689–90; and for a discussion of how Jesus transcends the Temple and in himself fulfils and replaces it see N. T. Wright, *Jesus and the Victory of God, Christian Origins and the Question of God* (London: SPCK, 1996), pp. 432–38.

57 For an example of this in practice see Dunn's treatment of how the *haustafeln* are reorganized in response to Christ and the activity of the Spirit. James Dunn, 'The Household Rules in the New Testament', in *The Family in Theological Perspective*, ed. Stephen Barton (Edinburgh: T&T Clarke, 1996), pp. 43–63. For a treatment consistent with Dunn's, but more radical in its implications see John Howard Yoder, *The Politics of Jesus*, 2nd edn (Grand Rapids: Eerdmans, 1994), pp. 162–92.

58 Fee, *God's Empowering Presence*, p. 150.

59 This is not to say that those outside the church can never bear witness to Jesus Christ. For an account of such secular 'parables of the kingdom', and how Christians might hear them, see Barth, *Church Dogmatics*, IV: 3, pp. 110–35. For an assessment of Barth's position see Nigel Biggar, *The Hastening That Waits: Karl Barth's Ethics*, (Oxford: Clarendon Press, 1993), pp. 147–61.

60 Barth, *Church Dogmatics*, IV: 3, pp. 740–41.

61 Whether this runs counter to models of church–world relations based on George Lindbeck's thesis concerning the cultural-linguistic model of doctrine is opaque. Cf., George Lindbeck, *The Nature of Doctrine* (London: SPCK, 1984). It is not the place of this book to explore this question.

62 Hebrew tradition clearly borrowed from the surrounding culture while radically transforming it. Brueggemann's study of the prophetic tradition locates it firmly in the covenantal tradition of Moses. However, he recognizes the influence of the surrounding culture, such as the Canaanite phenomenon of ecstasy echoed in 1 Samuel 10 and 19, on how Israel understood prophecy. Walter Brueggemann, *The*

Prophetic Imagination (Minneapolis: Fortress Press, 1978), p. 15. See also Jon Levenson, *Creation and the Persistence of Evil: The Jewish Drama of Divine Omnipotence* (Princeton: Princeton University Press, 1988).

63 Ezekial 16. See also Jacques Ellul, *The Meaning of the City* (Carlisle: Paternoster Press, 1997), pp. 94–97.

64 John Howard Yoder, 'A People in the World', in *The Royal Priesthood: Essays Ecclesiological and Ecumenical*, ed., Michael G. Cartwright (Grand Rapids, MI: Eerdmans, 1994), p. 81, n. 19.

65 For a parallel discussion of the relationship between social practices (or witness) and the acceptance by non-Christians of a Christian view of the world see Hauerwas, *With the Grain of the Universe*, pp. 210–15.

66 MacIntyre, 'Community, Law and the Idiom and Rhetoric of Rights', p. 110.

67 Cf. Eugene TeSelle, 'The Sojourner: Neither a Citizen nor an Alien', *Living in Two Cities: Augustinian Trajectories in Political Thought* (Scranton: University of Scranton Press, 1998), pp. 45–71.

68 For analyses of the church as a pilgrim see Geoffrey Preston, *Faces of the Church: Meditations on a Mystery and Its Images* (Edinburgh: T&T Clark, 1997), pp. 217–24.

69 Augustine, *City of God*, 18.51, in Gerard O'Daly, trans., *Augustine's City of God: A Reader's Guide* (Oxford: Clarendon Press, 1999), p. 159.

70 Cf., Michael Welker, *God the Spirit*, trans. John Hoffmeyer (Minneapolis: Fortress Press, 1992), pp. 232–33.

71 Marcus Borg, *Conflict, Holiness and Politics in the Teachings of Jesus*, Studies in the Bible and Early Christianity (Lampeter: Edwin Mellen Press, 1972), pp. 57–61. Cf., N. T. Wright, *The Climax of the Covenant: Christ and the Law in Pauline Theology* (Minneapolis: Fortress Press, 1992), p. 174.

72 Cf., Edward Casey, *The Fate of Place: A Philosophical History* (Berkeley: University of California Press, 1997), pp. 7–16.

73 Miroslav Volf, 'Soft Difference: Theological Reflections on the Relation Between Church and Culture in 1 Peter', *Ex Auditu*, 10 (1994), pp. 18–19. Cf., 'Epistle of Mathetes to Diognetus', in *Ante-Nicene Fathers*, trans. Alexander Roberts and James Donaldson, eds, Alexander Roberts and James Donaldson, 10 vols. (Edinburgh: T&T Clark, 1996), I, pp. 25–30 (ch. 5); hereafter *Ante-Nicene Fathers* is abbreviated to ANF.

74 This is arguably the mistake David Yeago makes. See David Yeago, 'Messiah's People'. Similarly, Rodney Clapp envisages the church as an ark – a separate and enclosed entity – in the troubled waters of the contemporary context. Rodney Clapp, *Families at the Crossroads: Beyond Traditional and Modern Options* (Leicester: InterVarsity Press, 1993), pp. 46–47.

75 Robert Markus understands Augustine to have a similar conception of the church. He states we can only draw a distinction between the 'world' and the 'church' eschatologically since in this age they are co-extensive. 'There is a real distinction to be drawn between them, but it is eschatological rather than sociological or historical. They are separable only in the final judgment, and their distinct – but not separate – being here and now in the *saeculum* consists of the relation they bear to that judgment. So in the last resort the Church *is* the world, the world reconciled to Christ.' Robert Markus, *Saeculum: History and Society in the Theology of St Augustine* (Cambridge: Cambridge University Press, 1970), p. 123. Similarly, Hütter establishes a parallel relationship between eschatology, ecclesiology and ethics in 'Ecclesial Ethics, the Church's Vocations, and Paraclesis', pp. 433–50.

76 In the light of a theological account of the relationship between Christians and non-Christians, attempts to characterize this relationship in terms of a 'clash of civilizations' or 'culture wars' are wholly inappropriate. For examples of such a construal see Samuel Huntington, *The Clash of Civilizations and the Remaking of World Order* (London: Simon & Schuster, 1996) and James Davidson Hunter, *Culture Wars: The Struggle to Define America* (New York: Basic Books, 1991).

77 A similar view is developed by William Werpehowski in 'Ad Hoc Apologetics', *Journal of Religion*, 66 (1986), 282–301.

78 For a review of the categories of 'alien', 'sojourner' and 'stranger' in post-exilic, New Testament and early Christian literature and how use of these categories in 1 Peter is consonant with this wider usage

see Reinhard Feldmeier, 'The "Nation" of Strangers: Social Contempt and its Theological Interpretation in Ancient Judaism and Early Christianity', in *Ethnicity and the Bible*, ed., Mark Brett (Leiden: E. J. Brill, 1996), pp. 241–70.

79 Bruce Winter, *Seek the Welfare of the City: Christians as Benefactors and Citizens* (Carlisle: Paternoster Press, 1994), p. 19.

80 *Contra* Wayne Meeks in *The Origins of Christian Morality* (New Haven, CT: Yale University Press, 1993), Winter draws a parallel between the exiled Jews in Babylon and the advice given in 1 Peter. He states: 'The parallels between Jeremiah 29 and 1 Peter are compelling. ... It is clear that as spiritual "sojourners" and "alien residents" they must withdraw from the self-indulgent lifestyle of their contemporaries (2:11) and seek the welfare of the society in which they live. They were instructed to spend their days in this earthly city seeking the blessing of its inhabitants (2:11ff).' Winter, *Seek the Welfare of the City*, p. 17.

81 Volf, 'Soft Difference', p. 26. See also RMO, p. 58 for a parallel exegesis of 1 Peter.

82 Ibid., p. 26.

83 Richard Niebuhr, *Christ and Culture* (London: Faber & Faber, 1952). For a critique of Niebuhr on this point see John Howard Yoder, 'How H. Richard Niebuhr Reasoned: A Critique of *Christ and Culture*', in *Authentic Transformation: A New Vision of Christ and Culture*, eds Glen Stassen, Diane Yeager and John Howard Yoder (Nashville: Abingdon, 1996), p. 55.

84 Cf., Winter, *Seek the Welfare of the City*, pp. 21–23.

CHAPTER 5

The practice of hospitality

This chapter is a response to a number of issues that have transpired in the previous chapters. These issues are the following: first, the insufficiency of MacIntyre's account of the relationship between Christians and non-Christians. Second, the contrast between MacIntyre's meta-theory for how incommensurable traditions can resolve ethical disputes that, in practice, generates conflict, and O'Donovan's account of the inherent incommensurability between Christian and non-Christian criteria of evaluation that, in practice, gives rise to an *ad hoc* commensurability. Third, the need to formulate a constructive account of how Christians should relate to their neighbours, one that takes into consideration eschatology and ecclesiology. I shall now seek to construct a model, not of how to resolve disputes between Christians and non-Christians, but of how Christians are to relate to non-Christians when ethical disputes arise. This is done by means of an assessment of the motif of hospitality, how it differs from other, contemporary ways of structuring difference, how it fits within a wider philosophical discourse, and how it can be understood within a specifically theological framework. On the basis of this analysis I will set out a model of the actual practice by which Christians have, do and should relate to their neighbours in such a way that these relations take account of the simultaneous continuity and radical discontinuity between them.

Hospitality, tolerance and Christian witness

The theological ground of the necessity of living 'betwixt and between' different traditions is set out in the doctrine of eschatology. According to this doctrine, while the Spirit makes present and available the restored and transformed creation now, creation will not be fully restored and transformed until Christ returns. The relationship between the ascended Christ and the Spirit, who makes Christ present to humans while we await Christ's *parousia*, emphasizes how Christians exist between two ages. As argued in the last chapter, the result of Christians self-consciously living between this age and the next is that they are marked off from non-Christians, not by race, or culture, or even by religious practice, but by their union with Christ whose ascension marks a relativization of this age and the inauguration of the new age. To be true to the presupposition of their faith, Christians must accept this situation of continuity and radical discontinuity with those around them. The implication of this is that the church is simultaneously like and unlike its neighbours in terms of its moral and social practices. The simultaneous similarity and dissimilarity between Christian and non-Christian moral and social practices does not mean we can make no generic statements about how Christians and non-Christians should relate with regard to moral disputes. There is still a need for some rubric by which to formulate and structure relations between Christians and non-Christians; that is, given that some of its neighbours will reject the church's response to moral issues, while at the same time, other neighbours will either share or take up the moral responses of the church (even though they may reject the belief on which that response is based), it must be asked what, theologically, is the best way to conceptualize and organize relations between the church and its neighbours.

In contemporary debate, analysis of how to cope with the fact of plurality and relate with those with whom one disagrees is framed in terms of tolerance, intolerance and freedom of expression and belief. A common assumption in the literature relating to tolerance and moral diversity is that tolerance and the willingness to live with difference is a phenomenon that emerged in the West after the Enlightenment.[1] However, the emphasis on the relative newness of tolerance as a concept can be overstated.[2] Discussions about questions of tolerance and freedom of conscience have been a constant theme in the Christian tradition. Two notable examples are Lactantius[3] and Aquinas.[4] It was, however, with the Enlightenment – and its search for a neutral arbiter between competing truth-claims and a growing emphasis on individual autonomy – that the notion of tolerance acquired increasing prominence. The emphasis on tolerance is seen also as a direct reaction against the allegedly religious wars of the post-Reformation era.[5] Acceptance of difference (or diversity), and the advocacy of toleration as a good, are now seen as the pre-eminent way of thinking about how those who disagree with each other should relate. Indicative of its prominence is the United Nation's annual International Day for Tolerance on 16 November which was inaugurated after the 1995 'Year for Tolerance'. The day forms part of the UN's efforts to promote human rights, mutual understanding, and social and economic development.[6]

Tolerance involves the willingness to accept differences (whether religious, moral, ethnic or economic) of which, at whatever level, one might, as an individual or as a community, disapprove.[7] For a person or group to be tolerant, three conditions must be met. First, there must be some conduct about which one disapproves, even if only minimally or potentially. Second, although such a person or group has power to act coercively against, or interfere to prevent, that of which they disapprove, they do not. Third, not interfering coercively must result from more than acquiescence, resignation, indifference or a balance of power. One does not tolerate that which one is not concerned about; nor is it tolerance simply to accept what one cannot, or is not willing to, change (either because one lacks power to effect change or because, for whatever reason, one fears to use one's power). Horton notes that toleration is particularly important and problematic when it involves a principled refusal to prohibit conduct believed to be wrong. He states: 'This gives rise to the so-called "paradox of toleration" according to which toleration requires that it is right to permit that which is wrong.'[8]

Following the assessment of MacIntyre's account of how incommensurable traditions may resolve ethical disputes, I concluded that there was no systematic way for Christians to resolve ethical disputes with non-Christians. Hence, the question arises as to how Christians are to relate to those with whom they disagree. The concept of tolerance constitutes one of the primary, contemporary ways in which this question is addressed.[9] This is true not just for society in general, but within the churches as well. However, it is my contention that it is not tolerance, but the practice of hospitality that constitutes the best way to address the question of how Christians are to relate to those with whom they disagree.

There is not the scope here for a full analysis of tolerance as a concept and a thorough consideration of its use within the Christian tradition.[10] I have made reference to tolerance in order to situate the consideration of hospitality as the best way for Christians to conceive of relations with those with whom they disagree in debates about how such relations are conceived at present. It suffices to say that the concept of tolerance does have a long pedigree in the Christian tradition. The work of Lactantius has already been noted, but another early example is Tertullian.[11] Both of these writers discuss the issue of religious freedom, sharing the view that belief is a matter of free will, and that faith cannot and should not be secured through coercion. From the Protestant Reformation onwards interest in the concept of tolerance intensified, especially as it related to the question of religious diversity.[12] In the modern period, the increase of relations between Western Christianity and other faith traditions, initially as a result of colonial expansion and then as a result of increased immigration, gave a renewed impetus to the question of religious tolerance. Subsequently, the increasing cultural diversity in democratic societies and substantive ethical disagreement both between Christians and between Christians and non-Christians, for example, over abortion and homosexuality, have led to assessments of how tolerance relates to the problem of ethical disputes.[13]

The theological justifications for tolerance are varied. One of the most striking theological defences of tolerance was given by the Anglican, Mandell Creighton, who saw it as condition of evangelical witness. After an account of how tolerance developed in the West, Creighton reflects on the need for tolerance to have a theological foundation, without which its exercise could easily become distorted.[14] For Creighton, the only sure basis for tolerance is theological. Furthermore, in Creighton's view, tolerance is part of the faithful witness of the church to the truth it has received from God. He states:

> The forbearance, the equitableness, the fairmindedness of Christ, – surely this should be the spirit of the Christian life, and this is what the Christian means by tolerance. It comes from the confidence of an assured hope, from the outlook on a vast horizon. The kingdom of heaven was to begin on earth; it has its place here and now, and before its contemplation the petty activities of actual life fall into due proportion. 'The Lord is at hand'; that is the great motive for forbearance.[15]

However, Creighton's analysis of the theological basis of tolerance in the light of the hope humans have in Christ is unusual. A more recent attempt to develop a constructive theological account of tolerance is given by David Fergusson who himself draws on Reformation theological justifications of tolerance such as that given by Sebastian Castellio, a contemporary and one time colleague of Calvin.[16] For the most part, the theological advocacy of tolerance is grounded in either an inherent capacity of humans as created in the image of God (for example, free will) or the fallibility and finitude of humans resulting from both their created and fallen nature.

Most defences of tolerance follow three, not specifically theological, arguments.[17] The first approach to tolerance centres on concern about human fallibility and the limits to human knowledge. However, the concern about human fallibility should not be seen as a form of relativism. Indeed, as Jay Newman argues, a certain kind of relativist is actually opposed to the concept of tolerance.[18] Neither does a concern about human fallibility imply that the tolerant person is completely sceptical about the possibility of knowing the truth about a particular question or issue. However, it can imply a limited scepticism that maintains belief in an ultimate horizon of truth which differing positions may shed light on. For example, Reinhold Niebuhr, for whom 'complete scepticism represents the abyss of meaninglessness',[19] contends, in relation to religious toleration, that while each religion should seek to proclaim its 'highest insights', it should preserve a 'humble and contrite recognition of the fact that all actual expressions of religious faith are subject to historical contingency and relativity.'[20] In his view: 'Such a recognition creates a spirit of tolerance.'[21] Arguments for tolerance on the pragmatic grounds of human fallibility can take a variety of forms.[22] These include the view that neither party has complete possession of the truth, truth will benefit from free investigation, and certainty in religious questions is difficult to achieve.

A second way of approaching the issue of tolerance seeks procedures that are tolerant. This is to say that arguments for limits to intervention and coercion are invoked when someone has power to change another's behaviour of which they disapprove. Procedural arguments are generally advocated in relation to the exercise of judicial and political authority. John Locke's *An Essay on Toleration* is an example of this approach.[23] Bernard Williams calls this model of tolerance 'liberal pluralism' and describes it thus:

> On the one hand, there are deeply held and differing convictions about moral or religious matters, held by various groups within society. On the other hand, there is a supposedly impartial state, which affirms the rights of all citizens to equal consideration, including an equal right to form and express their convictions.[24]

As has already been argued, via MacIntyre's genealogy of liberalism, and his critique of the modern state, the quest for neutral procedures based on reason has failed. The modern state is itself intolerant. As MacIntyre puts it: 'The modern state is never merely a neutral arbiter of conflicts, but is always to some degree itself a party to social conflict, and ... acts in the interests of particular and highly contestable conceptions of liberty and property.'[25] Thus, the foundation of, and procedures for, securing modern notions of tolerance has proved, in MacIntyre view at least, self-defeating.[26] However, the degree to which a political authority can or cannot be tolerant, and whether or not a state can be neutral between rival conceptions of the good, is not central to my argument. While these questions are important, my primary concern is with how tolerance can shape relations between Christians and non-Christians, and not with whether or not the state can act as a neutral arbiter between incommensurable moral standpoints.[27]

The third approach seeks to argue for tolerance as a substantive good. The arguments for tolerance in *On Liberty* by John Stuart Mill are an example of this approach. However, framing analyses of how one should live with difference in terms of tolerance as a substantive good, as distinct from a merely instrumental one, is conceptually problematic. As Bernard Williams comments: 'The difficulty with toleration is that it seems to be at once necessary and impossible.'[28] He points out that there is a difference between pragmatic tolerance and tolerance as a substantive value. Tolerance as a substantive value is based on a particular conception of the good: that is, the good of individual autonomy. This leads to the following problem: 'The practice of toleration cannot be based on a value such as that of individual autonomy, and also hope to escape from substantive disagreements about the good.'[29] Those who disagree with the liberal conception of the good will necessarily reject liberal conceptions of toleration and, as MacIntyre argues, they will reject liberal conceptions of rationality on which the particular good of toleration is based. There is a further conceptual problem with arguments for tolerance as a substantive good based on notions of human autonomy; it is a problem that lies at the heart of the so-called liberal–communitarian debate. As Susan Mendus puts it: 'We need to understand how people are *inter*dependent as well as *in*dependent. We need to explain how autonomy is formed, not solely from the internal nature of individuals, but also from the nature of the society in which they find themselves.'[30] To ground arguments for tolerance on individual autonomy is to ignore the ways in which an individual is embedded within a wider community of relations.[31]

Tolerance – whether understood in pragmatic or procedural terms or as a substantive good – is inadequate when addressing the question of how Christians should relate to those with whom they disagree and who have a different conception of the good. This is so for a number of reasons. First, while it is part of the tradition, tolerance has not been the primary way in which the question of how Christians should relate to those with whom they disagree has been conceived. The emphasis on tolerance since the early modern period overshadowed the notion and practice of hospitality within Christianity, eclipsing how hospitality shaped the ways in which Christians relate to those with whom they disagree. Second, not only does hospitality have more antecedents in Christian social practice than tolerance, but also, as a practice, it is founded on more explicitly biblical and theological imperatives. This is to say, even if we took into account pre-Enlightenment conceptions of tolerance within the Christian tradition, hospitality still constitutes a more specifically Christian way of thinking about and organizing relations with non-Christians. Third, the adequacy of tolerance as a way of framing relations between strangers in the context of deep religious and moral diversity is increasingly questioned. For example, John Gray argues:

> Liberal toleration arose from the divisions of monocultural societies. ... Yet it has a limited relevance to the circumstances of the contemporary world. Liberal toleration presupposed a cultural consensus on values even as it allowed for differences in beliefs. It is an inadequate ideal in societies in which deep moral diversity has become an established fact of life.[32]

The tradition-specific practice of hospitality opens up new ways of framing relations between strangers and can thereby provide a corrective to the narrow focus on tolerance that to many seems insufficient as the horizon of thought about the current context of 'deep moral diversity'. As Nederman and Laursen point out: 'One stimulus to enlarging the horizons of current toleration theorists may well be a careful examination and appreciation of how earlier thinkers dealt with similar issues concerning the diversity of human conviction and action.'[33] The analysis and assessment of hospitality within the Christian tradition given below constitutes precisely the kind of exercise that Nederman and Laursen call for.

Hospitality and the shape of relations between Christians and their neighbours

Hospitality is not an essentially domestic and apolitical kind of action. A number of philosophers have conceived of hospitality as a political practice, among them is Immanuel Kant, arguably the most influential Enlightenment thinker. Kant accorded hospitality (or in German 'hospitalität') a central significance in his account of how people from different cultures can 'enter into mutual relations which may eventually be regulated by public laws, thus bringing the human race nearer and nearer to a cosmopolitan constitution'.[34] MacIntyre, who as we have seen is a trenchant critic of the Enlightenment, also places hospitality at the centre of his account of what constitutes the good society.[35] Both thinkers realize that, for a society to avoid being engulfed by deadly conflict, hospitality of strangers is required in order for a society to be maintained and humans to flourish. Other philosophical treatments of hospitality can be found in Emmanuel Lévinas[36] and Jacques Derrida,[37] both of whom emphasize the relationship between hospitality and identity.

That both Kant and MacIntyre cite hospitality as an important political practice raises the question of whether they are talking about the same thing. Kant sees hospitality as a 'natural right' possessed of all humans 'by virtue of their right to communal possession of the earth's surface'.[38] He distinguishes the 'natural right of hospitality' from the 'right of a guest'. The guest makes a claim upon one to 'become a member of the native household for a certain time'.[39] By contrast, a stranger may only claim a 'right of resort': that is, the right to enter into relations with other inhabitants of the land or community. The converse of this is that the visitor may *only* attempt to enter into relations. It is on this basis that Kant gives a critique of the inhospitable and oppressive behaviour of the 'commercial states' that conquered, rather than merely entered into relations with, foreign countries and peoples, for example, the British in India.[40] However, Kant's conception of the hospitality we owe the stranger appears somewhat constricted when compared with MacIntyre's.

Like Kant, MacIntyre sees hospitality as a universal practice. It is central to the proper functioning of any society. He states:

> It is important to the functioning of communities that among the roles that play a part in their shared lives there should be that of 'the stranger', someone from outside the community who has happened to arrive amongst us and to whom we owe hospitality, just because she or he is a stranger.[41]

However, instead of grounding it in notions of a universal possession like Kant, he grounds it in a universal capacity: that is, the virtue of *misericordia*. He understands *misericordia* to denote the capacity for grief or sorrow over someone else's distress just insofar as one understands the other's distress as one's own. It is not mere sentiment; instead, it is sentiment guided by reason. Following Aquinas's definition of the term, he states: '*Misericordia* is that aspect of charity whereby we supply what is needed by our neighbour and among the virtues that relate us to our neighbour *misericordia* is the greatest.'[42] For MacIntyre, to understand another's distress as one's own is to recognize that other as a neighbour, whether they are family, a friend, or a stranger. Thus, *misericordia* directs one to include the stranger within one's communal relationships. It is thus the basis for extending the bounds of one's communal obligations, and thereby including the other in one's relations of giving and receiving characterized by just generosity. Therefore, in contrast to Kant's conception of hospitality, there is no such calculating and restricted understanding in MacIntyre's account. What transpires by briefly comparing and contrasting MacIntyre and Kant's conception of hospitality is that the implications of what they mean by hospitality are very different. Thus, while hospitality can be seen as a generic term, clearly it does not have a universal definition.

The practice of hospitality is central to most cultures. However, following the previous analysis of MacIntyre and O'Donovan, hospitality can only be understood within a particular tradition, and different traditions will have different forms of hospitality. Thus, living with those who are different, and framing relations with those who are different in terms of hospitality (rather than tolerance) entails understanding hospitality in the light of one particular tradition. It is the aim of this chapter to assess the conception of hospitality within the Christian tradition and then see how this conception of hospitality may shape relations between Christians and non-Christians with regard to ethical disputes.

A theologically specified account of hospitality

As already argued, the church seeks to follow after the Spirit who is constantly transfiguring the world. In its life together the church will bear witness to this transfigured reality. However, the dividing line between the church and its neighbours is always changing and no form of human sociality can claim finality or permanence. Rather, the church must constantly follow after the Spirit and recapitulate the Christ-event. However, reflection on resolving concrete ethical disputes does require a normative model of relations between Christians and non-Christians that furnishes us with a stronger basis for critical reflection on the present practice of the church in its relations with its neighbours.

The focal term for my conception of relations between the church and its neighbours is 'hospitality'. The motif of hospitality is a root metaphor and practice embedded in the Christian tradition that encapsulates its crucial elements with regard to how the church relates to its neighbours. This term is not used here to denote an abstract ideal, principle or middle axiom; rather, the term 'hospitality' arises out of the witness of scripture and the social practices and doctrines of the Christian tradition. Use of this motif is thus in line with the model for tradition-situated reflection and deliberation set out in previous chapters.

Importantly, the motif of hospitality maintains the key eschatological tensions of Christian specificity. It does not force a harmony either through abstraction: that is, the term does not dissolve the eschatological tension by appealing to some universal principle (love, justice, and so on); neither does it demand that Christians enter into relations with their neighbours on the basis of a rivalry between competing traditions. Rather, the motif highlights the central and substantial concerns already discussed; that is, it allows for Christians to retain their specific criteria for evaluating the veracity of moral claims, while at the level of moral practice experiencing both continuity and discontinuity with their neighbours. It is important to note that I am not claiming that the practice of hospitality precludes Christians relating to non-Christians via any form of philosophical argument; however, philosophical argument can neither be normative nor determinative of how Christians should relate to non-Christians.

Hospitality in scripture

There is a cycle of feasting parables and motifs within Luke's Gospel all of which form part of the justification for why Jesus is a *guest* of, and a *host* to, 'tax collectors and sinners'.[43] This cycle begins with Luke 14 and culminates in the banquet at the end of the Prodigal Son parable in Luke 15.[44] This table fellowship with sinners, and the reconfiguring of Israel's purity boundaries which this hospitality represents, signifies the heart of Jesus' mission. Jeremias notes that Jesus' eating with 'sinners', is an expression of the mission and message of Jesus (Mark 2.17), [these] eschatological meals [are] anticipatory celebrations of the feast in the end-time (Matt. 8.11 par.), in which the community of the saints is already being represented (Mark 2.19). The inclusion of sinners in the community of salvation, achieved in table-fellowship, is the most meaningful expression of the message of the redeeming love of God.[45]

Jeremias is not alone in New Testament scholarship in emphasizing Jesus' open commensality. While he (and Kenneth Bailey) may represent the so-called 'second quest' for the historical Jesus, even those in the 'third quest' (N. T. Wright, Markus Borg and Edward Sanders) and those of a very different view to the 'third quest' (for example, Dominic Crossan) emphasize this aspect of Jesus' ministry. As N. T. Wright points out: 'Most writers now agree that eating with "sinners" was one of the most characteristic and striking marks of Jesus' regular activity. ... Jesus was, as it were, celebrating the messianic banquet, and doing so with all the wrong people.'[46]

The great banquet depicted in Luke 14:15–24 is the high point of this cycle (although it is often overshadowed by the story of the Prodigal Son).[47] However, it needs to be set within the broader context of Jesus' ministry. The images of feasting and hospitality are abundant and vivid.[48] Among many there are: the wedding at Cana, Dives feasting while Lazarus starves at his gate, the joyous meal at Jericho with Zacchaeus, the woman washing Jesus' feet, Jesus washing his disciples' feet, the last supper, and the meals enjoyed with the risen Jesus. At various points his stories and actions challenge the religious, political, economic and social authorities of his day. Through his hospitality, which has as its focal point actual feasting and table fellowship, Jesus turns the world upside down.

There is both continuity and departure from the pattern of hospitality established in the Old Testament. The elements of continuity are very strong. God commanded his people to provide hospitality to strangers: 'The alien who resides with you shall be to you as the citizen among you; you shall love the alien as yourself, for you were aliens in the land of Egypt: I am the Lord your God, (Lev. 19:33–34).' The command in Leviticus 19 was echoed in a range of other legislation. The tithe, for instance, is fundamentally a command to be hospitable on a lavish scale (Dt. 12:17–19). Again, the commands concerning harvesting are demands that hospitality be observed: one who harvests a field must not seek to maximize his harvest, but must leave the gleanings for those who are in need (Dt. 24:19–22). Stories of hospitality constitute a leitmotif throughout the Old Testament; for example, Abraham and Sarah entertaining angels,[49] Abigail placating David, and the widow of Zarephath caring for Elijah.[50] At times this hospitality is not only offered but also demanded, as when Lot insists the Angels spend the night with him (Gen. 19:1–3).[51] At other times it is extended to enemies as a sign of the reconciling work of God, as when Isaac made a feast for Abimelech (Gen. 26:26–31), or Elisha mediated a peace between the Arameans and the Israelites (2 Kings 6:8–23). It is linked with the renewal of creation (Ecc. 10:16–17), and ultimately it comes to include all creation and all the nations at the messianic banquet, as depicted and anticipated in the prophets.[52] Jesus' ministry can be seen to draw together all these elements, intensify their application, and inaugurate their fulfilment.

Alongside this continuity, there is discontinuity.[53] There is much in the Old Testament that emphasizes how Israel is not to entertain its neighbours or have contact with those who are unclean. There are the numerous purity rituals set out in the Torah,[54] and most significantly, all the material relating to the conquest of those already living in Canaan in Joshua and elsewhere cannot be ignored. There is also the connection between being faithless to God and marrying foreign women expressed in both Nehemiah and Ezra.[55] It seems Israel is constantly in danger of being overwhelmed by pollution and sin (the two being distinct) and must constantly protect itself in order to maintain itself as holy and distinct among the nations.

Jesus does not resolve the tension between hospitality and holiness present in the Old Testament, but he does relate these two imperatives in a particular way. Jesus relates hospitality and holiness by inverting their relations: hospitality becomes the means of holiness. Instead of having to be set apart from or exclude pagans in order to maintain holiness, it is in Jesus' hospitality of pagans, the unclean, and sinners that his own holiness is shown forth. Instead of sin and impurity infecting him, it seems Jesus' purity and righteousness somehow 'infects' the impure, sinners and the Gentiles. As Borg puts it: 'In the teaching [and practice] of Jesus, holiness, not uncleanness was understood to be contagious.'[56] For example, the haemorrhaging woman has only to touch Jesus and she is healed and made clean.[57] Instead of Jesus having to undergo purity rituals because of contact with the woman, as any other rabbi would, it is the woman who is 'cleansed' by contact with him.[58] There is a similar dynamic when Jesus touches lepers, the dead, the blind, the deaf and dumb, or partakes of a meal with a tax collector. In discussing these acts N. T. Wright says: 'This means that Jesus' healing miracles must be seen clearly as bestowing the gift of *shalom*, wholeness, to those who lacked it, bringing not only physical health but renewed membership in the people of YHWH.'[59] Wright goes further and argues this holiness/wholeness was shown forth in Jesus' hospitality.

Jesus' speech and action announces a form of hospitality that, to some of his contemporaries, is shocking in relation to certain Old Testament precedents. Thus, his hospitality brings him into conflict with the custodians of Israel's purity, both self-appointed (the Pharisees, Zealot-types and so on) and actual (the Temple authorities). Borg contends that this conflict between Jesus and his contemporaries is about the shape and purpose of the people of God which is itself part of a wider debate about the response of Judaism to Roman political power and the encroachment of Hellenistic culture.[60] Through his hospitality Jesus rejected, and presented an alternative to, every other post-exilic programme for Israel's internal reform and quest for holiness. For all of these were based on the exclusion of 'sinners', separation from the 'world' (that is, Gentile uncleanness and rule), and solidarity formed by defining Israel's identity through opposition to sinners and Gentiles.[61] Jesus rejected also co-option by, and assimilation to, the pagan hegemony, and capitulation to sin. Rather, he advocated participation in the kingdom of God as enacted in his table-fellowship.

Jesus' hospitality is not to be isolated to himself: he calls his disciples to 'Go and do likewise' (Lk. 10:37). And, in accordance with Jesus' command, Christians have sought to mirror Jesus' pattern of hospitality. Although it is probably mistaken in its exegesis of the passage, Christians have constantly made use of the story of the great judgement given in Matthew 25:31–46 as a spur to follow Christ's call to 'Go and do likewise'. Christine Pohl goes so far as to say: 'This has been the most important passage for the entire tradition on Christian hospitality. "I was a stranger and you welcomed me" resounds throughout the ancient texts, and contemporary practitioners of hospitality refer to this text more often than to any other passage.'[62] Pohl herself thinks that the term 'stranger' is to be equated with the vulnerable. She states: 'This passage sets up a fundamental identification of Jesus with "the least of these" and personally and powerfully connects hospitality toward human beings with care for Jesus.'[63] However, many scholars argue that 'the least of these' does not refer to the poor and vulnerable, but to receiving the Gospel's messengers.[64] Nevertheless, the priority of providing hospitality for the vulnerable stranger is, Carig Keener notes,

> entirely consonant with the Jesus tradition (e.g. Mk 10:21; Lk 16:19–25) and biblical ethics as a whole (Ex 22:22–27; Prov 17:5; 19:17; 21:13). Jewish lists of loving works include showing hospitality and visiting the sick, though not visiting prisoners. Such acts were found praiseworthy on the day of Judgment (2 Enoch 63:1–2; b. Ned 39b-40a). ... One could thus understand Jesus' disciples as bringers of healing (10:8), caring for the least.[65]

Exegesis of the parable of the Great Banquet

I turn now to an exegesis of the Great Banquet parable in order to elucidate a theological understanding of hospitality. While the focus is on Luke's rendering of the Great Banquet parable, many of the same points could be made in relation to Matthew's version. However, Luke's version forms part of a wider development of the motif of hospitality throughout Luke–Acts.[66]

There is a parallel between the messianic feast depicted in Isaiah 25:6–9 and the Great Banquet parable told by Jesus in Luke 14:15–24. It is something akin to this messianic banquet that the pious guest had in mind when he exclaimed: 'Blessed is anyone who will eat bread in the kingdom of God!' (v.15). In Isaiah all the nations are envisaged as participating in the banquet and without even bringing gifts to honour Yahweh. The text contrasts God who swallows up death with the participants, from all nations, who swallow rich food and rejoice. Bailey points to the differences between this treatment of the messianic feast and how it is portrayed in the intertestamental period: in Enoch 1 the gentiles are excluded, and the Qumran community adds to this by rejecting all Jews who are unrighteous or physically blemished.[67] By contrast, the Isaiah presentation is reaffirmed in Luke. This reaffirmation is initially made in Luke 13:28–34 where Jesus declares that 'people will come from east and west, from north and south, and will eat in the kingdom of God. Indeed, some are last who will be first, and some who are first will be last' (Lk. 13:29–30). If Enoch and Qumran indicate the expectation of Jesus' contemporaries concerning the messianic feast, then the parable Jesus tells in response to the pious guest challenges and reconfigures these expectations.[68]

The parable of the Great Banquet portrays a time when the banquet is ready (Lk. 14:17); that is, when Jesus has inaugurated the eschaton. The invitation to this formal dinner is sent out to the host's peers. The invitation is met by insulting excuses that in effect are rejections.[69] These rejections are a self-conscious and systematic exclusion of the host by his peer group. Such rejection is not just a matter of a dented reputation: political power, economic well-being and, in the context of a shame culture, social identity, rested on maintaining one's prestige and honour.[70] Therefore, these 'guests' are not just rejecting the host's invitation, but they are portrayed as active enemies of the host.

The call to participate in the kingdom of God relativizes all social, economic, political and natural commitments, and not just those of the elite. This is confirmed in the following section (Lk. 14:25–33) which can be read as an elaboration on the preceding parable. As Bailey summarizes it:

> The parable says that as they reject Jesus (with these unacceptable excuses) they are rejecting the great banquet of salvation promised by God in Isaiah, that is, in some sense, even now set for them through the presence of Jesus in their midst. But not only do they reject the host, they also prefer other things.[71]

Thus, there is no simple rejection of Jesus. Rather, to refuse God's generosity is to prefer and attend to some other god or power. Likewise, acceptance of the invitation demands whole-hearted devotion: you must leave what you are doing and your present concerns, and without tarrying, you must go and participate fully in the banquet.[72] The invitation is a command and the command is an invitation.

The next part of the parable concerns the invitation to the outcasts. The host's anger is normal, but his response is not. Instead of seeking vengeance he makes the banquet open to outcasts: 'Go out at once into the streets and lanes of the town and bring in the poor, the crippled, the blind, and the lame' (Lk. 14:21). Braun reads this as the point of conversion of the host, the central character in this story. By inviting outcasts the host steps outside the accepted patterns of competitive social relations that preserve honour and prestige among the elite.[73] And instead of resorting to strategies of vengeance as would be expected, he inverts and subverts the existing patterns of social stratification and the moral order. By breaking with the 'ostentatious and agonistic rituals of dinner',[74] and not resorting to violence in order to preserve his name, the host reconfigures the existing degenerate patterns of human sociality and breaks the cycle of what René Girard calls 'mimetic rivalry'.[75] Instead of securing his identity, reputation, and economic well-being through mimesis of the conventional moral, social and economic norms, he rests them on identifying with the poor and outcasts. There is thus a conversion from one pattern of relating to another, and with this conversion the world itself is turned upside down. The final statement of the parable underscores this: the host severs himself completely from those with whom he previously sought table-fellowship and, by implication, expresses loyalty to those who now surround him (Lk. 14:24).[76] This reconfiguring is brought into sharp focus when the context in which Jesus tells this parable is understood to be not just a simple meal, but also a symposium characteristic of the Mediterranean world of Luke's time.[77] Jesus is the sage or teacher who is calling for the reigning symposium rules to be supplanted: the usual virtues are inverted – humility not pride is exalted (Lk. 14:10) – and the usual guests prove unworthy and instead it is the 'poor, the crippled, the lame, and the blind' who are honoured (Lk. 14:11–14).[78]

The identity of the outcasts themselves is significant. They are from the surrounding area, and so are part of the community, but are excluded from participating in the life of that community.[79] Thus a contrast is drawn between the notables of the world who both expect to be invited yet refuse the invitation, and those who do not consider themselves worthy or who are considered by others to be worthless, yet who are invited and accept.

There is a dramatic asymmetry at work here. Those who accept have nothing to bring. Braun notes that the language itself maximizes the sense of distance between the host and these guests. He states: 'This social awareness evident in the choice of invitational vocabulary indirectly yet unmistakably discloses the distance that separates these two parties.'[80] The host is in no way indebted to them and they cannot respond in kind; that is, they are undeserving guests, most probably either shocked or distrustful that such an invitation is extended to them. However, this dynamic requires careful interpretation. The conversion of the host can be read as the movement from an economy of gift the heart of which is agonistic rivalry and the maintenance of honour (such as that outlined by Marcel Mauss in his analysis of the 'potlatch' and gift cycle)[81] to an alternative economy of gift, or perhaps more accurately, an economy of blessing. In this economy of blessing nothing is expected in return (there is no perpetual cycle or flow of gifts as in Mauss's account) and no social, economic or political status is afforded the giver. However, the host of this parable is not to be confused with Aristotle's 'great souled' or 'magnanimous' man. The magnanimous man is disposed to confer benefits or offer gifts without expectation of a return, but these gifts serve to reinforce the superior status of the giver and his self-sufficiency and autonomy.[82] By contrast, the host of this parable does not remain self-sufficient. He actively pursues relationships with others, and it is pursued in such a way that the host is rendered vulnerable to rejection, while the recipients are blessed by participation in the feast. The host does not simply give a gift (the meal), nor does he identify or show solidarity with the poor and outcast in some notional or distant manner, rather, the host parties with them. Moreover, his actions are expressive of his need for and dependence on these people: a party, by definition, requires others. Thus the fruit of this feast is a communion of giver and receiver.[83]

The emphasis on inviting the poor and needy, in contrast with other patterns of hospitality, has been a principal virtue consistently echoed throughout the Christian tradition. It is the emphasis on inviting the outcast which, time and again, distinguishes Christian hospitality from other kinds of hospitality. For example, Lactantius criticizes classical philosophers who tied hospitality to advantage. He argues: 'Hospitality is a principle virtue, as the philosophers also say; but they turn it aside from true justice, and forcibly apply it to advantage.'[84] He then goes on to criticize Cicero in particular, stating, 'He has here committed the same error ... when he said that we must bestow our bounty on "suitable" persons. For the house of the just and wise man ought not to be open to the illustrious, but to the lowly and abject.'[85] Greek and Roman views of hospitality tended to emphasize reciprocity and the use of hospitality within a client-patron relationship from which both parties gained social, political and economic advantage.[86] For Lactantius, and other Christian writers, Christians were deliberately to welcome those who could offer little in return and from whom little prestige could be gained. By contrast, and as has already been noted, for the magnanimous man, hospitality and the giving of gifts underscores his superiority and accrues to him prestige. The views of Lactantius help explain the parable of the Great Banquet and illustrate how the conception of hospitality given in the parable is consistently echoed in the Christian tradition.

The last section of the parable intensifies the way in which the marginalized are included in the feast. The invitation to the celebration, which is at hand, is now extended to those outside the community.[87] Bailey envisages Jesus as having the mission to the Gentiles at the heart of his ministry. He states:

> Luke's interest in the gentiles is unmistakable. ... The genealogy [of Jesus] is traced to Adam (Luke 3.38) and not to Abraham (Matt 1.2). The quotation from Isaiah 40.3–5 in Luke 3.6 includes the phrase, 'And *all flesh* shall see the salvation of God,' and the commission of the disciples at the end of Luke specifically mentions the gentiles (24.47).[88]

The passage Jesus uses to declare his ministry makes this explicit (Lk. 4:16–19). Furthermore, this announcement is supplemented by reference to Elijah *going out* of Israel to help the gentile woman of Zarephath and Elisha ministering to the gentile Naaman who *comes into* Israel because he is attracted to what God is doing through Elisha (Lk. 4:25–27). The parable of the Great Banquet illuminates this dynamic. There is a simultaneously centrifugal and centripetal mission visualized: the servant is to go out so that others, whether outcasts or outsiders, can be drawn in. Bailey draws parallels to other passages in Luke: 'Again, as in Luke 4.16–30, the centripetal and the centrifugal forces of mission are set side by side. The city on the hill sends light *out* to *all the world*, and the lamp is seen only by those who are *in the house*.'[89] However, this dynamic is not restricted to Luke's Gospel. Parallels can be drawn with Jesus' encounter with the Syrophoenician woman depicted in Matthew 15:21–28 and Mark 7:24–30.[90] In addition, there is the story of the Centurion who calls on Jesus to heal his servant (Mt. 8:5–13): while Jesus was going about his ministry, this man comes to him. Furthermore, this soldier was not only a gentile, but also an oppressor, yet Jesus cites him as an example of faithfulness; that is, he is a true participant in the people of God.[91] These stories represent faithful responses (by outsiders) to the servant Lord who went out in their midst (meaning that he both literally walked around and that he departed from the accepted conventions of his day) so that the excluded might be included. They respond to the Lord as the servant who exorcizes creation, transforms their social, political and economic structures, and establishes a community of those who are to carry on this ministry, in his name, until he comes again. This going out and reconfiguring the existent order so that it becomes a feast, that is, a place of generative, fruitful relations, applies whether the context is first century Palestine or the remnants of Christendom at the dawn of the third millennium.

In summary, the parable of the Great Banquet articulates the nature and proper form of the church's relations with its neighbours. The church is to participate actively in the life of the world as slaves and envoys of the true King, in a manner akin to Jesus, extending an invitation to those, like they were previously, who are not worthy guests, who are marginalized in the wider society, who do not consider themselves invited, and who have not even heard there is such a banquet available. Some will reject the invitation, others will accept, and some will need encouragement to believe that such an invitation includes them. The invitation is not to revelry or idolatry, but to the messianic feast that has *already* begun. Like Jesus, the speech and action of the church is simultaneously centrifugal – they go out into the world – and centripetal – the world is drawn into participating in the banquet. Thus, the church, like Jesus, neither separates itself from the world nor becomes assimilated to the world.

Hospitality and Christian witness

The parable of the Great Banquet explains how we are to provide hospitality to our 'enemies' in the midst of them. It summarizes what Christ embodies in his life and ministry whereby he was the *journeying guest/host*. The very situation of the Great Banquet parable in the Lukan travel narrative emphasizes this. As Jesus travels to Jerusalem where he is the rejected guest who in turn becomes the gracious, crucified host, he tells this story of the hospitality he offers amid the rejection he receives. Moessner sees Christ's embodiment of the *journeying guest/host* as exemplified in the Emmaus road encounter: 'What is primary to the Emmaus episode and may be regarded as the interpretative key for all the meal scenes in Luke is the recognition of the journeying guest who is revealed at table as the Lord (v.35) and as Lord, the host of the banquet in the kingdom of God.'[92] He notes how Jesus journeyed with Cleopas and his friend on the road they were travelling, in dialogue with them about the kingdom of God. Jesus was then a guest at their home, who then became their host at the meal. At this meal strangers became friends and Jesus was understood to be the risen Lord. After this event these two disciples went out, leaving their home, journeying to the very heart of their social, political, and economic world – Jerusalem – in order to bear witness, with others, to the risen Christ.

Peter's meeting with Cornelius exemplifies how the church, as it follows after Jesus Christ, is itself a journeying guest/host and as such, this story portrays a picture of how Christians should relate to their neighbours. In Acts 10 we read first of the Spirit's work in the life of the Roman soldier Cornelius (Acts 10:1–8) signifying that God is already at work in the world drawing all things to him. The Spirit then gives Peter a vision of many varieties of food (Acts 10:9–16). It is a kerygmatic vision which echoes Jesus' call to Peter to love him and feed his sheep. It is a eucharistic vision of feasting wherein sacrifice, in this instance of animals, bears witness to a 'clean' or restored creation order represented by the four-cornered sheet and the cornucopia that fills it.[93] After three repetitions, this restored order, in a manner parallel to the ascension, is then taken up to heaven. This vision emphasizes that Christ has fulfilled the law and restored creation, and we are made clean in and through the ascended Christ. There is no longer any need for the People of God to distinguish themselves by purity rituals, such as not eating certain food, or avoiding the company of pagans and sinners. Our purity resides in Jesus Christ alone, not in any of our actions. Nothing can separate us from him (Rom. 8:35–9), and he has sent his Spirit through whom we participate in Christ's purity, and by which we are empowered to live according to this already established righteousness. Thus, contact with the pagan Cornelius will not 'infect' Peter; rather, through contact with Peter Cornelius will be enabled to appropriate his new identity more fully and Peter and Cornelius together, through the actions of the Spirit, will mutually constitute the People of God.

Peter is subsequently instructed to go with the men sent by Cornelius who lead him to where, in his immaturity, he would not want to go. After providing these strangers with hospitality (Acts 10:23), he journeys with them, along with some fellow believers, to Cornelius. At their meeting there is no demand that Cornelius bow to Peter (that is, those 'outside' the church bow to those 'inside'), they meet as equals, equally empowered by the Spirit to receive, through their encounter with each other, a fresh encounter and understanding of God. However, Peter, who is the guest of Cornelius at this point, becomes the host. It is he who interprets Cornelius's encounter with God, recognizing that God is at work outside the church (Acts 10:34–35) and frames Cornelius's experience in reference to the Gospel (Acts 10:34–43). As D'Costa says, the 'riches of the mystery of God are disclosed by the Spirit and are measured and discerned by their conformity to and in their illumination of Christ. ... In this sense, Jesus is the *normative* criteria for God, while not foreclosing the ongoing self-disclosure of God in history, through the Spirit.'[94] After this Christocentric naming of Cornelius's encounter with God, the Spirit is poured out on the Gentiles (Acts 10:45) and the church, represented by its practices (that is, baptism) and the presence of the Jewish believers, is reconfigured by the Spirit; and Peter and Cornelius live out this new understanding of who God is through Cornelius's hospitality towards Peter.[95] Thus, a reciprocity, or a giving and receiving from each, of a new understanding of who God is revealed to be by Jesus Christ, is matched by a giving and receiving of hospitality.

It is no coincidence that this encounter is followed by an account of the mission to the Gentiles and the subsequent dispute about circumcision: a dispute that centred on what it meant to be in but not of the world. The book of Acts proposes that by going out to the world, and actively participating in it, Peter was able to enjoy greater communion with God.[96] For a central dynamic of the church's neighbour relations, as articulated in this encounter, is that going out is the way of coming home. It is not just that Christians are to seek the welfare of the city, even though that city be Babylon (Jer. 27:9), but it is in the very act of going out to seek Babylon's welfare that they enjoy table fellowship with God: that is, holiness or purity is defined by communion with God (and not by separation from sinners and pagans) and communion is enjoyed by seeking the welfare of the poor, the impure and pagans. Furthermore, through going out to these people the life of the nations itself becomes transfigured into a proleptic celebration of the messianic banquet. Dulles captures the rhythm of this *single* movement well when he says:

> The Church's existence is a continual alternation between two phases. Like systole and exhalation in the process of breathing, assembly and mission succeed each other in the life of the Church. Discipleship would be stunted unless it included both the centripetal phase of worship and the centrifugal phase of mission.[97]

This single, simultaneously centripetal and centrifugal movement, is how the church is to remain righteous, holy and faithful to God's call when it is surrounded by enemies who wish to conquer and co-opt it and temptations and idolatries which threaten to seduce it. Equally, this centripetal and centrifugal movement is how the church ensures that it does not turn its back on its neighbours and deny that which it should accept from them.

In this encounter between Peter and Cornelius we see the Spirit at work outside the church, calling the church out from its settled place in order to follow God's mission to the world. Peter who is the guest of Cornelius becomes the host. But then the lives of both Peter and Cornelius are transfigured by the Spirit such that they both have to re-order their lives and their life together so that they embrace, and do not exclude each other. The re-ordering of their lives, so that it becomes a life together, is founded on their obedience to God whose self-revelation in Jesus Christ constitutes the criterion for evaluating what and whom to accept. In turn, the process whereby their patterns of life are transformed, and a new pattern emerges, bears witness to God's kaleidoscopic order. However, this new pattern of life formed in response to Jesus Christ neither erases nor destroys nor abandons all previous patterns of life. For example, Cornelius does not have to become a Jew. Instead, the decision as to whom to accept and whom to reject is evaluated in relation to whether or not the person bears witness to Jesus Christ. Thus, a measure of the hospitality of the church is how people are bound together and what boundaries are maintained or re-established between people. Truthful and generative binding and separating is a work of the Spirit who directs all things towards their eschatological fulfilment.[98]

At the heart of the process by which a new pattern of life emerges is the guest–host dynamic wherein Christians, like Christ, are both stranger and host. As Leviticus 19:34 reminds us, true hospitality requires we understand both the experience of being a vulnerable stranger and what it means to receive all things from God. To be sensitized to the needs and fears of a stranger we must remember the experience of being 'aliens in the land'. Yet it is not enough simply to shape our hospitality in the light of our own experiences as strangers. As Reinhard Hütter argues, true hospitality requires we remember the truth that we owe our existence not to ourselves or our own work, but rather to the Giver of Life.[99] We are the recipients of God's abundant and costly hospitality of us through the death and resurrection of Jesus Christ. Openness to the stranger requires constant remembrance of our strangeness to God and God's hospitality of us. Thus hospitality to the stranger is an evangelical imperative: it is a mark of the truthful disclosure of God's nature by a people who themselves are guests of God.

The book of Acts continues Jesus' journey, with the church recapitulating this guest–host dynamic of Jesus in its relations with the world. Moessner states: 'Thus the "Acts of the Apostles" are actually the stories of the journeying of the people of God whose leaders imitate their Prophet Messiah in proclaiming the glad tidings of the Kingdom.'[100] In effect, the verse Leviticus 19:34 is inverted. Far from the people of God being settled in the land and providing hospitality to strangers, the people of God are the sojourners in the world. Yet even though they are sojourners, Christians are to provide hospitality to the world. The church is not to be entertained by the degenerate forms of human sociality and thought enjoyed by the world. Rather, the church is to invite the world to participate in generative patterns of thought and action, and bear witness in its life together to the possibility of such patterns. Thus the church, through the social practice of hospitality, is to host the world even as it journeys as a stranger through the midst of the world, thereby bearing witness to the world's own eschatological possibilities. It is the Christocentric performance of hospitality that furnishes the world with the concrete, non-Utopian vision of 'just generosity' that MacIntyre sees as essential for human flourishing.[101]

Hospitality within the Christian tradition

The paradigm of hospitality set out in the biblical texts analysed above has informed the thinking and practice of the church throughout its history. From its earliest writings, right through to contemporary Christian practice, there is evidence for the centrality of hospitality as the practice that determines how Christians relate to their neighbours.

The *Didache* is an early example of both the exhortation to hospitality as an important Christian discipline and the tensions within the practice of hospitality. In an echo of Matthew 5:2, the *Didache* admonishes Christians to 'Give to anyone that asks you, and demand no return; the Father wants His own bounties to be shared with all.'[102] The document calls on Christians to be open-handed in their hospitality, especially towards the poor.[103] However, it tempers the exhortation to generosity with discernment by setting out a number of ways in which those who would abuse Christian hospitality, and those who threatened the life together of the community (for example, by their false teaching), can be discouraged.[104] The *Didache* represents an attempt to control abuses of hospitality while simultaneously encouraging its practice.[105] We see in the *Didache* a tension within the Christian tradition of hospitality that surfaces time and again; that is, the tension between recognizing Jesus in every stranger and the prudential consideration of discriminating between deserving and undeserving strangers.[106] However, the very existence of documents that attempt to address the problem of the abuse of hospitality points to how, in the early church at least, hospitality was considered a normative and necessary practice.[107]

Fears about the abuse of hospitality were not just focused on how guests might take advantage of it. There is also a strong emphasis in the tradition on admonishing hosts not to use hospitality to gain advantage. Already noted is the exhortation by many of the Church Fathers that Christians were deliberately to welcome those from whom little prestige could be gained. For example John Chrysostom wrote:

> Wherefore God bade us call to our suppers and our feasts the lame, and the maimed, and those who cannot repay us; for these are most of all properly called good deeds which are done for God's sake. Whereas if thou entertain some great and distinguished man, it is not such pure mercy, what thou doest: but some portion many times is assigned to thyself also, both by vain-glory, and by the return of the favor, and by thy rising in many men's estimation on account of thy guest.[108]

Within the Christian tradition the stranger to be welcomed is consistently defined as someone who lacks any resources to support themselves. The stranger is someone who lacks a 'place' in society because they are detached or excluded from the basic means of supporting and sustaining life – family, work, polity, land and so on – and are thus vulnerable. Pohl states: 'Through most of its history, the Christian hospitality tradition has expressed a normative concern for strangers who could not provide for or defend themselves.'[109] For example, in 1785 a group of Methodists founded the Stranger's Friends Society in London to aid the new class of urban poor. John Wesley described the Society as 'instituted wholly for the relief not of our society, but for the poor, sick, friendless strangers'.[110] In other words, following the parable of the Good Samaritan, the answer given to the question 'who is my neighbour?' (Lk. 10:29) has been that the neighbour to be welcomed is the 'friendless stranger'. Hence, what constitutes the abuse of hospitality by hosts is defined in terms of whether their hospitality ignores the vulnerable and friendless stranger.

The emphasis on welcoming the vulnerable stranger points to how Christian hospitality is often not simply a question of entertaining a stranger. To entertain a stranger implies the life of the host is relatively unaffected by the encounter. However, to accommodate (in the sense of adapt to and make space and time for) or host (in the sense of sacrificially offer oneself for) the stranger carries the implication that making room for the stranger requires the host to change their pattern of life. An emphasis on the readiness to change one's life in order that the vulnerable stranger may be accommodated is a constant theme in the tradition. Perhaps the most radical example of changing one's pattern of life in order that the vulnerable stranger might be accommodated is *The Rule of St Benedict*. Benedict's rule, and the forms of monasticism it inspired, sought a form of life in which humility and obedience were the means by which love of God and neighbour were accomplished. Benedict wrote: 'Renounce yourself in order to follow Christ.'[111] The renunciation he calls for is in order that the monk may 'relieve the lot of the poor, clothe the naked, visit the sick and bury the dead.'[112] For Benedict, hospitality of vulnerable strangers was directly linked to a readiness to change one's self-willed and pride-filled pattern of life in order that worship of God, and love of one's neighbour, might come first. To do this required training in 'a school for the Lord's service' and could not be achieved alone.[113] However, hospitality of vulnerable strangers was not simply the response of individual monks resulting from their training in the monastery. It was also part of the witness of the whole community. Echoing Matthew 25:35 Benedict writes: 'All guests who present themselves are to be welcomed as Christ, for he himself will say: "I was a stranger and you welcomed me." Proper honor must be shown to all, especially to those who share our faith and to pilgrims.'[114] Special provision for accommodating guests was made and this provision was central to the common life of the monastery which was, as Banner argues, designed to bear witness to the true peace of the City of God characterized by love rather than enmity.[115]

By the fourth century, more institutional, systematic and corporate forms of hospitality began to emerge. For example, John Chrysostom, acting in his capacity as Bishop, was instrumental in founding a number of hospitals in Constantinople.[116] These corporate forms of hospitality were often a response to particular crises. For example, Gregory Nazianzen praises Basil of Caesarea for founding hospitals that cared for the sick and poor after a terrible famine.[117] However, John Chrysostom constantly refers to the need for individual Christians to practise hospitality as well. In his forty-fifth sermon on the Acts of the Apostles, after a meditation on Matthew 25:39–42 and Abraham welcoming the Angels to his table, Chrysostom states: 'Make for yourself a guest chamber in your own house: set up a bed there, set up a table there and a candlestick. ... This do: surpass [the Church] in liberality: have a room to which Christ may come, say "This is Christ's cell; this building is set apart for Him".'[118] For Chrysostom there is both the hospitality undertaken by the Church itself and that undertaken by individuals within the church. He sees both as necessary.[119] What Chrysostom's sermon points to is the tension between the institutional and corporate nature of some instances of Christian hospitality, needed to address a certain scale of need, and how these instances can appear to obviate, and even militate against, the continuing responsibility for personal, particular and non-institutional hospitality by all Christians.[120]

The practice of hospitality continued to be a mark of Christian witness right up to the present day (even if it has not always been as forthcoming as it should have been). Calvin expressed anxiety about the loss of hospitality as a normative practice. Referring to the practice of hospitality, he states: 'This office of humanity has ... nearly ceased to be properly observed among men'.[121] Furthermore, he says of hospitality to refugees in Geneva: 'No duty can be more pleasing or acceptable to God'.[122] As Calvin's response to those Protestants fleeing persecution indicates, hospitality formed part of the church's faithful response to new social, political and economic developments and to particular historical crises. For example, while many Christians singularly failed to respond to the racist and violent persecution of the Jews by the Nazis, the response of those that did act faithfully was characterized by the practice of hospitality. A striking example is the story of the Protestant village of Le Chambon whose members, in their homes, and at great personal cost, protected thousands of Jews, and ensured their escape from the death camps.[123] A more contemporary example of the same practice of hospitality in response to racially motivated persecution were the actions of Fr. Sava and the monks of the Serbian Orthodox monastery at Dečani during the conflict over Kosovo in 1999. They sheltered Albanians from Serbian military forces and then, as NATO began taking control of the region, they sheltered Roma, Slav Muslims, and Serbs from Albanian militias.[124] The work of the largely Roman Catholic Sant'Egidio Community in resolving the civil war in Mozambique through welcoming and reconciling hostile neighbours is an example of the practice of hospitality in relation to deadly conflict.[125] In a very different area of activity, the work of Jean Vanier and the care given to those with severe learning disabilities in the L'Arche communities is yet another example of how hospitality shapes the response of Christians to vulnerable 'strangers' in relation to social and moral problems or crises.[126] These examples are but a few of the many that could be cited.

This brief review of ways in which hospitality has been conceived and practised emphasizes the centrality of hospitality within Christianity. Its centrality is further underlined by the way in which a concern for the proper practice of hospitality occurs in both exhortations to faithful witness and Christian renewal movements; for example, monasticism.[127] The above historical review also helps clarify how hospitality may shape relations between Christians and their neighbours. The neighbour is properly understood, within the Christian tradition, to be a stranger; moreover, the stranger is not simply someone who is different, instead, there is a consistent and special concern for the vulnerable stranger, for example, the poor, the sick, and the refugee. Moreover, as the witness of the village of Le Chambon demonstrates, the focus on the vulnerable stranger will, on occasion, mean the church finds itself actively opposed by those who would be, by Christian criteria of evaluation, inhospitable to the vulnerable stranger. As the exegesis of 1 Peter in the previous chapter made clear, a pattern of hospitality that bears witness to Jesus Christ will meet with a variety of responses, some of which will be very hostile. Conversely, because of its particular understanding of what hospitality requires, the church is not uncritically welcoming of everyone: a proper evaluation must be made of who, in any particular instance, is the stranger to be welcomed.

Care for the vulnerable stranger is not without its problems. A number of tensions have emerged within the practice of hospitality. There is the tension between greeting every stranger as Christ and discerning who would genuinely benefit from care, the tension of establishing institutional and corporate forms of hospitality and the need for hospitality to be personal, particular and practised by every Christian, and finally, the tension between provision and the capacity to provide wherein the integrity and resources of the community can be overwhelmed by the abuse of, or extensive need for, hospitality.[128] Despite these tensions, the practice of hospitality is a recurring and consistent activity throughout the Christian tradition and it is an activity shaped by response to the words and actions of Jesus Christ, given in Scripture, as Christians seek to bear faithful witness to God's hospitality of both them and their neighbours.

So far, I have deliberately resisted giving a formal definition of hospitality and have instead used the biblical material, and the history of the Christian tradition, to describe what the Christocentric performance of hospitality involves. As stated at the beginning of this chapter, the aim was to see how the Scriptural motif of hospitality portrays a concrete and generic pattern for relations between the church and its neighbours. What is required now is a definition of hospitality within a doctrinal framework in order to clarify what is meant by the term.

The doctrinal framework within which hospitality is situated

As a motif and social practice hospitality 'helps us trace the correspondence of the church's formal acts and observances to the shape of the Christ-event'.[129] While all the moments of the Christ-event are crucial to the proper mapping of ethics and evaluating moral problems, hospitality – as instantiated in the Scriptural motif and practised within the tradition – is the 'mark' by which we can identify properly Christian relations between the church and its neighbours: that is, relations which correspond to and recapitulate the Christ-event. As noted earlier in the discussion of O'Donovan's ecclesiology, recapitulation of the Christ-event is the structuring principle for all ecclesiology, including how the church relates to those around it. Hospitality is the social practice that corresponds to the church's recapitulation of Christ's ascension and the sending of his Spirit at Pentecost. This is to modify O'Donovan's schema slightly. O'Donovan includes in a single moment Christ's resurrection, ascension and Pentecost. I see these as two discrete moments rather than as a single one. Resurrection is a moment in itself as is the single movement of Christ to the right hand of the Father and the subsequent sending of the Spirit to commission the church. Relations between the church and its neighbours are properly situated in this latter moment because it is this moment that establishes the church and sets up the eschatological tension central to Christian specificity and how the church relates to its neighbours. At his ascension Christ's rule over 'the nations' is inaugurated and his 'kingdom' established. Thus the eschatological fulfilment of creation (restored at Christ's resurrection) is achieved. However, the ascension means Christ is not present on earth and the eschaton is not yet fully realized. However, at Pentecost the Spirit makes participation in the ascended Christ and the eschaton possible. The church bears witness to this possibility in its life together, while such witness-bearing inherently draws its neighbours into its common life.

At the heart of this doctrine is the eschatological tension between the reality that the eschaton is inaugurated, but is not yet made fully manifest. The church in its thought and action must take account of this tension. However, as Douglas Farrow describes at length, the church too often seeks to relieve this tension either by grasping at heaven in its own strength (thereby ignoring the actions of Christ and the Spirit), or by positing an over-realized eschatology (thereby forgetting Christ's absence), or even by a false pessimism (which overemphasizes Christ's absence and ignores the Spirit).[130] By contrast, true 'ecclesial being' balances the presence and absence of God.[131] The church, despite its sinfulness, enjoys communion with God, in Christ, through the Spirit, yet also waits expectantly for the full disclosure and perfection of that life with God at the *parousia*.

Hospitality is the social practice that structures relations between Christians and non-Christians in such a way that it recapitulates the ascension and Pentecost moments of the Christ-event. Specifically Christian hospitality is inaugurated at Pentecost and bears witness to the eschaton and corresponds to the tension at the heart of the eschaton, whereby it is established but not yet fully manifest. As an eschatological social practice, Christian hospitality is inspired and empowered by the Holy Spirit, who enables the church to host the life of its neighbours without the church being assimilated to, colonized by, or having to withdraw from its neighbours.

According to O'Donovan's schema each social practice that corresponds to a moment in the Christ-event has an accompanying sacrament. The accompanying sacrament embodies and symbolizes how the church is recapitulating the Christ-event. The sacramental enactment which accompanies the practice of hospitality is the single movement of feasting and fasting. This is not to deny the way in which the eucharist is in many ways paradigmatic for how Christians relate God's hospitality of us and our hospitality of each other, but it is to recognize that the feast days and festivals of the church encompass more than just a eucharist. Moreover, as noted earlier, the eucharist is related specifically to the Passion of Christ and the trial and martyrdom of the church, while feasting and fasting relate to the ascension and Pentecost moments of the Christ-event.[132]

Feasting and fasting as the sacramental enactment of hospitality

The church, in its moments and ministries of recapitulation, has always taken seriously the feast (or festival) and fasting as definitive in, and interpretative of, the shaping and expression of the Christian life. Such feasting and fasting is the sacramental enactment of the practice of hospitality; that is, feasting embodies a proleptic disclosure of the eschaton, while fasting ensures the eschatological tension is held. Apart from its instantiation of hospitality, we may well ask what relevance the analysis of feasting and fasting has to Christian ethics. The answer is that the framework of feasting and fasting set out below provides us with a lens through which to assess whether particular forms of life together undertaken by Christians bear faithful witness to Jesus Christ.

As set out above, in the Scriptural description of hospitality we see how actual banquets and feasts are a feature of the practice of hospitality. In addition, alongside the Eucharist and other sacraments, the Christian tradition always marked its anticipation of the eschaton/messianic banquet by feast days and festivals. These take many forms. They range from the catholic feasts that celebrate the central events of Christ's life, such as Christmas, Easter and Ascension, to the feast days of local saints.[133]

These feasts bear witness to the messianic feast that transforms the world of everyday work by breaking it open to new and true life.[134] Feasting, which celebrates the messianic feast, functions to create a space for true freedom and anticipates the time when this freedom will be fully established.[135] Feasts encompass and draw in every aspect of human sociality. Indeed, the feast envisaged, for example, in the parable of the Great Banquet allows no scope for this spiritual freedom to be etherealized or interiorized. As David Ford puts it: 'All the senses are engaged in a good feast. We taste, touch, smell, see, hear. Salvation as health is here vividly physical. Anything that heals and enhances savouring the world through our senses may feed into a salvation that culminates in feasting.'[136] To be drawn into the messianic feast, anticipated now in the feastings of the church, every area of life and every person must be transfigured. However, no new totality is created. There can be no overview or single principle that orders the feast. The myriad of conversations, encounters and exchanges, which in turn generate surplus to be exchanged, cannot be contained or directed. Neither is there a single pattern to conform to: each person has a gift, and each exchange takes place between distinct and unique persons whose particularity is established and enhanced through these exchanges. Thus, feasts and festivals are ways to anticipate and respond to the in-breaking messianic age that initiates true freedom and generates transfigured patterns of human sociality.

Before the *parousia*, the sacramental enactment which embodies hospitality has a double aspect: that is, feasting requires and is complemented by fasting. To embody hospitality through feasting alone would deny the absence of Jesus Christ and the cruciform nature of discipleship. Christians cannot ignore the words of invitation by which Christ invites them to enjoy his hospitality: 'If any want to become my followers, let them deny themselves and take up their cross and follow me' (Mk 8:34; cf., Mt. 16:24; Lk. 9:23). Neither can they ignore the reality that: 'the whole creation has been groaning in labour pains until now; and not only the creation, but we ourselves, who have the first fruits of the Spirit, groan inwardly while we wait for adoption, the redemption of our bodies' (Rom. 8:22–23). Moltmann states:

> The coming of Christ is looked for to bring the perfection of freedom to the whole of enslaved creation (Rom 8.19). In worship and in the eucharist men are taken up into this eschatological process of the setting free of the world to be the kingdom of glory. They celebrate this freedom in eschatological rejoicing and bring it into the world by taking up their crosses. The recollection of the suffering of the crucified rules out a view of the feast as an escape from the painful conditions of earthly life. ... Hope in the risen Christ rules out mere lamentation over this suffering without hope or denouncing its causes without joy. ... Joy at the presence of freedom through reconciliation is thus mixed with pain at the presence of unfreedom and hope of the world's release from it.[137]

Fasting is a way of embodying the pain of taking up our cross and physically entering into the expectation and longing for the full disclosure of God's rule. Feasting and fasting correspond to the different aspects of the eschatological tension: Christians both celebrate and invite others to participate in the resurrection hope, yet we wait for the fulfilment of that hope. There can be no true feasting without fasting: this would be to forget Christ's absence. Neither can there be true fasting without feasting: this would be to deny the freedom available now through what Christ has done.

The church in its liturgical year recognizes the intrinsic link between feasting and fasting. Thus, a period of fasting precedes the feast of Christmas and Lent precedes Easter.[138] Even within each week, there have traditionally been days of fasting, and Sunday, the feast-day. Hence, in its ordering of time itself the Christian tradition sought to mark the eschatological tension.

Without being bounded by fasting, the feast can quickly descend into Saturnalia or carnival. Parallels can be drawn between conceptions of carnival and the messianic feast. Within Christian practice the carnival has played a prominent part; for example, the tradition of holding carnivals before or on Shrove Tuesday that still continues. Mikhail Bakhtin even suggests that during the medieval era carnivals reconfigured official feasts that consecrated injustice.[139] However, the semi-sanctioned use of carnival within the liturgical year should not blind us to how it contrasts with Easter. Most obviously, Shrove Tuesday is not disciplined by a prior period of fasting.[140] This may seem trivial, but it points to the twofold rejection that lies at the heart of all forms of the carnivalesque. First, carnival denies Christ's affirmation of creation as good by contravening human limits (for example, through celebrating gluttony and excess) and overturning the established social order (for example, by celebrating anarchy).[141] Second, carnival constitutes a rejection of the future given by God (for example, by celebrating immediate gratification and reward). Bakhtin could well be right: carnivals can serve to disrupt an unjust social order. However, the manner of this disruption is wholly different in kind from the eschatological disruption of the messianic feast. Indeed, the treatment of carnival in literature (for example, in Rabelais's *Gargantua and Pantagruel*) and its depiction in art (for example, in the pictures of Hieronymus Bosch) suggests carnival is to be equated with a demonic parody of the messianic feast. In contrast to the messianic banquet, which enables generative, transfigured patterns of human sociality, marked in this age by feasting and fasting together, the Saturnalia or carnival is degenerate.[142]

In addition to its being the sacramental instantiation of hospitality, feasting and fasting provide us with a lens through which to analyse many forms of life together undertaken by Christians. The sacramental enactment of feasting and fasting thereby provides a means by which to assess whether or not particular forms of Christian life together constitute a faithful witness to Jesus Christ. An example of such an assessment might lie in a consideration of the monastic life as advocated by St Benedict; which fails to take sufficient account of the need for both feasting and fasting. St Benedict's 'little rule' has been a widely influential pattern of life since its inception in 530. However, while making worship central, the pattern of life together advocated by Benedict appears to have no place for feasting. He states: 'The life of a monk ought to be a continuous Lent.'[143] This sentiment is reflected in the rest of his rule: despite detailed prescriptions regarding the food and drink appropriate for monks, he gives no account either of how monks are to feast or what to do on feast days. Furthermore, there is nothing in the ascetic life he proposes which indicates that Christians may anticipate in the present age the resurrection life of Christ. While there is much to commend in the 'school for the Lord's service'[144] which St Benedict envisages, the curriculum of this school is too narrow. The lack of any account of feasting points to the loss of the eschatological tension that is so central to the Christian life. This critique of St Benedict's Rule is but one instance in which feasting and fasting can be used as a key to analyse patterns of life together which seek to bear faithful witness to God.

Following my previous analysis of MacIntyre and O'Donovan, I hold that hospitality can only be understood within a particular tradition and different traditions will have different forms of hospitality. In this chapter I have sought to assess the practice of hospitality within the Christian tradition and then see how this conception of hospitality both describes and defines the way Christians should relate to their neighbours with regard to ethical disputes. The assessment reveals that the hospitality of the church enables it to both be a guest and host of the life of its neighbours. This guest–host dynamic constitutes a recapitulation of the ascension and Pentecost moments of the Christ-event. Christian hospitality is inaugurated at Pentecost, bears witness to the eschaton, and corresponds to the tension at the heart of the eschaton, whereby it is established but not yet fully manifest. As an eschatological social practice, hospitality is inspired and empowered by the Holy Spirit, who enables the church to host the life of its neighbours without the church being assimilated to, or colonized by, or having to withdraw from the life of the world.[145]

Hospitality and tolerance contrasted

It is instructive to draw a contrast between Christian hospitality and tolerance. There is no clearly identifiable concrete social practice with which tolerance can be identified. Markham argues America itself constitutes an embodiment of tolerance derived from Christian commitments.[146] He states: 'The American democratic experiment can take much of the credit for showing the world that it is possible to be committed to both truth and plurality. Tolerance is an American virtue affirmed in the First Amendment and celebrated in its cities.'[147] However, David Hollenbach's critique of the impact of tolerance on social policy, especially urban social policy in America, stands as a stark rebuttal of Markham's claim.[148] Hollenbach states: 'Acceptance or tolerance of difference will certainly not knit up the tears in the flesh of the American body politic today. When acceptance of difference becomes acquiescence in deep social disparities and human misery it becomes part of the problem, not part of the solution.'[149] For Hollenbach: 'Tolerance as acceptance of differences is a psychological stance entirely inadequate for the development of a creative response to urban poverty today.'[150] What the American experience demonstrates is how difficult it is to translate a commitment to tolerance as either a pragmatic policy, or a substantive value, into concrete social practices. For example, the problems surrounding affirmative action policies, wherein to counter intolerance (that of racism) an intrinsically intolerant policy is employed (one which causes reverse discrimination), illustrates how difficult it is actually to establish tolerance in practical ways.

It seems tolerance acts as a break to any constructive action. Hollenbach notes that 'any form of genuine human action adds to or tries to change the direction of what is happening.'[151] Yet, tolerance, understood as never challenging opinions others hold, reduces us to silence and inactivity, because to add to and seek to change what others think is by definition intolerant. As Hollenbach notes, it is obviously a *reductio ad absurdum* to imply that a public philosophy built around tolerance aims to get people to stop talking and acting. However, this is the effect it has. The impact of tolerance on social policy has been to diminish the arena of public or social action. It does this because, as Hollenbach points out, modern conceptions of tolerance formulate 'the ideal of respect by only focusing on its importance for individuals regarded one at a time.'[152]

As has already been noted, when tolerance is a substantive value it is based on a particular conception of the good: that is, the good of individual autonomy.[153] The good of individual autonomy necessarily places the good of the individual before that of other persons and provides little warrant for moving beyond the individual good and seeking the good of others. Markham recognizes that a commitment to tolerance can only guarantee a minimal level of social peace. He states: 'We need to move beyond tolerance, to active engagement and concern in the life of others, to dialogue, to collaborative truth-seeking and the enrichment of life through the insights of others.'[154] Yet the way in which tolerance frames relations between persons precisely acts as a block to such movement. By contrast, inherent within the Christocentric performance of hospitality is the call to welcome the stranger: that is, within the Christian practice of hospitality there is the imperative to enter into relationship with, and accommodate, those who are different.

The move beyond mere acceptance of a stranger's existence is not simply a move actively to welcome a stranger, but is a move actively to welcome those with the least status. The imperative to welcome the weak and the vulnerable serves as a constant reminder to see and hear those members of society who are most easily marginalized, oppressed and rendered invisible. As will be seen in the discussion of euthanasia, in contemporary society the suffering-dying are a good example of those who are likely to be neglected or oppressed because they lack the means to protect themselves. Other examples include the homeless, the severely disabled and the refugee. Tolerance involves no equivalent imperative to attend to and actively help those without a place or a voice in society; indeed, a tolerant society can be deeply oppressive for many of its members. By contrast, while the Christian commitment to hospitality has often been ignored, it has also been consistently invoked and acted upon in relation to the treatment of the socially excluded and, moreover, the diverse and wide-ranging legacy of its practice, for example, in hospitals, the provision of asylum, and the work of groups such as the Salvation Army, demonstrates how hospitality has inspired a wide variety of concrete social practices.

A good illustration of the contrast between tolerance and hospitality in relation to protecting and aiding the vulnerable is the issue of immigration. In an analysis of the debate surrounding Enoch Powell's 'Rivers of Blood' speech in 1968, Markham notes that the response of the churches called for integration, but failed to take account of any notion of tolerance. Markham states that tolerance 'does not require complete integration and acceptance, which is why many Christians are unhappy with it.'[155] He goes on to say:

> But toleration accommodates Powell's realism. ... Tolerance is a call for different communities to live together in peaceful coexistence. It is true that these communities will disagree about religion; and there are numerous differences in terms of history and custom; but these different communities need to discover tolerance as the half-way house between whole-hearted acceptance and outright hostility.[156]

Markham is not alone in advocating tolerance as the principle governing the reception of immigrants. John Locke, on the basis of an economic rationale, rather than a theological one, similarly appeals for the tolerance of refugees.[157] However, in the light of the theological account of hospitality given above, neither Markham's nor Locke's advocacy of tolerance as a 'half-way house' will suffice. The church has no place accommodating Powell's 'realism'. As the story of the encounter between Peter and Cornelius illustrates, and Paul constantly emphasizes, Christ breaks down the barriers between different races and nations. The Church has no stake in preserving the kind of unity Powell advocated, one based on language or race.

Instead, the unity the Church seeks to bears witness to is the eschatological unity given by the Spirit at Pentecost.[158] Neither should the churches have adopted tolerance as the principle governing their response to refugees and immigrants as Markham and Locke advocate. Christ's demand is for hospitality towards the stranger and not, as the principle of toleration allows, mere acceptance or 'peaceful coexistence'.[159] Christian hospitality requires the active welcome and making a place for immigrants (whether these immigrants accept Christianity or not) and this hospitality includes the support of public policies that echo Christ's imperative to make a place for the stranger.[160]

Christians are not only commanded to welcome the vulnerable stranger, but to see the vulnerable stranger as representing Christ. The ground of welcoming strangers is Christ himself. To warrant hospitality the stranger neither has to be deserving in some way, nor do they have to earn the right to it, nor must they possess some innate capacity that renders them worthy of acceptance among the human community, nor is welcome dependent on a well meaning humanitarian impulse on the part of the giver. To be a recipient of Christian hospitality one does not have to do or be anything; one's status as a guest is received as a freely given gift from Christ. Conversely, hospitality of the stranger constitutes part of the church's witness to the Christ-event, especially the hospitality each sinner receives from God in and through Christ. The call to welcome strangers as if they were Christ contrasts with the commitment to tolerance as a substantive good, founded as it is on a commitment to the good of individual autonomy.[161] As will be argued in relation to the issue of euthanasia, placing a value on human autonomy in no way guarantees the acceptance of the vulnerable stranger. In many instances it can lead to the neglect and oppression of those who are not autonomous, for example, the unborn and the terminally ill.

Tolerance can, by its very commitments, be oppressive. The contrast between Porphyry and Lactantius illustrates how this oppression may come about. In addition to being a disciple of Plotinus, Porphyry provided philosophical legitimation to Diocletian's policy of repressing Christianity in the work now known as *Against the Christians*.[162] Robert Wilken states: 'Porphyry was an exponent of an inclusive religious outlook that held that there were many ways to God; he even attempted to find a way of integrating Christ into the pantheon of Romans gods by honouring him as a sage.'[163] However, his very commitment to a demythologized polytheism formed the basis of his opposition to Christianity's claim to have found the true way to God.[164] In Porphyry's view, those people who made such an exclusive claim were opposed to and threatened the Roman religio-civil order and thus they were unpatriotic and should be punished accordingly.[165] For example, in his attack on Christian baptism, Porphyry states: '[The Christians] would bring us a society without law. They would teach us to have no fear of the gods.'[166] By contrast, Lactantius, a contemporary of Porphyry, believes Christianity to be the only way to God and that its way has been definitively revealed in Jesus Christ.[167] It is on the basis of specifically Christian claims that Lactantius argues against the use of coercion. Lactantius held that coercion was inimical to true religion as instantiated in the Christian faith. He states:

> There is no occasion for violence and injury, for religion cannot be imposed by force; the matter must be carried on by words rather than by blows, that the will may be affected. ... For true religion is to be defended, not by putting to death, but by dying; not by cruelty, but by patient endurance; not by guilt, but by good faith: for the former belong to evils, but the latter to goods; and it is necessary for that which is good to have place in religion, and not that which is evil.[168]

It is no coincidence that Lactantius counted hospitality as a principal virtue and associated its practice with the exercise of true justice and the ordering of relations between Christians and strangers (notably, the destitute, orphans, widows, captives, the sick and the dead in need of burial).[169] It is the very demand for a pragmatic tolerance, instantiated in a policy of an inclusive civil religion, that leads Porphyry to support persecution of those he views as threatening the Roman religio-civil order. By contrast, it is the specific claims of Christianity, and its related practices, that grounds Lactantius' advocacy of freedom of conscience in matters of religion.

Summary

I have defined hospitality as a Christian social practice that recapitulates the ascension/Pentecost moment of the Christ-event. As a social practice hospitality is central to shaping relations between the church and its neighbours and takes many forms in the Christian tradition. Care for the sick and the poor, hospitality to strangers, educational initiatives, and peace-making endeavours are all examples of ways in which the church hosts the life together of its neighbours and enables that life to bear witness to its eschatological possibilities. Many of these initiatives are responses to moral problems the church is confronted with. Some of these problems are old and some arise from new questions. The church will develop patterns of thought and action in response to such moral questions (as it does in response to questions that are not specifically moral). However, the response of the church is not developed in isolation from the life together of its neighbours. As it develops its response, the church will be engaged with the life of those around it, who will inevitably be involved with and inform its discernment. In its interaction with the life of its neighbours, the church will also seek to establish patterns of sociality which bear witness to how a particular moral issue is transfigured by God. The patterns of thought and action that constitute the response of the church to a particular issue are constantly open to further specification in the light of who Jesus Christ is. Such specification and alignment is a constant and ever-present task (one that will often involve Christians testing their claims against the claims made by other traditions). Furthermore, and as the exposition of 1 Peter in the last chapter clarified, some of its neighbours will participate in the church's response to the issue, some will reject it, some will ignore it, and some will actively oppose it. Mediating disputes over moral problems which confront Christians and non-Christians is never simply a question of each accommodating the other's view, nor of compromise between two positions, nor of rivalry as one tradition seeks to vindicate its answer against the answer given by other traditions. The only criterion by which the church can accept or reject the thought and action of its neighbours is whether such action accords with thought and action directed to God. The only response the church can make to moral problems is to bear witness to their resolution in and through Jesus Christ and to invite its neighbours to participate in those patterns of thought and action that bear witness to this resolution. At times this invitation will involve the church changing its pattern of life together as it discerns in the life of its neighbours patterns of thought and action that bear more truthful witness to Jesus Christ.

Retaining Jesus Christ as the criterion of evaluation and advocating hospitality as the form of engagement is not to deny the possibility of conversation or philosophical argument with non-Christians. This is so for four reasons. First, retaining Jesus Christ as the criterion of evaluation and advocating hospitality as the form of engagement sets up the possibility of real conversation wherein the church will have something distinctive to contribute. Second, it ensures that the conversation is not shaped decisively by one or other of the church's conversation partners. Third, faithful witness to its own presuppositions depends on the church reaching out to and entering into conversation with the thought and action of non-Christians. Fourth, the church embodies the eschatological possibilities of its neighbours' life – thus, through the actions of the Spirit, the life of the church intrinsically involves the life of its neighbours. In short, retaining Jesus Christ as the criterion of evaluation and advocating hospitality as the form of engagement necessarily directs the church into conversation with its neighbours; that is, to the 'action of living or having one's being in, among' its neighbours.[170]

Notes

1 One of the most influential accounts of the view that tolerance and acceptance of diversity are recent historical phenomena is that given by John Rawls's introduction to *Political Liberalism* (New York: Columbia University Press, 1993), pp. xxiii–xxvii. See also, John Horton, 'Toleration', in *Routledge Encyclopedia of Philosophy*, ed., Edward Craig (London: Routledge, 1998), pp. 429–33. For a critique of Rawls's historical and conceptual reconstruction of toleration see Will Kymlicka, 'Two Models of Pluralism and Tolerance', in *Toleration: An Elusive Virtue,* ed. David Heyd (Princeton, NJ: Princeton University Press, 1996), pp. 81–105.

2 Nederman and Laursen argue that the conventional picture of how the principle of toleration emerged in the West has been challenged by a considerable body of historical scholarship that demonstrates both the longevity and diversity of approaches to tolerance. Cary Nederman and John Laursen, 'Difference and Dissent: Introduction', in *Difference and Dissent: Theories of Toleration in Medieval and Early Modern Europe*, eds, Cary Nederman and John Laursen (London: Rowman & Littlefield, 1996), pp. 1–16.

3 Lactantius, *The Divine Institutes*, in ANF, trans. William Fletcher, eds, Alexander Roberts and James Donaldson, 10 vols. (Edinburgh: T&T Clark, 1994), VII, pp. 9–223 (bk. V, ch. 19–21)

4 *Summa Theologica* II–II, Qu. 10–12.

5 For example, see John Horton and Susan Mendus, 'Introduction', in *Aspects of Toleration: Philosophical Studies*, eds John Horton and Susan Mendus (London: Methuen, 1985), pp. 1–15 (pp. 1–2). However, Michael Howard argues that the wars of the sixteenth century resulted from the breakdown of the

established political order and the emergence of nation-states. Michael Howard, *The Invention of Peace: Reflections on War and International Order* (London: Profile Books, 2000), pp. 14–19. See also Cavanaugh, '"A Fire Strong Enough to Consume the House:" The Wars of Religion and the Rise of the State'.

6 See 'Plan of Action to follow up the United Nations Year for Tolerance (1995)', www.unesco.org/tolerance/planeng.htm

7 It is related to, but distinct from, notions of freedom of belief. Put simply, only to tolerate something falls short of and does not necessitate granting or advocating freedom of expression to the action or belief tolerated.

8 Horton, 'Toleration', p. 431.

9 Drawing on a range of sociological surveys David Hollenbach notes that: 'Tolerance of difference ... has become the highest social aspiration of American culture.' Hollenbach, *The Common Good and Christian Ethics*, p. 24.

10 For a review of justifications given by theologians for using the notion of tolerance in determining relations between Christians and non-Christians see Ian Markham, *Plurality and Christian Ethics* (Cambridge: Cambridge University Press, 1995), pp. 178–88.

11 See Tertullian's *Apology* and 'Letter to Scapula', ANF, vol. 3.

12 On this see Wilbur Jordan, *The Development of Religious Toleration in England*, 4 vols (Cambridge: Cambridge University Press, 1932–40).

13 See for example, Reinhold Niebuhr, *The Children of Light and the Children of Darkness* (London: Nisbet & Co., 1945), pp. 84–104.

14 Mandell Creighton, *Persecution and Tolerance* (London: Longmans, Green & Co., 1895), pp. 115–16.

15 Ibid., p.135.

16 David Fergusson, *Church, State and Civil Society* (Cambridge: Cambridge University Press, 2004), pp. 72–93.

17 The tripartite division set out here is heuristic. In practice, the three kinds of argument for tolerance frequently overlap.

18 Jay Newman, *Foundations of Religious Tolerance* (Toronto: University of Toronto Press, 1982), p. 22.

19 Reinhold Niebuhr, 'The Test of Tolerance', in *Religious Pluralism in the West*, ed. D. Mullan (Oxford: Blackwell, 1998), p. 293.

20 Reinhold Niebuhr, *The Children of Light*, p. 88.

21 Ibid.

22 An earlier justification of tolerance on the grounds of the fallibility of human knowledge appears in Pierre Bayle, *Treatise on Universal Tolerance* (1686). For an account of Bayle's thought see Preston King, *Toleration* (London: Allen & Unwin, 1976), pp. 90–99.

23 John Locke, *An Essay on Toleration*, in *Locke: Political Essays*, ed., Mark Goldie (Cambridge: Cambridge University Press, 1997), pp. 134–59. For an assessment of Locke's account of toleration see Susan Mendus, *Toleration and the Limits of Liberalism* (London: Macmillan, 1989), pp. 22–43.

24 Bernard Williams, 'Toleration: An Impossible Virtue', in *Toleration: An Elusive Virtue*, ed. David Heyd (Princeton: Princeton University Press, 1996), p. 22.

25 Alasdair MacIntyre, 'Toleration and the Goods of Conflict', in *The Politics of Toleration: Tolerance and Intolerance in Modern Life*, ed. Susan Mendus (Edinburgh: Edinburgh University Press, 1999), pp. 138–39.

26 For an assessment of the five dominant 'regimes of tolerance' and what they do not tolerate and exclude see Michael Walzer, *On Toleration* (New Haven: Yale University Press, 1997), pp. 14–36.

27 Putting to one side questions about the relationship between political authority and tolerance does not constitute an implicit acceptance of 'liberal pluralism' as the necessary context of relations between Christians and non-Christians. It does constitute a recognition that in the West it is the liberal democratic polity, in one form or another, that is the present context within which Christians and non-Christians have to relate to each other.

28 Bernard Williams, 'Tolerating the Intolerable', in *The Politics of Toleration*, p. 65.
29 Ibid., p. 73. Cf. Thomas Nagel, *Equality and Partiality* (Oxford: Oxford University Press, 1991), pp. 154–68.
30 Mendus, *Toleration and the Limits of Liberalism*, pp. 67–68.
31 For further consideration of the relationship beween tolerance and autonomy and how tolerance can militate against genuine respect for the other see Luke Bretherton, 'Tolerance, Hospitality and Education: A Theological Proposal', *Studies in Christian Ethics*, 17.1 (2004), pp. 86–91.
32 John Gray, 'Pluralism and Toleration in Contemporary Political Philosophy', *Political Studies*, 48.2 (2000), p. 323. See also Susan Khin Zaw, 'Locke and multiculturalism: Toleration, Relativism, and Reason', in *Public Education in a Multicultural Society*, ed. Robert K. Fullinwider (Cambridge: Cambridge University Press, 1996) pp. 121–55.
33 Nederman and Laursen, 'Difference and Dissent: Introduction', p. 12.
34 Immanuel Kant, 'Perpetual Peace: A Philosophical Sketch', in *Kant: Political Writings*, trans. H. B. Nisbet, ed. Hans Reiss (Cambridge: Cambridge University Press, 1991), p. 106.
35 DRA, pp. 122–28.
36 For example, Emmanuel Lévinas, 'Responsibility for the Other', in *Ethics and Infinity*, trans. Richard Cohen (Pittsburgh: Duquesne University Press, 1985).
37 For example, Jacques Derrida and Anne Dufourmantelle, *Of Hospitality*, trans. Rachel Bowlby (Stanford: Stanford University Press, 2000).
38 Kant, 'Perpetual Peace', p. 106.
39 Ibid.
40 Ibid.
41 DRA, p. 123.
42 Ibid., p. 125.
43 For an analysis of this meal cycle see Arthur Just, *The Ongoing Feast: Table Fellowship and Eschatology at Emmaus* (Collegeville, Minnesota: The Liturgical Press, 1993), pp. 165–95. For an analysis of the term 'sinners' in the gospels see N. T. Wright, *Jesus and the Victory of God, Christian Origins and the Question of God* (London: SPCK, 1996), pp. 264–68. For an assessment of why tax collectors were singled out as a category for reprobation see Marcus Borg, *Conflict, Holiness and Politics in the Teachings of Jesus* (Lampeter: Edwin Mellen Press, 1972), pp. 83–86.
44 Borg sees the related parables of the lost sheep, the lost coin and the prodigal son as both a defence of Jesus' actions and an invitation to join in the celebration of the return of the outcasts to the People of God. *Conflict, Holiness and Politics*, p. 91.
45 J. Jeremias, *New Testament Theology*, p. 115. Quoted in Kenneth Bailey, *Poet and Peasant and Through Peasant Eyes: A Literary-Cultural Approach to the Parables of Luke* (Grand Rapids: Eerdmans, 1983), p. 143.
46 Wright, *Jesus and the Victory of God*, p. 431. For a discussion of the different 'quests' for Jesus see *Jesus and the Victory of God*, pp. 3–124. Cf., Borg, *Conflict, Holiness and Politics*, p. 79.
47 Just sees the Great Banquet parable as the climax of the meal cycle. Just, *The Ongoing Feast*, p. 178.
48 For a treatment of the theme of hospitality in Luke-Acts see John Koenig, *New Testament Hospitality: Partnership with Strangers as Promise and Mission, Overtures Biblical Theology* (Philadelphia: Fortress Press, 1985), pp. 85–123.
49 For an exegesis of Genesis 18 that draws out the theological implications of the hospitality motif in the story of Abraham and Sarah receiving the angels see Gavin D'Costa, *Sexing the Trinity: Gender, Culture and the Divine* (London: SCM Press, 2000), p. 157–61.
50 Gen. 18; 1 Sam. 25; 1 Kings 17:18–24.
51 For an exegesis of this passage in relation to hospitality see Eugene Rogers, *Sexuality and the Christian Body* (Oxford: Blackwell, 1999), pp. 257–60. Rogers contrasts the hospitality of Abraham with the violent inhospitality of the Sodomites.
52 Texts relating to the messianic banquet include: Is. 25, 54; Ez. 39; and Joel 2–3. For an analysis of Israel's relationship to the land see Walter Brueggemann, *The Land: Place as Gift, Promise, and*

Challenge in Biblical Faith, 2nd edn (Minneapolis: Augsburg Fortress Publishers, 2002); and for an assessment of the prophetic texts in relation to the messianic hope see idem, *Hopeful Imagination: Prophetic Voices in Exile* (Philadelphia: Fortress Press, 1986).

53 For a study of the diversity of views on the issue of the treatment of strangers in the Old Testament see Daniel Smith-Christopher, 'Between Ezra and Isaiah: Exclusion, Transformation, and Inclusion of the "Foreigner" in Post-Exilic Biblical Theology', in *Ethnicity and the Bible*, ed. Mark Brett (Leiden: E. J. Brill, 1996), pp. 117–42.

54 For an assessment of the relationship between Israel's holiness, the Temple cult and Israel's distinctive identity in relation to other nations see Jacob Milgrom, *Leviticus 1–16*, 3 vols, *Anchor Bible* (New York: Doubleday, 1991), III.

55 Josh. 23:11–13; Ez. 10:2–4, 10:10; Neh. 13:26–27.

56 Borg, *Conflict, Holiness and Politics*, p. 135.

57 Mk 5:25–34; Lk. 8:43–48.

58 Borg, *Conflict, Holiness and Politics*, p. 135–36.

59 Wright, *Jesus and the Victory of God*, p. 192; cf., Borg, *Conflict, Holiness and Politics*, p. 93.

60 Borg, *Conflict, Holiness and Politics*, pp. 2–4.

61 A parallel may be drawn between such programmes of exclusion and some contemporary expressions of Protestant 'fundamentalism' whose definition of faithful practice and belief requires that the identity of believers be defined over and against non-believers. See Robert Wuthnow and Matthew P. Lawson, 'Sources of Christian Fundamentalism in the United States', in *Accounting for Fundamentalisms: The Dynamic Character of Movements*, eds Martin Marty and R. Scott Appleby (Chicago: University of Chicago Press, 1991), pp. 39–43.

62 Christine Pohl, *Making Room: Recovering Hospitality as a Christian Tradition* (Grand Rapids: Eerdmans, 1999), p. 22.

63 Ibid.

64 See Graham Stanton, *A Gospel for a New People* (Edinburgh: T&T Clark, 1992), pp. 207–30; and Craig Keener, *A Commentary on the Gospel of Matthew* (Grand Rapids: Eerdmans, 1999), p. 604–606.

65 Keener, *A Commentary on the Gospel of Matthew*, p. 605.

66 For a commentary on the motif of hospitality throughout Luke's Gospel see Brendan Byrne, *The Hospitality of God: A Reading of Luke's Gospel* (Collegeville, Minnesota: Liturgical Press, 2000).

67 Bailey, *Peasant Eyes*, p. 91.

68 Cf., Koenig, *New Testament Hospitality*, p. 17.

69 Bailey, *Peasant Eyes*, p. 96–99. See also Borg, *Conflict, Holiness and Politics*, p. 80.

70 Willi Braun, *Feasting and Social Rhetoric in Luke 14* (Cambridge: Cambridge University Press, 1995), pp. 110–11. It should be noted that Braun emphasizes the Greco-Roman context, as distinct from the Jewish context, of Luke-Acts.

71 Bailey, *Peasant Eyes*, p. 99.

72 Cf., Jesus calling Peter, Andrew, James and John from their fishing nets (Mt. 4:17–23; Mk 1:14–20; Lk. 5:1–11).

73 Braun, *Feasting*, p. 105.

74 Ibid, p. 106.

75 René Girard, 'Mimesis and Violence', in *The Girard Reader*, ed. James G. Williams (New York: Crossroad Publishing, 1996), pp. 9–19. See also: Gil Baillie, *Violence Unveiled: Humanity at the Crossroads* (New York: Crossroad, 1997), pp. 111–32. For a summary and critique of Girard's work in general see Gerard Loughlin, 'René Girard (b. 1923): Introduction', in *The Postmodern God: A Theological Reader*, ed., Graham Ward, (Oxford: Basil Blackwell, 1997), pp. 96–104.

76 Braun, *Feasting*, p. 122 and p. 131.

77 Ibid., pp. 43–61.

78 This draws attention to the difference between classical, aristocratic virtue and Christian virtues, and between Socratic dialectic and Christian rhetoric, and the kind of peace each envisages. See Milbank, *Theology and Social Theory*, pp. 327–32 and pp. 359–64.

79 Cf. MacIntyre's discussion of hospitality to, and *misericordia* for, the stranger as central virtues for human flourishing in community in DRA, pp. 122–28.

80 Braun, *Feasting*, p. 97.

81 Marcel Mauss, *The Gift: The Form and Reason for Exchange in Archaic Societies* (London: Routledge, 2002). For a theological critique of Mauss's suspicion that the reciprocal exchange of gifts is necessarily unfree and ethically compromising see Alan Jacobs, *A Theology of Reading: The Hermeneutics of Love* (Cambridge, MA: Westview Press, 2001), pp. 77–90.

82 Aristotle, *Nicomachean Ethics*, trans. Roger Crisp (Cambridge: Cambridge University Press, 2000), p. 70 (1124b). For a critique of Aristotle's conception of the 'magnanimous man' see Milbank, *Theology and Social Theory*, pp. 351–52 and Jacobs, *A Theology of Reading*, pp. 84–90. MacIntyre's critique of Nietzsche also applies in this respect. As MacIntyre points out, to cut oneself off from shared activities and isolate oneself from a wider community of shared practices is 'to condemn oneself to that moral solipsism which constitutes Nietzschean greatness.' AV, p. 258.

83 The interrelationship between host and guest in the Parable of the Great Banquet has suggestive parallels with how Emmanuel Lévinas conceives the summons to moral existence wherein, through an encounter with the face of the Other, my egoism is called into question and I learn to take the Other into account. Like the relationship between the host and the guests, for Lévinas, there is a double asymmetry at work in the relationship between the Other and myself. The Other is both higher and lower than me. Thomas Ogletree summarizes Lévinas's view thus: 'The person I meet in a moral mode is both higher and lower than I am: higher in the sense that she summons me to conscience and judges the arbitrariness of my freedom; lower in the sense that she approaches me not with the power to coerce, but in destitution and with supplication, offering no resistance other than a moral one.' Thomas Ogletree, 'Hospitality to the Stranger: the Role of the "Other" in Moral Experience', in *Hospitality to the Stranger: Dimensions of Moral Understanding* (Philadelphia: Fortress Press, 1985), p. 48. The Other/guest is my master or teacher who opens up a new world of meaning to which I as host otherwise have no access; encounter with them is the point of conversion to moral existence. Yet the Other/guest is lower than me because they are vulnerable and dependent on my hospitality.

84 Lactantius, *The Divine Institutes*, p. 176.

85 Ibid.

86 Winter, *Seek the Welfare of the City*, pp. 45–60. Winter emphasizes how Paul, in the letters to the Thessalonians, criticizes and seeks to re-constitute the classical practice of the patron–client relationship. For a study of patron–client relations in the ancient world see Moses Finley, *The Ancient Economy*, 2nd edn (London: Hogarth, 1985).

87 Bailey argues that to justify something akin to the Inquisition or the Crusades on the basis of the statement 'Go out into the roads and lanes, and compel people to come in, so that my house may be filled (v.23)' is an incorrect interpretation. Rather, the statement is meant to indicate the asymmetric and unexpected character of the invitation. The servant must persist in actively persuading the astounded and incredulous strangers that the invitation is genuine until he has drawn the strangers into the banquet. Bailey, *Peasant Eyes*, p. 108. Ford goes further, and reads this parable as an explicit rejection of contemporary Jewish notions of 'holy war', especially those linked with the messianic banquet. Massyngbaerde Ford, *My Enemy is My Guest: Jesus and Violence in Luke* (New York: Orbis, 1984), pp. 102–105.

88 Bailey, *Peasant Eyes*, p. 102.

89 Ibid., p. 107.

90 Ibid.

91 Hays sees this dynamic at work throughout Mark's gospel. Richard Hays, *The Moral Vision of the New Testament: A Contemporary Introduction to New Testament Ethics* (Edinburgh: T&T Clark, 1996), pp. 89–90.

92 David Moessner, *Lord of the Banquet: The Literary and Theological Significance of the Lukan Travel Narrative* (Minneapolis: Fortress Press, 1989), p. 184. Cf., Just, *The Ongoing Feast*, p. 261.

93 Cf., Ian McDonald, *The Crucible of Christian Morality* (London: Routledge, 1998), pp. 19–20.

94 Gavin D'Costa, 'Christ, the Trinity, and Religious Pluralism', in *Christian Uniqueness Reconsidered: The Myth of a Pluralistic Theology of Religions*, ed. Gavin D'Costa (New York: Orbis Books, 1996), p. 23. Cf., Fergusson, *Community, Liberalism and Christian Ethics*, pp. 166–67.

95 For a parallel interpretation cf., Lesslie Newbigin, *The Open Secret: An Introduction to the Theology of Mission*, rev. edn (London: SPCK, 1995), pp. 59–60; and Hays, *The Moral Vision*, p. 440.

96 We can see a similar dynamic at work in the story of Paul's mission.

97 Avery Dulles, *Models of the Church: A Critical Assessment of the Church in all its Aspects*, 2nd edn (Dublin: Gill and Macmillan, 1989), p. 220.

98 Cf., Yoder, 'Binding and Loosing', in Cartwright, *The Royal Priesthood*, pp. 323–58.

99 Reinhard Hütter, 'Hospitality and Truth: The Disclosure of Practices in Worship and Doctrine', in *Practicing Theology: Beliefs and Practices in Christian Life*, eds, Miroslav Volf and Dorothy C. Bass (Grand Michigan, MI. Eerdmans, 2002), p. 206–27.

100 Moessner, *Lord of the Banquet*, p. 296.

101 DRA, p. 126.

102 *Didache* 1.3.

103 *Didache* 4.5

104 Simon Tugwell, *The Apostolic Fathers* (London: Geoffrey Chapman, 1989), pp. 1–5, 8–9.

105 Pohl, *Making Room*, p. 147.

106 Cf., *Constitutions of the Holy Apostles*, in ANF, trans. William Fletcher, eds Alexander Roberts and James Donaldson, 10 vols. (Edinburgh: T&T Clark, 1994), VII, p. 397; Benedict, *The Rule of St Benedict*, trans. Timothy Fry (New York: Vintage Books, 1998), ch. 53; and see Pohl, *Making Room*, pp. 93–94 for comments by Luther and Calvin on the problem of discriminating between deserving and undeserving strangers.

107 Ample evidence for this is given in the extensive collation of early Christian literature relating to the theology and practice of hospitality in Amy Oden, ed., *And You Welcomed Me: A Sourcebook on Hospitality in Early Christianity* (Nashville: Abingdon Press, 2001).

108 John Chrysostom, 'Homily 20 on 1 Corinthians', *Epistles of Paul to the Corinthians*, in *Nicene and Post-Nicene Fathers*, trans. Talbot Chambers, ed., Philip Schaff, First Series, 14 vols (Edinburgh: T&T Clark, 1989), XII, p. 117. Hereafter abbreviated to NPNF.

109 Pohl, *Making Room*, p. 87.

110 Wesley, *Works of John Wesley*, vol. 4: *Journals* (Grand Rapids: Baker Book House, 1979), p. 481. Quoted in Pohl, *Making Room*, p. 88.

111 Benedict, *The Rule*, p. 12 (ch. 4).

112 Ibid.

113 Banner notes how Benedict, in contrast to the Desert Fathers, resolves the tension between communal and eremitic forms of monasticism in favour of the communal. Michael Banner, '"Who are my Mother and my Brothers?": Marx, Bonhoeffer and Benedict and the Redemption of the Family', in *Christian Ethics and Contemporary Moral Problems*, pp. 235–38.

114 Benedict, *The Rule*, p. 51 (ch. 53).

115 Banner, '"Who are my Mother and my Brothers?"', p. 241–44.

116 Timothy Miller, 'Hospital: Medieval and Renaissance History', in *Encyclopedia of Bioethics*, ed. Warren Reich (New York: Macmillan, 1995), p. 1160.

117 Gregory Nazianzen, *Panegyric on St Basil*, in NPNF, trans. Charles Brown and James Swallow, eds, Philip Schaff and Henry Wace, Second Series, 14 vols (Edinburgh: T&T Clark, 1996), VII, p. 407.

118 John Chrysostom, *Homily 45 on The Acts of the Apostles*, in NPNF, trans. J. Walker and J. Sheppard, ed., Philip Schaff, 14 vols (Edinburgh: T&T Clark, 1989), XI, p. 277.

119 For an example of how both the tension between institutional and personal hospitality and the tension between recognizing Jesus in the stranger and the need to discriminate were successfully negotiated, see the assessment of care for the sick, pilgrims and urban poor in medieval Paris centred on the Cathedral of Notre Dame in Richard Sennett, *Flesh and Stone: the Body and the City in Western Civilization* (London: Faber & Faber, 1994), pp. 173–83.

120 Chrysostom's crucial insight may be developed in relation to what MacIntyre identifies as the inherent tension between the ideals and creativity of a practice – such as hospitality – and the competitiveness of its institutional form (AV, p. 194). Similarly, Ivan Illich has argued that beyond a certain threshold, institutions may prove counterproductive to the very purposes they seek to achieve (hospitals damage health more than improve it, or communication systems create more noise than understanding); moreover, beyond a certain size institutions militate against the sustaining of personal, hospitable relationships or 'conviviality'. See Ivan Illich, *Tools for Conviviality* (New York: Harper & Row, 1973) and *Medical Nemesis: The Expropriation of Health* (London: Marian Boyars, 1976).

121 John Calvin, *Commentaries on the Epistle of Paul the Apostle to the Hebrews* (Grand Rapids: Eerdmans, 1948), p. 340. Quoted in Pohl, *Making Room*, p. 36.

122 John Calvin, *Commentary on the Prophet Isaiah*, vol. 1 (Grand Rapids: Eerdmans, 1948), p. 484. Quoted in Pohl, *Making Room*, p. 6.

123 For an account of what happened in Le Chambon see Philip Hallie, *Lest Innocent Blood Be Shed* (New York: Harper & Row, 1979).

124 Based on interviews with Fr. Sava and representatives of Brit-For during a visit to Kosovo, 9–12 July, 1999.

125 For an account of the critical role the Sant'Egidio community played in the 1993 peace settlement in Mozambique see R. Scott Appleby, *The Ambivalence of the Sacred: Religion, Violence, and Reconciliation* (Oxford: Rowman & Littlefield, 2000), pp. 158–64; and Andrea Bartoli, 'Forgiveness and Reconciliation in the Mozambique Peace Process', in *Forgiveness and Reconciliation: Religion, Public Policy and Conflict Transformation*, eds, Raymond G. Helmick and Rodney L. Petersen (Radnor, PA: Templeton Foundation, 2001), pp. 361–81.

126 See Jean Vanier, *An Ark for the Poor: The Story of L'Arche* (New York: Crossroad, 1995).

127 Pohl notes that a critique of lax hospitality and a call for its proper practice was also part of the Protestant Reformation. Pohl, *Making Room*, p. 52.

128 As we shall see, each of these tensions occurs in our assessment of hospice care.

129 *Desire*, p. 173.

130 Farrow, *Ascension*, pp. 87–254.

131 Farrow thinks this balance is played out most clearly in the eucharist. See: Farrow, *Ascension*, p. 150.

132 For an analysis of how the eucharist relates to the trial and martyrdom of the church as a body see William Cavanaugh, *Torture and Eucharist: Theology, Politics, and the Body of Christ* (Oxford: Blackwell Publishers, 1998), pp. 222–72.

133 On the formation of the liturgical calendar and the shaping of time see Edward Muir, *Ritual in Early Modern Europe* (Cambridge: Cambridge University Press, 1997), pp. 55–80.

134 For a history of the development of patterns of feasting in the Christian liturgical year see Adolf Adam, *The Liturgical Year*, trans. Matthew O'Connell (Collegeville: The Liturgical Press, 1990), pp. 23–31.

135 Jürgen Moltmann, *The Church in the Power of the Spirit* (London: SCM, 1977), pp. 274–75.

136 David Ford, *Self and Salvation: Being Transformed* (Cambridge: Cambridge University Press, 1998), p. 267.

137 Jürgen Moltmann, 'The Liberating Feast,' *Concilium*, 10.2 (1974), p. 79. Cf., idem, *The Church in the Power of the Spirit*, pp. 112–13.

138 On the relationship between Lent and Easter and Advent and Christmas, see Adam, *The Liturgical Year*, pp. 91–94; pp. 130–32.

139 For a discussion of carnival, and Bakhtin's theory in particular, see John Docker, *Postmodernism and Popular Culture: A Cultural History* (Cambridge: Cambridge University Press, 1994), pp. 168–244; see also Peter Stallybrass and Allon White, *The Politics and Poetics of Transgression* (London: Methuen, 1986).

140 From a theological perspective, the problem with contemporary forms of carnival is that they are not disciplined by the subsequent cycle of fasting and feasting given in Lent and Easter. Indeed, they

absolutize the carnival as the pre-eminent form of life together. In extending the fool's reign beyond a day, the lordship of misrule becomes a tyranny that menaces the just ordering of society. Contemporary patterns of consumerism could be seen as an example of this, as could many post-1789 political revolutions.

141 I am not suggesting that the established social order is always right or just: all social orders are in need of transfiguration. It is rather that carnival seeks to over-turn and erase all anterior forms of human sociality and tradition, whether they are just or not.

142 It must be recognized that much feasting and fasting wholly fails to bear witness to the messianic feast. However, the ineptitude and iniquity of much Christian feasting should not tempt us to entertain its demonic parody as somehow better.

143 Benedict, *The Rule*, p. 49.

144 Ibid., p. 5.

145 For a systematic doctrinal account of the relationship between divine and human hospitality see John Navone SJ, 'Divine and Human Hospitality', *New Blackfriars*, 85.997 (2004), 329–40.

146 Markham, *Plurality and Christian Ethics*, pp. 83–126.

147 Ibid., p. 188.

148 Hollenbach, *The Common Good and Christian Ethics*, pp. 32–42. It should be noted that Hollenbach sees a re-invigorated notion of the common good, rather than hospitality, as the best response to the problem of ethical diversity.

149 Ibid., p. 41.

150 Ibid., p. 40.

151 Ibid., p. 70.

152 Ibid.

153 Williams, 'Tolerating the Intolerable', p. 73.

154 Markham, *Plurality and Christian Ethics*, p. 188. Markham provides no justification for why there is a need to move beyond tolerance.

155 Ibid., p. 69.

156 Ibid.

157 John Locke, 'For a General Naturalisation', in *Locke: Political Essays*, pp. 322–26.

158 Welker, *God the Spirit*, pp. 232–33.

159 Maurice Cranston counts it as a merit that Locke appealed for tolerance of Huguenot refugees. However, while it is to the credit of Locke that he did not share the xenophobia of his peers, his essentially utilitarian arguments still constitute a singular failure of Christian vision. See Maurice Cranston, 'John Locke and the Case for Toleration', in *On Toleration*, eds Susan Mendus and David Edwards (Oxford: Clarendon Press, 1987), pp. 114–15.

160 The tragedy is that most churches singularly failed to live in accord with the realism of the Gospel and followed a false account of reality as exemplified by Enoch Powell. For example, see the account of the racially motivated rejection of Afro-Caribbean Anglican immigrants in Anglican churches in London in Clifford Hill, *West Indian Migrants and the London Churches* (Oxford: Oxford University Press, 1963); Glynne Gordon-Carter, *An Amazing Journey: The Church of England's Response to Institutional Racism* (London: Church House Publishing, 2003), pp. 8–14.

161 It could be argued that the virtue of tolerance, based as it is on a commitment to the good of individual autonomy, is the mark, not of the Christian host, but of the self-sufficient magnanimous man.

162 Only fragments exist of Porphyry's original writings. Following Harnack, Joseph Hoffman's text of *Against the Christians* uses Marcarius Magnes's *Apocriticus* as the primary source for Porphyry's text. For a discussion on the text and the controversy surrounding it see Joseph Hoffmann, ed. *Porphyry's Against the Christians: the Literary Remains* (Amherst, NY: Prometheus Books, 1994), pp. 21–23; 164–66.

163 Robert Wilken, 'In Defense of Constantine', *First Things*, no. 112 (2001), p. 38. See also, Hoffmann, *Porphyry's Against the Christians*, p. 169.

164 Hoffmann argues that Porphyry viewed the gods as symbols of the powers operating in and through nature and understood religious myths as parables of philosophical truth. Hoffmann, *Porphyry's Against the Christians*, pp. 160–61.

165 Ibid., pp. 18–19.

166 Ibid., p. 81.

167 Lactantius, *The Divine Institutes*, pp. 105–107. For an account of the historical relationship between Lactantius and Porphyry see Elizabeth Digeser, *The Making of a Christian Empire: Lactantius and Rome* (Ithaca, NY: Cornell University Press, 2000).

168 Lactantius, *The Divine Institutes*, pp. 156–57.

169 Ibid., pp. 175–78.

170 'Conversation', *Shorter Oxford English Dictionary*.

CHAPTER 6

Hospitality, hospice care and euthanasia – a case study in negotiating moral diversity

To further understand how the social practice of hospitality may determine the relationship between Christians and non-Christians with regard to moral problems this final chapter develops an analysis of how hospitality shapes a response to a particular dispute. The ethical dispute addressed is whether euthanasia is an appropriate response to the terminally ill or, as Paul Ramsey calls them, the 'suffering-dying'.[1]

The focus will be on the question of whether or not euthanasia is an appropriate response to the suffering-dying; that is, whether the act of euthanasia can, in certain circumstances, constitute good care for the suffering-dying. The debate surrounding this question is a paradigmatic instance of the problem first identified by MacIntyre: that is, the problem of whether we can come to common judgements over a particular moral question when there appear to be radically divergent ways of thinking about that issue and no common tradition or criteria that is authoritative for determining moral judgements.

The issue of euthanasia and treatment of the suffering-dying is highly contentious in Britain. There have been a number of attempts to legalize voluntary euthanasia and there is periodic public debate about the issue both in response to proposed Parliamentary Bills and particular cases; for example, in response to the conviction for manslaughter of Dr Nigel Cox in 1992.[2] Although voluntary euthanasia remains illegal, that it will remain so for much longer is not certain. The most serious recent parliamentary consideration of euthanasia was conducted by the House of Lords' Select Committee on Medical Ethics established in 1993.[3] This Committee unanimously agreed there should be no change in the current law. However, since 1994 there has been a continued campaign to legalize voluntary euthanasia and a number of legislative proposals that some would argue allow for euthanasia in certain cases, for example, the 2004 Mental Incapacity Bill. There are also a number of other factors that combine to create a climate more amenable to the legalization of voluntary euthanasia. These factors are the following: the advance in healthcare technology that enables more people to live longer who would otherwise have died at a much earlier stage of an illness; the practice and subsequent statutory backing for doctors to use euthanasia in the Netherlands since 1993 (and further strengthened in 2001) and the legalisation of voluntary euthanasia in Belgium since 2002, both of which set precedents for other European countries;[4] the political pressure to restrict public healthcare expenditure and ration resources;[5] and the demographic shift in Western Europe whereby the numbers of those retired will exceed those in paid employment leading to a reduction of tax revenue with a simultaneous increase in the need for public expenditure.[6]

Despite the ruling of the House of Lords' Select Committee in 1994, there is no prevailing consensus and the rights or wrongs of euthanasia, like those of abortion, are vigorously contested.[7] Given the conflict over whether euthanasia constitutes good care for the suffering-dying, the contemporary debate surrounding euthanasia lends itself to being a test case for an assessment of our constructive proposal for how Christians are to relate to non-Christians when faced with a dispute about what is the right answer to a particular moral problem.

Defining euthanasia

Before proceeding with an analysis of why euthanasia is contested as a response to the suffering-dying a definition of what is meant (and not meant) by the term 'euthanasia' must be given. This is in itself problematic. As John Finnis states: 'The term euthanasia has no generally accepted and philosophically warranted core of meaning.'[8] Therefore, as a result of the imprecision and lack of a widely accepted definition, great care is necessary when formulating a definition of the term 'euthanasia'.

Paul Ramsey notes that the term 'euthanasia' stems from the Greek for a 'good death': that is, a death without suffering.[9] However, the term has come to denote the deliberate and intentional killing by act or omission of a person whose life is considered not to be worth living.[10] This shift is reflected in how John Finnis defines euthanasia. He states, it is the 'adopting and carrying out of a proposal that, as part of the medical care being given someone, his or her life be terminated on the ground that it would be better for him or her (or at least no harm) if that were done.'[11] John Harris, in his debate with Finnis about the moral legitimacy (or otherwise) of euthanasia, uses the term 'euthanasia' to mean 'the implementation of a decision that a particular individual's life will come to an end before it need do so – a decision that a life will end when it could be prolonged'.[12] However, neither of these brief definitions of the term 'euthanasia' tells us much about either what kind of action is involved, or how this kind of action is to be distinguished from many of the other justifications given for ending an individual's life.

Grisez and Boyle set three conditions for an act to qualify as an act of euthanasia. These conditions are the following: the patient (the one being killed) either is suffering and dying, or is suffering irremediably; the agent (who does the killing) sincerely believes that the patient would be better off dead: that is, that no further continuance of the patient's life is likely to be beneficial for the patient; and lastly, the agent deliberately brings about the patient's death in order that the patient shall have the benefit of being better off dead: that is, they shall no longer suffer.[13] Tom Beauchamp outlines a similar list of conditions for a death to be considered an act of euthanasia. The conditions he sets are the following:

(1) The death is intended by at least one other person whose action is a contributing cause of death; (2) the person who dies is either acutely suffering or irreversibly comatose (or soon will be), and this condition alone is the primary reason for intending the person's death; and (3) the means chosen to produce the death must be as painless as possible, or a sufficient moral justification must exist for a more painful method.[14]

These conditions help to distinguish the action of euthanasia from others types of action that involve bringing about an individual's death, for example, self-defence and capital punishment.

From the definitions given so far and from these two sets of conditions given by Grisez and Boyle and Beauchamp, a picture emerges of who is the subject of euthanasia. It seems that to bring about the death of someone and to describe it as an instance of euthanasia is to bring about the death of an individual who is a patient (and is therefore, in some way, claimed to be a subject of medical care), who is innocent (that is, the reason for bringing about their death is not in response to any criminal, bad or immoral action by the individual), and whose death is considered to be a benefit (or at least no harm) to the individual. We can conclude that the subject of euthanasia is an innocent patient for whom death is considered preferable to suffering.

In relation to the status of the action of the agent administering euthanasia, Dan Brock states: 'The claim that any individual instance of euthanasia is a case of deliberate killing of an innocent person is, with only minor qualifications, correct.'[15] He goes on to say: 'Unlike forgoing life-sustaining treatment, commonly understood as allowing to die, euthanasia is clearly killing, defined as depriving of life or causing the death of a living being.'[16] Brock makes the further distinction between euthanasia and forms of treatment that foreshorten the life of the patient:

> While providing morphine for pain relief at doses where the risk of respiratory depression and an earlier death may be a foreseen but unintended side effect of treating the patient's pain, in a case of euthanasia the patient's death is deliberate or intended even if ... the physician's ultimate end [is to respect] the patient's wishes.[17]

The distinctions Brock makes between euthanasia and forgoing treatment and treatment that unintentionally foreshortens life are important and need explaining further in order to establish clarity about exactly what is meant by the term 'euthanasia'.

It is necessary to distinguish the action of euthanasia from letting die and forgoing treatment. Critical to making these kinds of distinction is the principle of double effect. It is this principle that allowed Brock to make the distinction, in the above quotation, between a 'foreseen but unintended side effect' and deliberately causing the death of a patient. The principle of double effect makes the claim that a single act can have two effects or consequences one of which is foreseen but not intended, the other of which is deliberately intended. Where these effects have a moral import, it is the deliberately intended effects that are decisive in determining the moral significance of the act (although the agent may also be held responsible for the foreseen but unintended effects). Beauchamp outlines four conditions that must be satisfied for an act to be morally permissible despite one or more bad effects. These conditions are the following: first, the act must be morally good or morally neutral, independent of its effects; second, the agent must intend the good effect only (that is, the bad effects can be foreseen and permitted, but not intended); third, the bad effects must not be a means to the good effect (that is, one cannot do bad that good may come of it); and fourth, the good effect must proportionally outweigh the bad effects.[18] Critics of this principle tend to focus on the second condition, calling into question both whether there is a morally relevant difference between foreseeing and intending, and whether, if a doctor foresees an effect, he is not morally responsible for it. There is not the space to engage with these criticisms here; however, these criticisms tend to ignore the long tradition of nuanced moral language that allows precisely for distinctions between intended and foreseen effects, as well as between intention, desire and motivation.[19] Suffice to say, it is use of the principle of double effect that allows euthanasia to be distinguished from, for example, the administering of analgesic drugs to relieve pain even if the administering of these drugs shortens the life of the patient concerned.[20] The morally significant factor is the intention of the agent; for example, both martyr and suicide recognize in advance that the result of their choice and act will be death; however, the martyr does not aim at death.[21] As Pellegrino points out, however:

> The moral quality of accidental [or foreseen but unintended] effects depends on the degree to which we foresee their probability or avoidability. The more certain, the more probable and the more avoidable the accidental effect, the more carefully must the moral quality of the act be assessed.[22]

Yet, as Pellegrino goes on to say: 'We are responsible for the whole event but culpable only for those parts of it we intend.'[23]

By focusing on the question of intention not only can we distinguish euthanasia from acts which foreshorten life, but also, from those acts that constitute forgoing treatment or 'letting die'. This distinction has sometimes been made on the basis of the distinction between acts of omission and acts of commission. However, as both Finnis and Harris point out, there is 'no morally relevant distinction between employing deliberate omissions ... *in order to* terminate life ("passive euthanasia") and employing "a deliberate intervention" for the same purpose ("active euthanasia").'[24] In other words, if the intention is to kill the patient, then it is *morally* irrelevant whether it is by an act of omission or an act of commission.

If it is the case that the patient's disease or injury or condition is the cause of death and neither the patient nor physician intended the patient's death then it is not an instance of euthanasia but of 'letting die'. However, there are many cases in which it would be specious to say that when technology is removed a natural death occurs. If the patient's death is intended by removing the technology and occurs not merely by natural causes, then, as Beauchamp argues: 'The patient's decision and the physician's intentional action play an important causal role in the outcome in the circumstance in which death occurs.'[25] For example, to withhold nutrition and hydration so that a patient starves to death is both a necessary and a sufficient condition of death by starvation at the time death occurs. Correspondingly, if the patient is suffering from a condition such as severe brain damage or cancer, these conditions (the reason for refusing treatment) are neither a necessary nor a sufficient cause of death by starvation. They are not the cause of death as it occurs and when it occurs.[26] Therefore, it is the intention of the parties involved that is crucial in distinguishing natural causes of death, letting die and euthanasia.

It is important to clarify that what is physically possible (for example, keeping a patient alive) is not always ethically necessary. There is enormous scope for discretion when it comes to withdrawing or withholding treatment and allowing a patient to die while continuing to care for (rather than attempting to cure) the patient. The omission of life-sustaining treatment which a person has refused or which a physician for some other reason has no duty to provide is not necessarily an instance of euthanasia. In Ramsey's view, in just or only omitting treatment (as distinct from omitting treatment with the intention of causing death): 'We cease doing what was once called for and begin to do precisely what is called for now. We attend and company with [the patient] in this, his very own dying, rendering it as comfortable and dignified as possible.'[27] Thus, the omission of treatment does not include denying care we owe all humans, whether living or dying, for example, providing sufficient food and water to someone in a persistent vegetative state.

Omitting life-saving remedies and letting a patient die is sometimes justified on the grounds of the distinction between ordinary and extraordinary treatments. However, it is not clear whether defining what constitutes ordinary and extraordinary treatment and drawing a line between them is of moral significance. For example, Peter Singer cites the question of whether the employment of a respirator constitutes ordinary or extraordinary care. He makes two points: 'Firstly, the very description of the respirator as "extraordinary" depends on a judgement already having been made to the effect that it is not worthwhile prolonging the life of a patient in [a persistent vegetative state].'[28] For Singer, the attempt to claim factual specificity for the distinction between extraordinary and ordinary care masks a prior moral judgement. He states: 'Labelling a means of treatment as "extraordinary" serves to disguise a judgment about the quality of life of the patient on whom the means of treatment is being used.'[29] Singer's second point is that the distinction between extraordinary and ordinary means can disguise, but cannot ultimately conceal, the fact that it is intention that is the critical issue not the means used to carry out the intention. Singer gives the example of the Tony Bland case as one that clarifies the issue. In the Bland case the distinction between ordinary and extraordinary was not used and it was admitted that the intention of the doctors in withholding nutrition and hydration was to bring about the death of an innocent human being.[30]

By focusing on the question of intention the distinction some make between assisted suicide and euthanasia is shown to be morally irrelevant. While there may be a practical distinction, there is no moral distinction between euthanasia and assisted suicide. In assisted suicide the action of the person whose death is brought about must be the final cause of death (the final link in a causal chain leading to death), whereas in euthanasia the final cause of one person's death must be another person's action. However, as Beauchamp points out, both assisted suicide and euthanasia involve some form of assistance in bringing about another's death.[31] Furthermore, in both assisted suicide and euthanasia, it is the intention of those directly responsible for the causal chain leading to death that is morally significant, and not the final cause of death.

Having defined euthanasia in broad terms and distinguished euthanasia from a variety of other similar and related kinds of action, the different types of euthanasia must be delineated. Harris distinguishes various kinds of euthanasia. He contends that if a patient consciously decided to end their life or expressly approves the decision by another to end their life, that is called *voluntary euthanasia.* He goes on to say: 'Where the individual concerned does not know about the decision and has not consciously and expressly approved it in advance, I will call this non-voluntary euthanasia even where he or she is believed or presumed to be in accord.'[32] Furthermore, if the patient is competent to give informed consent and does not give it, or if the agent assumes the patient would not consent if competent, then the act of euthanasia is involuntary.[33] Those who advocate legalization of euthanasia support voluntary and non-voluntary euthanasia (for example, of anencephalic infants), but there is a widespread consensus against involuntary euthanasia.[34] For the purposes of this chapter, these different types of euthanasia are not significant. The focus is on euthanasia as a broadly defined type of action denoting the deliberate and intentional killing by act or omission of an innocent person whose life is considered not to be worth living, and whether this kind of action should be considered good care for the suffering-dying.

Brock identifies the moral problem with the proposal that euthanasia constitutes a form of good care for the suffering-dying. He states: 'If the deliberate killing of an innocent person is wrong, euthanasia would be nearly always impermissible.'[35] So the question is raised as to whether medical care and practice may, in certain circumstances, legitimately involve the deliberately killing of the innocent, or is it 'always impermissible' in medicine?

The practice of medicine and euthanasia

Albert Jonsen states:

> The contemporary proposals for assisted suicide or medical killing are, in essence, proposals to inaugurate a social practice. It is misleading, I think, to say that they have the intention of alleviating pain; this is a motive, not an intention. The intention is the innovative moral practice itself ... whereby medical care, already accepted as a moral good, is given an expanded definition of its task and

practitioners are charged with a responsibility they have not previously had. The proposal is to endorse medical killing as a practice integral to the practice of medicine.[36]

The question addressed in this section is whether Jonsen is right or whether, contrary to Jonsen's statement, the action of euthanasia is consonant with the history and tradition of medical practice. It is important to address this question in order to understand what is driving the call for euthanasia: the internal logic and coherence of medicine itself, or some other factor external to medicine. It is important to be clear about the source of what is driving the call for euthanasia in order to identify the real point of conflict between Christians and non-Christians over what constitutes good care for the suffering-dying. There are many instances of conflict between Christians and non-Christians that result from either confusion about, or misunderstanding of, the real point at issue. The question is whether the point at issue is the nature of medicine itself or something else. If the point at issue does not arise within medicine itself, but is driven by something else, then we can proceed to identify and assess what that 'something else' might be.

It is legitimate to call medicine a 'practice' in MacIntyre's sense of the term. There are rules and technical skills and certain virtues are required for its proper performance. Furthermore, there is a tradition in which medicine is situated and this tradition involves an on-going conversation about what constitutes good medicine. This conversation and tradition is itself situated within a wider narrative about what the good of human life is. The roots of the Western medical tradition lie in ancient Greece, notably in those physicians who followed the Hippocratic Oath and in the philosophers who gave a theoretical account of medicine. Georgios Anagnastopoulos states:

> The ancient Greek philosophical tradition is in complete agreement with what we find in the extant writings from the Hippocratic medical tradition. Plato and Aristotle see medicine as a practical/productive *science* that seeks to understand a certain subject matter as well as realize a certain end, i.e. health.[37]

Anagnastopoulos points out that according to Plato, medicine '"is the science of health" (*Charmides 165d*) or "the science of health and disease" (*Republic* iv 438e) and according to Aristotle "the science of things connected with health" (*Nichomachean Ethics* vi 10.1143a3) or "science of producing health" (*Topics* ii 3.110b18-19).'[38] Anagnastopoulos counters the claim made by Ludwig Edelstein that the Hippocratic Oath reflected merely the beliefs of a fringe Pythagorean sect and is not representative of either the practice or views of the mainstream of medical practitioners in the ancient Greek world.[39] Instead, Anagnastopoulos argues that the Hippocratic Oath is indicative of, and consistent with, not only ancient Greek medical practice, but also with the views and practice of physicians over many centuries. Allen Verhey's view concurs with that of Anagnastopoulos. Verhey states that the point of the Hippocratic Oath:

was not that one would fail to be a good Pythagorean if one violated these standards, although that is true enough, but rather that one would fail to be a good medical practitioner. The good medical practitioner is not a mere technician; he is committed by the practice of medicine to certain goods and to certain standards.[40]

What are the goods and standards that medicine pursues as a practice with standards of excellence implicit in it? As already stated, Plato and Aristotle viewed the *telos* of medicine as health. Anagnastopoulos notes that: 'The essentialist conception of the goals of medicine that Plato and Aristotle expound does not allow for any considerations other than the health of the patient to determine physicians' actions.'[41] The Hippocratic Oath identifies the chief good as seeking 'the benefit of the sick' and keeping the patient from harm and injustice.[42] For the Hippocratic Oath, seeking the benefit of the sick in a way that causes them no harm or injustice inherently involves a number of other related ends, for example, confidentiality. Verhey comments that because

> the ends intrinsic to medicine are to heal the sick, to protect and nurture health, to maintain and restore physical well-being, limits could be imposed on the use of skills within the practice. The skills were not to be used to serve alien ends, and the destruction of human life – either the last of it or the first of it [i.e. euthanasia or abortion] – was seen as an alien and conflicting end.[43]

Therefore, in accord with what Verhey and Anagnastopoulos argue, the intentional killing of innocent life is antithetical to the proper practice of medicine. Thus, the call for euthanasia is not consistent with the internal logic and coherence of medicine itself.[44]

If the goal of medicine is health then the question arises as to what is meant by the term 'health'? Grisez furnishes us with a good working definition. He states health is 'well-integrated, harmonious, psychosomatic functioning'.[45] By implication, the term 'health' does not include the totality of human well-being, nor should it be reduced solely to biological or somatic functionality. Grisez points out that while health is a good in itself, it is also an instrumental good: that is, it is a 'more or less important condition for the intellectual, moral and cultural fulfilment of the person'.[46] However, without a clear idea of what human fulfilment consists of one cannot say what health seeks and thus one cannot say what constitutes good health. It is at this point that the reasons begin to emerge as to why it is plausible for euthanasia to be considered a form of good care for the suffering-dying.

For MacIntyre, since the Enlightenment, it is precisely any sense of what human fulfilment consists of that is now lost. The loss of any wider *telos* for human life means that any sense of what medicine as a practice is trying to achieve in seeking the 'health' of a patient is lost and medicine either over-reaches itself (and denies its proper limits) or it stops short of that which it should properly undertake.

To seek a patient's well-being is to presuppose some framework of meaning already in place. When such a framework is absent for either the patients or physicians or both, then clinical medicine, however scientifically well-founded its judgements, can enhance a patient's well-being only by accident. According to MacIntyre, it is precisely notions of the human good and narratives which make sense of life within a wider framework of meaning that modernity undercuts, and in the process it renders the very notion of 'sound clinical judgement' problematic. It renders them problematic because medicine lacks any ability to ground questions about what constitutes 'better' or 'worse' treatments for any particular patient.[47] Medicine now shares the irrationality of modernity since it is situated both within the Enlightenment narrative about unlimited progress through technical mastery of nature and economic growth, and the liberal tradition which vaunts individual autonomy and denies the possibility of any ultimate human good.[48] By being situated thus, medicine becomes incoherent as a practice. Crucially, a proper understanding of what constitutes 'health' becomes unobtainable. As a result, rather than seek the benefit of the sick and keeping the patient from harm and injustice, as the Hippocratic Oath exhorts, medicine has, in many instances, become unjust and oppresses the weak. The loss of a wider notion of the human good renders medicine itself incoherent and it is this incoherence that enables the proposal suggested by Albert Jonsen, namely that we should 'endorse medical killing as a practice integral to the practice of medicine', even to be considered.[49]

As is now clear, it is developments external to medicine that have allowed an action – euthanasia – that is essentially alien to the good practice of medicine to be seen as a legitimate part of medicine. Therefore, to understand why euthanasia is considered a form of good care for the suffering-dying, and why this view is incommensurable with a Christian account of what good care for the suffering-dying consists of, it is necessary to look beyond medicine and attend to the philosophical presuppositions of those who endorse euthanasia.

Philosophical defences of euthanasia

Perhaps the most influential of these philosophical trends driving the call for euthanasia is the increasing emphasis on individual human autonomy as something that determines what is good or in the best interests of a person. For example, R. G. Frey, in his case for legalizing voluntary euthanasia, states: 'Control over our own life is one of the most important goods we enjoy. ... It is our life and how we live it and what we make of it is up to us.'[50] Dan Brock defines autonomy as 'the freedom to decide for ourselves as we see fit what direction our life will take, even when others may with good reason disagree.'[51] The freedom to choose is framed in terms of the 'rights' of the patient. These rights, which 'belong' to the patient, protect the patient's ability to exercise her freedom of choice and her interests as against, say, the interests of the medical profession or the wider community. This shift towards emphasizing the autonomy of a patient in medical decisions is such that Brock now notes:

> A common model of the doctor–patient relationship is one in which the doctor is viewed as the agent of the patient and who is to act in the interest and for the welfare of the patient alone. The physician should adopt what has been called a patient-centred ethic.[52]

A good example of how the notion of autonomy is employed in supporting arguments for euthanasia is that set out by Ronald Dworkin. Dworkin takes it to be 'generally agreed' that 'adult citizens of normal competence have a right to autonomy, that is, a right to make important decisions defining their own lives for themselves.'[53] Dworkin recognizes that the notion of autonomy is far from simple. For example, he asks when the right to autonomy is lost and 'why we should ever respect the decisions people make when we believe that these are not in their interests'?[54] After dismissing what he terms the 'evidentiary view of autonomy' (that is, the claim that we should respect an individual's decisions because that person generally knows his own best interests),[55] Dworkin makes a case for what he calls the 'integrity view of autonomy'. Dworkin states that 'the value of autonomy, on this view, derives from the capacity it protects: the capacity to express one's own character – values, commitments, convictions, and critical as well as experiential interests – in the life one leads.'[56] Dworkin goes on to say:

> Recognizing an individual right to autonomy makes self-creation possible. ... We allow someone to choose death over radical amputation or a blood transfusion, if that is his informed wish, because we acknowledge his right to a life structured by his own values.[57]

Dworkin here is clearly not suggesting that the moral worth of what we choose is that which is important, but rather, the moral worth lies in the act of choosing and ascribing value to something.[58] When the capacity to choose is impaired, the value of the life is endangered because self-creation is restricted.

One implication of Dworkin's view of autonomy is that human beings are not equal in possessing basic dignity. Human life is valued insofar as the person whose life it is is in a position to value things and projects and activities and does value them. The requirement that a person possess certain abilities in order to possess dignity underlies the distinction Dworkin makes between 'biological life' and 'human life'. For Dworkin, 'human life' is constituted by 'personal choice, training, commitment and decision'.[59] On this account those who cannot generate choices, commitments or decisions can no longer be counted as possessing 'human life'. Thus, to deny them 'biological life' is not to kill them; rather, it is not to prolong a form of life no longer worth living. Mary Warnock makes a similar distinction between 'simply being alive' and 'the specifically human consciousness of having a life to lead'.[60] Only those who possess 'fully human consciousness' have value or dignity.

The corollary of the view that an individual's ability to make decisions and exercise choice is determinative of her human worth is that her choices should be determinative of what constitute good care. This is to say, the patient's autonomy – their choice – takes precedence over medical possibility, the judgement of those medical practitioners involved, and the concerns of the family and wider community of the patient. Therefore, if the patient expresses her will in a choice for euthanasia (specifying under what conditions this choice is to be applied in a 'living will') the doctor and family are morally obliged to follow the patient's prior choice, even if the patient is currently no longer able to exercise that choice. Moreover, Dworkin states that: 'A competent person's right to autonomy requires that his past decisions about how he is to be treated if he becomes demented must be respected even if they contradict the desires he has at that later point.'[61] Dworkin calls this 'precedent autonomy'.

I have pointed to how the notion of autonomy is employed to legitimize the action of euthanasia as morally licit. However, a notion of autonomy like Dworkin's does not fully justify, or give decisive weight to, the conception of euthanasia as good care for the suffering-dying. There are many actions which may be warranted on grounds of autonomy that would not thereby be considered good actions, for example, smoking cigarettes. There are, thus, two further factors, that combine together with the conception of autonomy (and its concomitant, the dualistic divide between human and biological life) outlined above, to give weight to the idea that euthanasia is a form of good care for the suffering-dying.

The first of these other factors is the contemporary conception of death. William May draws attention to how, in contemporary Western culture, death is both hidden away and on prominent display. He states: 'On the one hand death is a taboo subject, the unmentionable event; on the other, death (and violence) is an obsession at every level of our culture.'[62] Death's concealment, whether it is in hospitals or the hushed tones of polite conversation, excludes death from on-going human community. Yet precisely at the point of its concealment there is an obsession with violent death manifested in the 'pornography of death' that so many contemporary films, books, computer games and television programmes display.[63] Like all forms of pornography, the pornography of death objectifies the action and abstracts it from its proper human response; that is, grief. Popular advocates of euthanasia, for example, Derek Humphry, seek to challenge the contemporary taboos surrounding death. Humphry states that the 'right-to-die credo ... aims to share the dying experience.'[64] However, contrary to what Humphry asserts, the concealment of death and the concomitant obsession with violent death are embodied in the action of euthanasia. Euthanasia is an act which both excludes death (by hurrying it on in order to get it over with) and inflicts violence on the body (by denying the body its own time and pace of death). Furthermore, Humphry's need to insist that, for example, assisted suicide, should only be done by those who have 'a bonding of love or friendship, and mutual respect' with the patient is evidence of the rarity of what he calls 'self-deliverance' being situated in a 'bonding of love'.[65] More often than not, assisted suicide and euthanasia represent an abstraction of death from the bonds of human community in their refusal of dependence on others and the claims for on-going care.[66]

Whether death is viewed with horror or as 'natural' and inevitable, death still represents the termination of an individual's direct involvement in all that they value. Many advocates of euthanasia take the view that if death cannot be defeated, then it can at least be painless, planned and dignified, so that the random encroachment of death is defied and the last word of a human is self-assertion. Furthermore, given the inevitability of death there comes a point for every human when medical care cannot cure the patient and extending the patient's life becomes futile. In effect, death is the point at which medicine reaches its limit. At this point the patient is in danger from one of two eventualities. These are, over-treatment or neglect. The former constitutes a perpetuation of suffering through medical treatment that is intrusive and unnecessary in the light of death's inevitability. The latter exacerbates suffering unnecessarily by abrogating any care at all so that the patient is left to die a painful and degrading death because medicine can no longer cure the patient. Given that pain is considered an affront to human dignity euthanasia emerges as the most loving response given these two other possible ways to respond to the suffering-dying.[67] Dworkin is representative of those who present euthanasia as the optimum way of avoiding either over-treatment or neglect of the suffering-dying.[68]

While contemporary attitudes about death are an important factor, they are less significant in legitimizing euthanasia than the second factor; that is, contemporary attitudes to suffering. Within modernity illness, pain and suffering are pointless: that is, they can play no role in helping us live our lives well. O'Donovan notes that suffering became unintelligible in contemporary society because it is a society orientated towards the individual and the exercise of the individual will. He states: 'The role society, on earth and in heaven, could play in justifying the individual's suffering is removed. The late-modern age, accordingly, is in perpetual rebellion against the "pointlessness", the "waste" of suffering.'[69] Both the valuing of compassion over wisdom and the resort to technological means to 'solve' (meaning to 'eliminate') any perceived suffering exacerbates this. O'Donovan points out that within the logic of modernity, and spurred on by compassion, suffering in any form must be eliminated through technical means.[70] As Hauerwas notes in relation to O'Donovan's insight: 'Illness is an absurdity in a history formed by the commitment to overcome all evils that potentially we can control.'[71]

Those who advocate euthanasia view a planned and regulated death as preferable to one that involves suffering. Indeed, assisting someone to die is considered an act of mercy when she is suffering in her dying, because the quality of human life is more important than life itself. The assumption behind this is that certain forms of life are not worth living, either because they do not constitute human life, or because the quality of life is so impaired as to make death preferable. An example of the former is someone with no higher brain functions but who is 'biologically' alive. This is thought to be a non-human form of life. An example of the latter is someone who is considered to be fully human, but is enduring great pain.

Relating autonomy, death and suffering within a theological account of good care

Christians have a view of autonomy, death and suffering that diverges completely from that of those who seek to have euthanasia recognized as part of good medicine. In what follows I try to clarify the roots of the incommensurability between the view of Christians and the views of those who advocate euthanasia by analysing why, according to the logic of their own tradition, Christians reject the central assumptions that underpin arguments for euthanasia: that is, the preference for death over suffering and the move to emphasize patient autonomy. I contend that, in contemporary society, the suffering-dying are an instance of the vulnerable stranger whom Christ admonishes the church to welcome.

The modern view of suffering contrasts directly with Christian approaches to suffering. For Christians the question is not whether suffering has a point in and of itself. Instead, the experience of suffering is located in a wider framework and narrative in which suffering has a place. John Paul II summarizes an approach to suffering that seeks to locate it within a wider framework of meaning, when he states:

> According to Christian teaching ... suffering, especially in the final moments of life, has a special place in God's plan of salvation. It is a sharing in the passion of Christ and unites the person with the redemptive sacrifice which Christ offered in obedience to the Father's will.[72]

However, as Nigel Biggar points out, the notion of suffering at work in the above statement (and elsewhere in John Paul II's treatment of suffering) as somehow redemptive is too broad.[73] After giving a critique of John Paul II's conception of suffering, Biggar concludes:

> It is possible ... to regard human suffering as redemptive, but only of a certain kind; namely, the compassionate and forgiving suffering of injury. Other kinds of human suffering – such as terminal illness and chronic pain – cannot be regarded as redemptive in the strong sense of imitating the compassion and forgiveness of God in Christ.[74]

Biggar points out that this is not to say that terminal illness and chronic pain cannot be 'redemptive' in a weaker sense. For Biggar, the kind of suffering involved in terminal illness can be 'redemptive' as part of both a duty to endure it for the sake of fulfilling a responsibility (for example, reconciliation with an estranged family member), and as part of Christian faithfulness. With regard to this latter point, Biggar states:

> A life is valuable not only for what it builds, but also for what it says. So in the faithful, hopeful, charitable manner of my suffering I may be able to demonstrate salvific truths about, for example, the contingent value of the human individual, the gracious goodness of God, and the humanising prospect of eternal life.[75]

But witnessing to truths such as these is not the same as saying the suffering endured in, for example, chronic illness, is redemptive in any strong sense (that is, constituting a witness to or participation in God's redemption of humanity). Situating suffering within the narrative framework of the Gospel does not mean that suffering is redemptive in a strong sense; however, following Biggar, it does enable one to say that suffering may be redemptive in the weaker sense. Thus situating suffering within the Gospel narrative can enable men and women to abide patiently in, and bear patiently with, suffering: by enabling them to interpret their experience within a framework that does not make suffering pointless or meaningless.

Situating suffering in the narrative of the Gospel does not eliminate the need for attempts to alleviate it. Meilaender clarifies why this is the case when he states:

> The principle that governs Christian compassion ... is not 'minimize suffering.' It is 'maximize care.' Were our goal only to minimize suffering, no doubt we could sometimes achieve it by eliminating *sufferers*. But then we refuse to understand suffering as a significant part of human life that can have meaning or purpose. We should not, of course, pretend that suffering in itself is a good thing, nor should we put forward claims about the benefits others can reap from their suffering. ... The suffering that comes is an evil, but the God who in Jesus has not abandoned us in that suffering can bring good from it for us as for Jesus. ... Our task is therefore not to abandon those who suffer but to 'maximize care' for them as they live out their own life's story. We ought 'always to care, never to kill.'[76]

He goes on to point out that if suffering cannot be relieved, we must remember that even God does not really 'solve' or take away the problem of suffering; rather, God lives and bears with suffering. Within such an approach to suffering the idea that we can balance or calculate how much suffering is preferable to death in order to make medical decisions is wholly mistaken.

The basis of this Christian conception of suffering is a particular vision of life and death. The Christian vision of life and death is wholly different in kind from that embodied in the action of euthanasia. The Christian lives in response to Jesus' call to seek not life for its own sake, but to seek first the kingdom of God (Mt. 6.33). Karl Barth puts it thus: 'Life is no second God, and therefore the respect due to it cannot rival the reverence owed to God.'[77] Barth points out that the respect owed to life as a good in itself has as its limitation 'the will of God the Creator Himself who commands it, and the horizon which is set for man by the same God with his determination for eternal life.'[78] What Barth says points also to how Christians understand the basis of their life: it is not their own but received as a gift and loan from God which can only be fulfilled in communion with God. Thus Christians seek to live within these limits, recognizing that between these limits lies the sphere of true freedom. They bear their life in trust for a certain time. They are neither to prolong, nor protect, nor seek its fulfilment, at all costs. In Christianity, life is a good, but it is not the greatest good.

The approach to life outlined above determines a particular conception of death.[79] As noted previously, advocates of euthanasia see death as the termination of all human goods and to be accepted as inevitable; and in its inevitability, death is considered 'natural'. Euthanasia encapsulates this approach to dying in its shrill indifference to death. By contrast, Christianity views death as a deeply ambivalent phenomenon. For Christians, death is an evil, but it is not the greatest evil humans can suffer. Death is both a proper limit established by God, and an enemy God defeats. This ambiguity brings to the fore the seeming contradiction at the heart of the Christian vision of life. As Meilaender puts it:

> We are created from the dust of the ground – finite beings who are limited by biological necessities and historical location. We are also free spirits, moved by the life-giving Spirit of God, created ultimately for communion with God – and therefore soaring beyond any limited understanding of our person in terms of presently 'given' conditions of life.[80]

The ambivalence towards death is manifested in the Bible by the tension between Ecclesiastes and Romans. Paul Ramsey, after an extended meditation on the understanding of death in Ecclesiastes, concludes that while dying is part of life, it is always an indignity. Ramsey states:

> So the grandeur and misery of man are fused together in the human reality and experience of death. To deny the indignity of death requires that the dignity of man be refused also. The more acceptable in itself death is, the less the worth or uniqueness ascribed to the dying life.[81]

As Ramsey points out, death is an indignity which causes us to 'number our days' and probe the depths of life while there is still time.[82] For Ramsey, Ecclesiastes leads us to conclude that without death human life would be a condition of endless boredom. However, the vision in Ecclesiastes does not exhaust the Christian conception of death. As O'Donovan argues, Ramsey underplays the evangelical proclamation of the resurrection.[83] It is this proclamation that forms the foundation of Paul's understanding of death set out in Romans. For Paul, the dominion of death (and sin) was broken by the death and resurrection of Jesus Christ, so that death is no longer an enemy that sets the limit of our life. As Paul writes: 'For the law of the Spirit of life in Christ Jesus has set you free from the law of sin and of death' (Rom. 8:2). O'Donovan notes: 'The Christian Gospel, therefore, proclaims a reconciliation of humanity with mortality, for it proclaims that eternal life is present here and now, even under the conditions of mortality.'[84] Hence, as Paul phrases it: 'Christ will be exalted now as always in my body, whether by life or by death' (Phil. 1:20).

It is the resurrection that should properly determine the Christian understanding of death.[85] Death, which formerly deprived us of future possibilities, can do so no more. After the resurrection we may now live in the security that 'neither death, nor life, nor angels, nor rulers, nor things present, nor things to come, nor powers, nor height, nor depth, nor anything else in all creation, will be able to separate us from the love of God in Christ Jesus our Lord' (Rom. 8:38–39). O'Donovan states that 'resurrection unmasks the pretensions of death to be a Last Thing, by superseding it as a Later-than-last Thing, and so demonstrating that it was never more than a penultimate thing.'[86] Thus death no longer determines life's dignity; now it is the new life we have in Christ that establishes the value of human life. This is not to say that life has no limit; rather, as the earlier quotation from Barth indicates, its limit is now the eschatological horizon. It is this *telos* for human life that gives life its meaning and purpose. Furthermore, as O'Donovan points out, death can only properly be understood in the relation to this horizon. In relation to the eschaton, death can be seen as a form of judgement, but not as a final sentence. O'Donovan states:

> To see death as the emblem of divine judgment requires that we have first seen life as an emblem of divine acquittal. Because God has said his final 'Yes' to the world, we may understand the mysterious and world-denying absurdity of death as God's penultimate 'No', the No which supports the Yes by refusing all forms of uncreation and destruction in the human will.[87]

By understanding death in the shadow of the resurrection Christians are directed to a very different response to death and dying. In relation to our death, instead of the defiance 'which aims to "surmount our fate" by a moment of human assertion',[88] of which euthanasia may often be an expression, Christians approach death with hope for a future given in Jesus Christ. In relation to those who are dying: 'The resurrection of Christ frees a man for approach to the dying not because it arms him with a possession to give, but because it frees him from all this worry and confusion about possessions.'[89] In other words, the resurrection of Christ frees us to abide with and care for the suffering-dying without either over-treating them, or neglecting them, or intending their death.

Just as Christians reject the assumption that death is preferable to suffering, so they also question the conception of autonomy that is such a central premise in arguments for euthanasia. As previously noted, the conception of autonomy proposed by advocates of euthanasia presupposes a dualism: that is, a belief that we can separate the mind and the body. However, the Christian tradition presupposes a very different anthropology, in which humans are conceived of as psychosomatic wholes. Life is unitary; it is not vegetable life supplemented by animal life supplemented by an intellectual life.[90] Augustine represents the Christian tradition when he states that: 'A man's body is no mere adornment, or external convenience; it belongs to his very nature as a man.'[91] Unlike Dworkin, Singer, Warnock and others, Christians cannot argue for a separation of 'human life' from 'biological life'. Thus, within a theological anthropology, even if one's brain has been so damaged that one is no longer capable of intellectual acts, one does not cease to be human; instead, one is a damaged human.

The refusal of a dualism between 'human life' from 'biological life' is premised, in the first instance, on the doctrine of creation. Central to the doctrine of creation is the insistence that God did not need to create. Conversely, what God does create is free to be itself for no reason other than God's gratuitous giving of it to be itself. The doctrine of creation *ex nihilo* means that human being, which is also to say human bodies, are not *for* anything. Bodies are good in and of themselves. Furthermore, God loves and desires our bodies precisely as that which is not God, as that which is created, bodily, limited and so on. Thus we value our bodies not simply because they are the means by which we are able to carry out our life projects, but because they have intrinsic value as created goods.[92] As Banner argues:

> The conviction that Jesus Christ is the first is the conviction that the grace of God shown in Jesus Christ is shown in creation. It is in virtue of this conviction, ... that Augustine commends all those practices which honour and cherish the body (of the self, the other, the unborn, and of the dead) rather than repudiate it. These practices value the body as itself a gift from the hand of the creator, and not as a thing of indifference, as it were, of which truly valuable human life simply makes use.[93]

Furthermore, as creatures of God, our existence and value is not determined by any human action or capacity. Instead, our bodily existence is a gift and loan from God of which we are stewards and in respect of which we at once owe a duty to our Creator and to one another. Hauerwas puts it thus: 'For our creaturely status is but a reminder that our existence is not secured by our own power, but rather requires the constant care and trust in others.'[94] Thus, for the Christian, our life is not ours to dispose of as we see fit. It is not our property and we are not autonomous.[95] We come to be through God and others, and whether we like it or not, we are always dependent on God and others.

The status of humans as creatures is not all Christians have to say about the body. Our bodies are also destined for participation in a new creation. As Eugene Rogers notes: 'Salvation is itself bodily. It depends, for Gentile Christians, upon the crucifixion of God's body, and it depends on their human bodies' getting taken up into God's body.'[96] Thus the coming of the kingdom of God, which Jesus both announces through miracles that restore and heal bodies, and the resurrection of his own body, speaks of the goodness and future of human bodies. The human body has value and a future in and of itself and not merely as a thing of which 'human life' makes use of for a time. The action of euthanasia, by contrast, not only views the body in solely instrumental terms, but also expresses hopelessness about the future of the body. Banner points out that these contrasting anthropologies lead to very different kinds of medical practice:

> If the goodness of human life includes the goodness of bodily life and if this body is itself to be caught up in the redemption for which the Christian hopes, then medicine is permitted, vindicated and honoured. It is hereby commanded and summoned to serve the good of the body which genuinely is a human good, belonging to our past, present and future. We find, however, that medicine refuses this calling either by withdrawing altogether from the service of the body, or by converting service into manipulation.[97]

Implicit in and underlying a specifically Christian anthropology is the doctrine of recapitulation. The grace of God revealed in the redemption of humans through Jesus Christ is a renewal of the grace given in creation. Thus, the Christian vision of human life as a psychosomatic whole, wherein the body is cherished in and of itself, is founded upon the reality that 'Christ does not come as the last to redeem us from a world for which he was not the first, but comes to restore and reconcile this world to its creator.'[98]

The contrast with a Christian conception of life suggests that an emphasis on patient autonomy and calls for euthanasia misconstrue the nature of freedom. It is a misconstual because even those philosophers who were ambivalent about or opposed to Christianity did not think that the decision to terminate one's life could be a free act. For example, John Stuart Mill, who is often held to be a forebear of those who argue for euthanasia on the grounds of personal liberty,[99] argued that one could not in the name of freedom choose unfreedom. Mill states that in relation to one who wishes to sell himself into slavery: 'The principle of freedom cannot require that he should be free not to be free. It is not freedom, to be allowed to alienate his freedom.'[100] The same can be said for the person who chooses euthanasia and in doing so uses (or abuses) his freedom to give up freedom. As O'Donovan notes: 'For freedom as there exercised encompasses its own annihilation.'[101] It is thus a 'destructive and defiant attack upon the nature of the free agent himself, who [like the slave] is permitted thereafter to make no more free choices.'[102] O'Donovan goes on to point out that freedom is never merely a means to an end which can then disappear. Rather, freedom has a teleological structure, 'in which freedom-given serves freedom-to-be-achieved'.[103] To choose death is to choose unfreedom and that is a false exercise of autonomy.

The contrast between the notion of autonomy central to advocacy of euthanasia and a Christian vision of life raises a further issue that is specifically Christian in content. The specifically Christian insight is that freedom is not constituted by the autonomous exercise of the human will. Rather, as Barth puts it: 'Life is the freedom which is bestowed by God. To will it is to will what we are permitted. It is to will in the freedom in which man is not sovereign or solitary, but always has God above him as the Creator, Giver and Lord of his life.'[104] Thus, to the Christian, the action of euthanasia far from constituting a free act is in fact an instance of alienation and bondage to sin.

Autonomy should not form the ground on which Christians protect patients against the encroachments of medical technology or the neglect of their appointed carers. Christians must seek to situate care for the suffering-dying within the narrative of the Gospel and the practice of hospitality. On this basis medical practice is exhorted to 'maximize care' rather than 'minimize suffering'. Implicit in such an exhortation is the view that dependence on others is not of itself a bad thing.

Within the framework of their own tradition, Christians have a completely divergent view from those who advocate euthanasia as a form of good care for the suffering-dying. While euthanasia may seem a loving option to some, against the background of Christian belief and practice, euthanasia cannot constitute an act of love and care. Meilaender notes:

> Such action cannot be loving because it cannot be part of the meaning of commitment to the well-being of another human being within the appointed limits of earthly life. The benevolence of the euthanatizer is enough like love to give us pause, to tempt us to call it love. And *perhaps* it may even be the closest those who feel themselves to bear the full responsibility for relief of suffering and production of good in our world can come to love. But it is not the creaturely love which Christians praise, a love which can sometimes do no more than suffer as best we can with the sufferer.[105]

Christians can say to those who advocate voluntary euthanasia: 'All honour to the well-meaning humanitarianism of [your] underlying motive!'[106] However, as Barth goes on to say, such a call is derived not from what Christians take to be authoritative, but 'from another book'.[107] And while Christians may applaud the humanitarian sentiment that inspires calls for euthanasia, they must conclude that those who make such calls are tragically colluding in their own bondage.[108] Furthermore, in contrast to those who advocate euthanasia, Christians should recognize the suffering-dying as vulnerable strangers under threat of being neglected, oppressed, or killed off, and thus in need of a 'place' within the church so that they might be welcomed and cared for.

The incommensurability between the view held by Christians and that held by those who advocate euthanasia makes the issue of what constitutes good care for the suffering-dying a test case for the conception of hospitality set out above.[109] Having mapped the incommensurability between the beliefs of Christians and those who advocate euthanasia the following question needs addressing: if Christians should reject euthanasia, what is a Christian response to care for the suffering-dying that accords with the model of hospitality set out in the previous chapter? Furthermore, given their rejection of euthanasia, how are Christians to relate to those neighbours whose view is incommensurable with a Christian account of what care for the suffering-dying should consist of? It is to these questions that I now turn. What follows also constitutes a recapitulation of the central arguments of this book.

MacIntyre's response to the care we owe the suffering-dying

MacIntyre's work suggests one possible response for Christians to make to the suffering-dying. He argues that the good society (that is, one which embodies relationships of giving and receiving through which our individual and common goods can be achieved) is one in which

> it is taken for granted that disability and dependence on others are something that all of us experience at certain times in our lives ... and that consequently our interest in how the needs of the disabled are adequately voiced and met is not a special interest ... but rather the interest of the whole political society.[110]

Thus, MacIntyre places care of the disabled and weaker members of society (of which the suffering-dying are an instance) at the centre of determining what constitutes a good society.[111] Care for the weak is also central to determining what is rational. He states:

> We discover ... in our encounters with the disabled hitherto unrecognized sources of error in our own practical reasoning. And, insofar as these derived from hitherto dominant norms of our social environment, we will have to transform that environment as well as ourselves, if we are to be freed from such errors in our shared deliberative reasoning.[112]

MacIntyre is in effect calling for something very like what St Benedict advocates; that is, a society governed by the dictum that: 'Care of the sick must rank above and before all else, so that they may truly be served as Christ.'[113] For MacIntyre, a society in which such care is a priority will be a society characterized by the kind of just generosity and acknowledged dependence that MacIntyre advocates is crucial for developing independent rational agency.

Opposition to euthanasia would seem to be consistent with MacIntyre's account of the good society and what constitutes rational deliberation. Euthanasia constitutes a denial both of acknowledged dependence (by both agent and patient) and of the importance of care for the radically disabled. MacIntyre explicitly recommends care of those with 'extreme forms of disability and dependence'; that is, those human beings whose 'potentialities for rationality or affective response have been permanently frustrated'.[114] An example of such a person is someone in a persistent vegetative state. MacIntyre sees such care neither as a burden nor as an opportunity for benevolence, but as a form of education through which we might learn what it is for someone else to be wholly entrusted to our care (so that we are answerable for their well-being).

MacIntyre's approach to determining what is good and rational contradicts the view of 'human life' advocated by Dworkin and others: that is, in MacIntyre's view, the exercise of the will and autonomy are not paramount. Against views which separate 'human life' from 'biological life' MacIntyre urges us to recognize the centrality of the body to our humanity. He states that an 'attitude of denial towards the facts of disability and dependence presuppose either a failure or a refusal to acknowledge adequately the bodily dimension of our existence.'[115] As previously argued, euthanasia constitutes just such a refusal. MacIntyre argues for a proper acknowledgment of the role our animal and bodily nature play in constituting our rationality by calling for a recognition of 'how our thinking is the thinking of one species of animal'.[116]

When MacIntyre is contrasted with a theological account of the psychosomatic unity of human life a fundamental difference emerges. O'Donovan points out that the positing of a psychosomatic or body–soul unity is not enough to rule out, 'on the one hand, an Aristotelian settlement which accepts individual perishability for the sake of species survival; and it will not rule out, on the other, a defiance of natural mortality (by technique, if it can be done).'[117] Thus, even though MacIntyre's account of dependent rational animals is consistent with opposition to euthanasia, the arguments he might put forward against advocates of euthanasia lack the explanatory force and secure ground such a position demands. By contrast, a Christian anthropology does not ground the psychosomatic unity of human life in arguments about 'how our thinking is the thinking of one species of animal'; instead, arguments for the psychosomatic unity of human life rest on the claim God has made upon the bodily life of humans by the resurrection of Jesus Christ. As O'Donovan puts it:

> The principle of psychosomatic unity, then, has no *free-standing* authority for Christian thought, but rides on the principle that the resurrection of Christ is central to Christian faith and the resurrection of all mankind to Christian hope. It is in this context that the Christian will wish to give his assent to the saying, 'Embodiment is the end of all God's works.'[118]

Thus, we are to respect the body and care for the suffering-dying neither because we share an animal nature with them (even though we do) nor because we might learn something (even though we might), but because care (and only care) is owed to this dying person as someone who is called 'to an irreplaceable presence before the judgment seat of God.'[119]

For MacIntyre, the modern nation-state cannot embody the kind of just society he envisages. It can only be realized in relatively small-scale communities. It is at this point that his call for a politics of the local community comes into play. It would be some form of this politics – in which this vision of acknowledged dependence and care for the radically disabled was embodied – that would form the basis of a practical response, derived from MacIntyre's work, to calls for legalizing voluntary euthanasia. However, as I argued in the last chapter, while the response of Christians to ethical disputes with their neighbours might well (and probably should) involve something like the local politics MacIntyre calls for, such a politics cannot constitute the whole or only response of Christians. It cannot do so because, as this chapter has discussed at length, the views of those who advocate euthanasia are incommensurable with a Christian view of care for the suffering-dying. The divergent nature of these two views forestalls the point of the kind of 'local politics' MacIntyre envisages; that is, the gradual convergence and overcoming of incommensurability. As previously argued, because of the nature of the incommensurability between the views of Christians and non-Christians any gradual convergence between them cannot be achieved by following the prescriptions of MacIntyre's meta-theory.

Grisez's understanding of the care we owe the suffering-dying

Grisez vehemently opposes euthanasia as a form of care for the suffering-dying. His suggestion for what does constitute good care for the suffering-dying is known by his advocacy of hospice care. In his view, hospice care constitutes good care for three reasons: the patient as a person is respected, so that they are not merely treated as a patient, and the demands of their community are given priority over those of medical intervention; the dying person is recognized as dying, and thus no irrelevant treatment is given; and the dying person is not neglected, but cared for in every way possible.[120] This would seem to conform to Meilaender's principle that Christians should 'maximize care' rather than 'minimize suffering'.

Interestingly, Grisez presents two quite different kinds of argument against voluntary euthanasia. In *Life and Death with Liberty and Justice* he excludes theological considerations from his argument. He excludes them because he seeks to present arguments acceptable to the general public.[121] Yet in volume two of *Living a Christian Life* he uses an explicitly theological framework to make his case. In arguing that killing of the innocent is always wrong he states:

> The serious wrongness of killing the innocent follows not only from the inherent goodness of human life but from the order of creation (humans made in the image of God) and the purpose of redemption (the covenant communion, which will be perfected in heavenly communion, to which humankind is called). The order of creation and the purpose of redemption are central to divine revelation. Hence Scripture makes it clear that divine revelation teaches that killing the innocent is wrong.[122]

Furthermore, he argues that in the current secularized climate non-believers lack the hope of the resurrection. This lack of hope causes them to either dread death or undervalue it.[123] He holds that their lack of relationship with God leads them both to deny the sanctity of life and the essential evil of acts against human life.[124] He then cautions that: 'Christians who live in cultures largely shaped by nonbelief must be careful not to adopt this non-Christian attitude toward life and death.'[125] However, the grounding of his arguments against euthanasia in 'divine revelation' seems to have no purchase on the strategy he adopts for engaging non-Christians (who he recognizes do not share the views of Christians) in relation to what is or is not appropriate care for the suffering-dying.

Grisez holds that 'a just regard for liberty in a pluralistic society forbids any such appeal to Christian moral norms to justify public policies.'[126] Therefore, he excludes explicitly Christian witness from the proposals he gives for how Christians are to relate with non-Christians over the issue of care for the suffering-dying. Instead, he presents an argument relating to jurisprudence and what does and does not constitute an appropriate law. His argument rests on the assumption that it is the law, rather than morality (the two being related but distinct) that should determine what ought to be accepted as public policy in a pluralistic society.[127] In other words, Grisez holds that the apparatus of the state can be neutral between competing claims; however, as previously argued in relation to MacIntyre's account of the modern nation-state, Grisez's position is inherently flawed.

In his calls for a legislative approach to resolving conflicts Grisez does not admit any notion of the common good as relevant to or foundational for determining proper legal rights and duties. He seeks to determine what minimum standards the law should uphold in relation to care for the suffering-dying by way of notions of liberty and justice alone. Yet in response to this approach a question inspired by MacIntyre suggests itself: that is, whose vision of justice is Grisez referring to? As MacIntyre argues, we cannot determine what constitutes justice or liberty without recourse to some conception of the *telos* they serve. In practice, Grisez does refer to a specific *telos* by ultimately grounding his argument about why euthanasia is unjust on notions of the person as directed to communion with God and neighbour.[128] Furthermore, Grisez recognizes that the concept of 'the person', on which both he and John Finnis rest their notion of the psychosomatic unity of human life (and thereby their opposition to dualistic accounts of human life which ground calls for euthanasia) is a distinctively Christian concept.[129] Grisez states:

> The pagans of ancient times lacked the concept of person, which was developed by Christians to articulate the mysteries of three persons in one God and a divine person who also is human. … From its theological roots, the concept gathered meaning in its application to human individuals, considered as beings made in God's image and called to be his children.[130]

Yet Grisez, in his argument against euthanasia in public discourse, continues to appeal to non-Christians to accept a concept he recognizes can be wholly alien to them. At the same time, he does not link Christianity with the one form of practice – hospice care – which bears witness to the kind of care he considers appropriate for the suffering-dying. Yet without such a link being made, appeals to terms like 'person', and advocacy of the kind of care he considers to be appropriate, are bound to be misunderstood. This is to say, unless Christians point to embodiments of what they are talking about then what Christians advocate can easily be misconstrued.

Grisez sees hospice care as an alternative to calls for euthanasia. He states:

> If the legalization of voluntary active euthanasia is to be rejected in the interest of protecting the lives and respecting the liberty of members of society who do not wish to be killed and to kill, then this alternative to death by active euthanasia must be promoted. Indeed, it seems to us, there is some duty of society to make available to all quality palliative care.[131]

However, his call for the promotion of hospice care takes no account of the explicitly Christian witness on which such care is based. Nor does his advocacy of hospice care play a central role in his account of how Christians are to relate to non-Christians with regard to the dispute over what constitutes good care for the suffering-dying.

Like Grisez, I argue that hospice care is the best form of care for the suffering-dying. However, it is my contention that it embodies a particular, Christian vision of hospitality in relation to care for the suffering-dying. Furthermore, the practice of hospitality (as embodied in hospice care) and not recourse to the law or the state as Grisez suggests, represents the best response to the disagreement Christians have with their neighbours about what constitutes good care for the suffering-dying.[132]

The acceptance of hospice care amid continuing disagreement about what constitutes good care for the suffering-dying is a paradigm instance of how, despite the incommensurability between their evaluative criteria for what is good and just, Christians and non-Christians may share an *ad hoc* commensurability at the level of social practices. Contrary to expectation non-Christians take up the Christian approach: many non-Christians attend hospices. Yet disagreement is not 'solved' or eliminated, but neither is the particular approach of Christians found to exclude others or be marginalized by non-Christians. Instead, what Christians advocate has become accepted as defining what constitutes good care for the suffering-dying. A good example of the acceptance of hospice care amidst fundamental disagreement over the issue of euthanasia is Derek Humphry who supports hospice care yet argues vociferously for euthanasia.[133] Thus the phenomenon of the acceptance of hospice care by non-Christians illustrates how the church is simultaneously alien to, and a host of, its neighbours, in relation to ethical disputes.

Hospice care as an embodiment of Christian hospitality

Hospice care is a paradigmatic instance of how the Christian social practice of hospitality is the primary way in which Christians should relate to non-Christians with regard to ethical disputes. Contrary to MacIntyre's model of relations between Christians and non-Christians, the differences between Christians and non-Christians seem incapable of being resolved either over time, along the lines MacIntyre sets out in his meta-theory, or by recourse to some universal criteria of evaluation as Grisez argues. Rather, hospice care, as an embodied and institutionalized form of hospitality, recapitulates the ascension/Pentecost moments in the Christ-event and retains specifically Christian criteria for evaluating what is good and just in relation to the determination of what constitutes good care for the suffering-dying. However, hospice care, in its recapitulation and retention of specifically Christian criteria of evaluation, allows for commensurability with non-Christians at the level of social practice. What follows is an account of how and why hospice care constitutes a paradigmatic instance of Christian hospitality.

A definition of hospice care

The term 'hospice care' has come to mean a programme (rather than a place) of care for terminally ill patients and their families.[134] For the purposes of the following discussion, the term 'hospital' refers to an institution that focuses on caring for patients and, if possible, curing them. The term 'hospice' (signifying an institution carrying out such care) is distinguished from a hospital in that it does not maintain specific services to cure patients, only to care for them. Neither does the term 'hospice care' refer to a specific regimen of medical treatment. The term 'palliative medicine' refers to that technical aspect of hospice care that aims to relieve pain through the use of specific drugs.[135] Hospice care, on the other hand, refers to an approach to care for the suffering-dying that is much wider than simply relief of pain. While it provides an approach to care that includes the effective and holistic relief of patients from pain and other distressing symptoms of their condition, it also offers psychological and spiritual care for patients so that they may come to terms with and prepare for their own death as fully as they can, a support system to help them live as actively and creatively as possible until death (thereby promoting independence, personal integrity and self-esteem), and the provision of help to families so they can cope during the patient's illness and in bereavement.[136] A further central tenet of hospice care is that it seeks neither to hasten nor to postpone death.

In its approach to care for the suffering-dying, hospice care attempts to provide a type of care that incorporates the technical and scientific expertise of medicine within a broad vision of hospitality. The primary focus is neither the treatment nor the disease, but the person and her family, and instead of each patient being treated as part of a uniform system of medicine, the particularity of each patient, her condition, family and background are considered. Thus, hospice care seeks to take the whole person (and the relationships within which she is embedded) seriously, and to structure the treatment around her rather than the reverse.[137] For example, intrusive surgery and treatments are used only when their benefits clearly outweigh any potential burdens. As Cicely Saunders puts it: 'In the hospice movement we continue to be concerned both with the sophisticated science of our treatments and with the art of our caring, bringing competence alongside compassion.'[138]

The form of hospice care was shaped by a rejection of a number of trends in medicine: the focus on cure rather than care, the emphasis on technique and technology instead of on the patient, and the increasing advocacy of euthanasia.[139] James comments that:

> The early hospice 'vision' emerged from individuals' personal convictions to become a descriptive ideal, dedicated, critical of former practice and with the intention of disrupting former patterns of care of the dying. Committed to listening to patients, to perceiving death as a time of growth, to offering an alternative to euthanasia by providing skilled, compassionate care for people dying of cancer, hospice aspirations were on a grand scale.[140]

A brief history of the hospice movement

The modern hospice movement is generally recognized as being initiated by Dame Cicely Saunders, who founded St Christopher's Hospice, London, in 1967. The name 'hospice' was chosen deliberately for the connotation of being a place of rest and hospitality for travellers and pilgrims. Margaret Manning places the hospice movement within a wider Christian tradition of care for strangers, the sick and the dying.[141] Moreover, Clark and Seymour state: 'In retaining the name, modern hospices have sought self-consciously to rekindle the tradition of devotion, calling and the ethic of service which was enshrined in the religious foundations of their predecessors.'[142] As Clark and Seymour point out, early Christian and medieval hospices were not specifically for the care of the dying; although there are many such precedents. For example, in 361 Emperor Julian wrote about Fabriola, a wealthy Roman matron and Christian convert who turned her villa into a refuge for the sick and dying pilgrims returning from Africa.[143] However, the decisive influence on the modern hospice movement is the consistent practice of care for the poor, sick and dying within the Christian tradition, and this practice informs the work of hospices still.

The practice of hospitality for the sick and dying in Christianity forms the common patrimony of both hospices and hospitals. By 320 the church in Antioch was operating a hospice to feed and shelter the poor and sick of Syria. In the 370s Basil of Caesarea opened an institution where physicians and nurses treated patients. Twenty years later, John Chrysostom founded hospitals in Constantinople where doctors tended the sick. By 410, the monk Neilos of Ankyra considered the hospital physician a common figure in the Greek Christian world.[144] Miller holds that these identifiably medical institutions were distinguished from the Classical Greek *asklepieia* and the Roman *valetudinaria* by their emphasis on care for the poor. He notes the inspiration for this emphasis came directly from the New Testament teaching on hospitality.[145] The distinctiveness of Christian care for the sick and needy is highlighted by the Emperor Julian, who in his attempt to re-establish Hellenic religion in the empire and withdraw imperial patronage given to the church by Constantine, attested to the significance of Christian institutions of care for strangers, the sick and the poor.[146] The hospice movement self-consciously appropriated this long tradition of Christian care for the sick and the outcast in its attempt to address the question of what constitutes good care for the suffering-dying.

Manning and Saunders trace the modern form of hospice care to the renewal of the medieval practice of establishing hospices by the French Sisters of Charity, founded by Vincent de Paul, and their Protestant counterpart, the sisters of Kaiserworth.[147] The Sisters of Charity founded Our Lady's Hospice, Dublin specifically for the incurably ill in 1879.[148] It was this establishment that 'paved the way for a new perspective on the needs of those facing death.'[149] The Irish Sisters subsequently opened further hospices; for example, they established St Joseph's in London in 1905. Another major influence on the modern hospice movement was St Luke's, founded by Howard Barrett and the West London (Methodist) Mission in 1893. Goldin notes that St Luke's 'To a far greater degree than any institution of its time in London ... was a protohospice, using the word *hospice* in its contemporary sense.'[150] It established many precedents for contemporary care of the suffering-dying. The founding of St Christopher's Hospice was the final step in the development of the modern form of the hospice in Britain and throughout the world.[151] The modern hospice is thus situated in a tradition of Christian hospitality, medical practice and care for the dying, while at the same time being a particular response to the contemporary context.

Hospice care as Christian hospitality

The hospice movement does represent a genuinely and self-consciously Christian response to care for the suffering-dying. Margaret Manning comments that the ideal of Cicely Saunders 'was to build a Christian hospice, but one unattached to any single denomination and grounded in the Christian awareness that God's will was being actualised in a tangible way in her work.'[152] Saunders herself stated in her explanation of St Christopher's that it was 'a Christian Foundation, ecumenical and practical, searching for God's plan for its work and development.'[153] Clark and Seymour conclude: 'Matters of the spirit, and of Christianity in particular, thus have a crucial influence on the development of hospice thinking from the outset.'[154]

Hospice care constitutes a witness to the Christ-event through its practice. It constitutes a witness by answering those forms of medical treatment that made euthanasia appear a form of loving care for the suffering-dying with a constructive alternative. Hospice care re-situates medicine as a practice within a specifically Christian vision of human well-being. Furthermore, hospice care sought to re-situate the response to the suffering-dying within a Christian conception of suffering and death. By re-situating medical practice, and specifically, care for the suffering-dying, within a wider, Christian account of what the purpose of such care is, the hospice movement generated new forms of care that are genuinely good medical practice (that is, they seek neither to cure nor kill the suffering-dying, but to maximize care) and help patients to enjoy a 'good death' (that is, a death in which a person is neither neglected nor over-treated but attended to in this, her very own dying, rendering it as comfortable and dignified as possible). Noted already is the threat modern medicine poses to the weak, how modern conceptions of the person marginalize the suffering-dying as merely 'biological life', and how contemporary society excludes death and the dying. Following the Christian tradition of care for the weak and the marginalized, hospice care is an attempt to bear witness to the need to include, care for, and abide with the suffering-dying, who, in contemporary society, find themselves excluded from the bounds of human society and either neglected, oppressed by over-intrusive medical treatment, or under threat of being unjustly killed. In short, by recognizing, accommodating, and creating a 'place' for the suffering-dying, hospice care gives hospitality to vulnerable strangers.

The manner in which hospice care gives a place to the suffering-dying bears the marks of feasting and fasting that are a sign of properly Christian hospitality. Hospice care neither denies the absence of Christ nor the possibilities, even in dying, of the freedom available now through the actions of God (even dying is not a continual fast, but may encompass times of joyful feasting). Hospice care gives space and time for the celebration of the life now dying, and yet, in the care it gives, it expects and longs for the full disclosure of God's rule when 'he will wipe every tear from their eyes. Death will be no more; mourning and crying and pain will be no more, for the first things have passed away.'[155] Hospice care incorporates both joy at the presence of freedom through reconciliation (the joy of the feast) and pain at the presence of unfreedom and hope of the world's release from it (the longing of the fast).

The critique of contemporary medical practice hospice care embodies, and the alternative patterns of care it developed, are widely recognized and accepted. For example, George Young, speaking as the then Government Under-Secretary for Health and Social Security, stated:

> By its very existence it offers a wider challenge to the health professions. ... It reminds staff that there is an additional dimension to their patients; that we should not be so busy developing curative medicine that we forget to care for people as individuals. ... The hospice movement seems to offer us a much needed antidote to a too heavy reliance on technological medicine. It certainly does not reject technology but it begs us to reassess its role in medicine and patient care.[156]

Indeed, it seems the existence of hospice care has been a central defence against changing the legislation regarding euthanasia. For example, Lord Raglan, the sponsor of the euthanasia bill debated in the House of Lords in 1969, admitted in reference to St Christopher's Hospice: 'It might be said that if everyone could spend his last days in such surroundings there would be no need for this Bill.'[157] People of other faith traditions and of no faith tradition have responded positively to and participated in hospice care (in a manner that echoes the response of non-Christians to Christian witness outlined earlier in relation to the exegesis of 1 Peter). The 1998 Hospice directory states: 'Although it is true that many hospices may have a Christian foundation, patients and staff are from any faith or none. Hospice and palliative care try to meet the needs of people from all cultures and religions and of those with no faith at all.'[158] Thus, even advocates of euthanasia and those who share no sympathy with the Christian faith, have recognized the value of the social practice of hospice care while disagreeing with the premises on which it is founded. This response is characteristic of what was argued previously; that is, while many non-Christians will disagree with the criteria Christians use to determine what is good and just, this disagreement does not preclude them participating in specifically Christian social practices. Furthermore, that hospitality is at the core of hospice care necessarily entails hospice care being orientated towards enabling non-Christians to participate in it.

In the previous chapter I reviewed the Christian tradition regarding the practice of hospitality, and then analysed how this conception of hospitality both describes and defines the way Christians should relate to their neighbours with regard to ethical disputes. In this chapter I sought to show how the hospitality of the church, as instantiated in hospice care, enables the church to be both a guest (the treatment of the suffering-dying in hospice care is, more often than not, alien to that of its neighbours) and a host of the life of its neighbours (many non-Christians participate in hospices and, moreover, many non-Christians have had their attitude and treatment of the suffering-dying shaped by the Christian practice of hospice care). In theological terms, this guest-host dynamic constitutes a recapitulation of the ascension and Pentecost moments of the Christ-event.

Christian hospitality is inaugurated at Pentecost and bears witness to the eschaton and corresponds to the tension at the heart of the eschaton, whereby it is established but not yet fully manifest. There is a parallel dynamic in hospice care wherein the eschatological hope for the future of the body is borne witness to in the proper cherishing of the body, but it is recognized that the eschaton sets a limit to this life, and so life is not prolonged at all costs. Likewise, that the eschaton is not yet fully established is borne witness to by the fact that hospice care is precisely a response to the recognition of the suffering of the suffering-dying, and the need to establish ways of faithfully bearing with and caring for the dying in their suffering, and neither attempting to deny the suffering of this age nor masking the continued power of death by excluding death from the midst of human community.

As an eschatological social practice, hospitality is inspired and empowered by the Holy Spirit, who enables the church to host the life of its neighbours without the church being assimilated to, or colonized by, or having to withdraw from, the life of its neighbours. Hospice care is a testimony to how the church can open up new possibilities and radically change the status quo through a deep engagement with the life of its neighbours in a way that both demands a change in the life together of the church and the life of its neighbours. The hospice movement achieved this by refusing to accept euthanasia as the only response to the problems of neglect and over-treatment of the suffering-dying. In place of euthanasia it created new ways of relating with the suffering-dying that are consistent with the particular, personal communion we will enjoy with God and each other in the age to come. A further aspect of how hospice care changed contemporary practice and opened up new possibilities is seen in its reaction to, and contrast with, the character of care in contemporary hospitals. In contrast to the often institutionalized, homogeneous and impersonal treatment provided in many hospitals, in hospice care strong emphasis is given to the relationship of the patient with God, with their family, and with themselves, and the tailoring of care to the particular situation of the patient. Furthermore, it is still the case that many hospice care programmes are reliant on a large number of non-professional voluntary staff whose contribution to the care of the suffering-dying is a costly gift rather than a contractual obligation.

Future developments

While its thinking and practice is rooted in the Christian tradition, hospice care is no longer exclusively a Christian venture. Ann Bradshaw details how hospice care is becoming increasingly secularized and goes so far as to suggest that: 'The original spiritual ethic and its influence on the history and development of the hospice movement is virtually ignored.'[159] This may be overstated. However, the further hospice care moves away from its roots, due to its rapid growth and integration into established systems of healthcare (and, according to Bradshaw, a sense of taboo about its Christian foundation), the more vulnerable it is to co-option by the very trends it opposed. For example, James notes that due to an increasing emphasis on the medical aspects of palliative care there is a trend towards intervention and a 'technical' approach to care.[160] Samuel Klagsbrun, reflecting on the future of the hospice movement in 1981 noted: 'The proliferation in America of hospice courses and training programmes and the focus on techniques is a glaring example of misunderstanding of what hospice is all about.'[161] In addition, to use MacIntyre's terms, there is a real danger that the 'goods of excellence' are becoming subordinate to the 'goods of effectiveness'. James states: 'As economic constraints on health authorities increase, the question of "standards" and compromise will inevitably affect hospices.'[162] She goes on to say that 'cost efficiency indicators running through a bureaucratic formula' will increasingly determine the 'good death'.[163] There is thus the danger that, like Peter and John confronted with Simon Magus (Acts 8:9–24), there are those who will misconstrue the nature and basis of what is being offered, and who, like Simon Magus, will seek to make of it 'magic': that is, a technical manipulation reproducible by solely human means and measured in terms of money alone. For the present, however, the hospice movement remains a faithful, albeit fragile, form of Christian hospitality.[164]

In conclusion, one can see in the new patterns of sociality generated by the hospice movement a faithful response to the reconfiguring work of the Holy Spirit and a recapitulation of Jesus Christ in the form of life together instantiated by hospice care. By going out to and embracing the suffering-dying and providing a constructive alternative to the call for euthanasia, hospice care is a proleptic disclosure of the messianic banquet amidst a suffering world that is increasingly hostile to the terminally ill.

Notes

1 As Ramsey puts it: 'The claims of the "suffering-*dying*" upon the human community are quite different from the claims of those who, though suffering, still may live, or who are incurably ill but not yet dying.' Paul Ramsey, 'On (Only) Caring for the Dying', in *The Essential Paul Ramsey: A Collection*, eds Paul Ramsey, William Werpehowski and Stephen Crocco (New Haven: Yale University Press, 1994), p. 209.

2 Dr Cox was convicted of manslaughter at Winchester Crown Court for the killing of Lillian Boyes. For a summary of the case see Peter Singer, *Rethinking Life and Death: The Collapse of Our Traditional Ethics* (Oxford: Oxford University Press, 1995), pp. 139–40. Singer cites similar landmark cases from Canada, Australia and America, Ibid., pp. 133–42.

3 Proposals to legalize voluntary euthanasia have come before House of Lords in 1936, 1950, 1969 and 1994.

4 In 1993, with the support of the Royal Dutch Medical Association, the Dutch Parliament voted to allow voluntary euthanasia for the incurably ill. On 11 April, 2001 the Dutch senate gave approval to a bill formally legalizing euthanasia. Strict conditions still apply to the use of euthanasia; however, under the 1993 law euthanasia remained a criminal offence in the penal code, whereas the 2001 law formally legalizes euthanasia.

5 David Clark and Jane Seymour, *Reflections on Palliative Care* (Buckingham: Open University Press, 1999), pp. 52–53. Beauchamp perceives this kind of view to be behind what he calls the 'slippery slope' argument against euthanasia: Tom Beauchamp, 'Introduction', in *Intending Death: The Ethics of Assisted Suicide and Euthanasia*, ed., Tom Beauchamp (New Jersey: Prentice Hall, 1996), pp. 14–15.

6 *Euthanasia, Clinical Practice and the Law*, ed. Luke Gormally (London: The Linacre Centre for Health Care Ethics, 1994), pp. 32–33. Cf., Stanley Hauerwas, *Naming the Silences: God, Medicine, and the Problem of Suffering* (Edinburgh: T&T Clark, 1993), p. 103.

7 For an account of how opinions are divided and the contentious nature of the debate about euthanasia see Ronald Dworkin, *Life's Dominion: An Argument About Abortion and Euthanasia* (London: HarperCollins, 1993), pp. 179–83.

8 John Finnis, 'A Philosophical Case Against Euthanasia', in *Euthanasia Examined: Ethical, Clinical and Legal Perspectives*, ed. John Keown (Cambridge: Cambridge University Press, 1995), p. 23.

9 Ramsey, 'On (Only) Caring for the Dying', p. 215.

10 For a history of attitudes towards suicide and euthanasia in the classical and Christian traditions and the development of contemporary calls for the legitimization of euthanasia from the nineteenth century onwards see Hugh Trowell, *Euthanasia: The Unfinished Debate on Euthanasia* (London: SCM Press, 1973), pp. 1–22.

11 Finnis, 'A Philosophical Case Against Euthanasia', p. 24. Cf., John Paul II, 'Euthanasia: Declaration of the Sacred Congregation for the Doctrine of the Faith (May 5, 1980)', in *On Moral Medicine: Theological Perspectives in Medical Ethics*, eds Stephen Lammers and Allen Verhey, 2nd edn (Grand Rapids: Eerdmans, 1998), p. 652.

12 John Harris, 'Euthanasia and the Value of Life', in Kewosn, *Euthanasia Examined*, pp. 6–7.

13 Germain Grisez and Joseph Boyle, *Life and Death with Liberty and Justice: A Contribution to the Euthanasia Debate* (Notre Dame: University of Notre Dame Press, 1979), p. 139. Cf., Gilbert Meilaender, 'Euthanasia and Christian Vision', in *On Moral Medicine*, p. 656.

14 Beauchamp, 'Introduction', p. 4.

15 Dan Brock, *Life and Death: Philosophical Essays in Biomedical Ethics*, (Cambridge: Cambridge University Press, 1993), p. 208.

16 Ibid.

17 Ibid.

18 Beauchamp, 'Introduction', p. 12.

19 For an analysis of how and why intention counts see: Finnis, 'A Philosophical Case Against Euthanasia', pp. 25–30. For an account of how intention relates to its effect, how it is distinguished from desire and motivation, and how the concept of intention has been used in moral philosophy see Edmund Pellegrino, 'The Place of Intention in the Moral Assessment of Assisted Suicide and Active Euthanasia', in *Intending Death*, pp. 163–83.

20 Grisez and Boyle, *Life and Death*, p. 141.

21 Meilaender, 'Euthanasia and Christian Vision', p. 656–57. For an account of the difference between suicide and martyrdom see Michael Banner, 'Christian Anthropology at the Beginning and End of Life', in *Christian Ethics and Contemporary Moral Problems*, pp. 71–76.

22 Pellegrino, 'The Place of Intention', p. 166.

23 Ibid.

24 Finnis, 'A Philosophical Case Against Euthanasia', pp. 25; John Harris, 'The Philosophical Case Against the Philosophical Case Against Euthanasia', in *Euthanasia Examined*, p. 36. See also Gormally, *Euthanasia, Clinical Practice and the Law*, pp. 46–48.

25 Beauchamp, 'Introduction', p. 5.

26 Ibid.

27 Ramsey, 'On (Only) Caring for the Dying', p. 218.

28 Singer, *Rethinking Life and Death*, p. 71.

29 Ibid., p. 72.

30 Ibid.

31 Beauchamp, 'Introduction', p. 4.

32 Harris, 'Euthanasia and the Value of Life', pp. 6–7.

33 Brock, *Life and Death*, pp. 108–109. For a summary of the critique of distinctions between voluntary and involuntary euthanasia see Banner, 'Christian Anthropology', pp. 69–70.

34 Nigel Biggar notes: 'If any doubt remains about the centrality of the value of individual autonomy to the public debate, then the complete absence of any effective public promotion of involuntary or compulsory euthanasia should help to dispel it.' Nigel Biggar, 'God, the Responsible Individual, and the Value of Human Life and Suffering', SCE, 11.1 (1998), p. 29, n.1.

35 Brock, *Life and Death*, p. 208.

36 Albert Jonsen, 'Criteria That Make Intentional Killing Unjustified', in Beauchamp, *Intending Death*, p. 51.

37 Georgios Anagnastopoulos, 'Euthanasia and the Physician's Role: Reflections on Some Views in the Ancient Greek Tradition', in *Bioethics: Ancient Themes in Contemporary Issues*, ed. Mark Kuczewski and Ronald Polansky (Cambridge, MA: MIT Press, 2000), p. 258.

38 Ibid.

39 Ibid., pp. 261–66. Anagnastopoulos argues that the central thesis of Pythagorean beliefs were also central to those of many later philosophers, notably Plato and Aristotle. Cf., Ludwig Edelstein, 'The Hippocractic Oath: Text, Translation, and Interpretation', in *Cross Cultural Perspectives in Medical Ethics*, ed. Robert Veatch (Boston: Jones and Bartlett, 1989), pp. 6–24.

40 Allen Verhey, 'The Doctor's Oath – and a Christian Swearing It', in Lammer's and Verhey, *On Moral Medicine*, p. 111.

41 Anagnastopoulos, 'Euthanasia and the Physicians Role', p. 271.

42 'The Hippocratic Oath', in Lammer's and Verhey, *On Moral Medicine*, p. 107.

43 Verhey, 'The Doctor's Oath – and a Christian Swearing It', p. 111.

44 Pellegrino argues that to act against the good of medicine and repeatedly intend the death of patients not only affects the virtues necessary to be a doctor, but compromises the virtues of medicine itself and 'if enough moral agents in a society have wrong intentions about killing in the medical context the attitudes of the whole profession and society will be affected with a disvaluation of human life itself.' Pellegrino, 'The Place of Intention', p. 166.

45 LCL, p. 519.

46 Ibid., p. 521.

47 See Alasdair MacIntyre, 'Can Medicine Dispense with a Theological Perspective on Human Nature', in *Knowledge, Value and Belief*, eds T. Engelhart and D. Callahan (Hastings-on-Hudson: Institute of Society, Ethics and the Life Sciences, 1977), pp. 25–43; and idem, 'Patient as Agent', in *Philosophical Medical Ethics: its Nature and Significance*, eds, Stuart Spicker and H. Tristram Englehardt (Dordrecht: Reidel, 1977), pp. 197–212. See also, Stanley Hauerwas, 'Salvation and Health: Why Medicine Needs the Church', in Lammer's and Verhey, *On Moral Medicine*, pp. 77–78.

48 Clear and obvious parallels can be drawn between the general points MacIntyre highlights for opprobrium in his critique of the contemporary context and the particular issues surrounding calls for euthanasia. In short, MacIntyre's critique is directed at exactly the kinds of positions taken by those who call for the legalization of euthanasia. Such positions represent a paradigm case of what MacIntyre takes to be the irrationality and miasma prevalent in modern moral discourse.

49 Jonsen, 'Criteria That Make Intentional Killing Unjustified', p. 51.

50 R. G. Frey 'Distinctions in Death', in *Euthanasia and Physician Assisted Suicide: For and Against*, eds Gerald Dworkin, R. G. Frey and Sissela Bok (Cambridge: Cambridge University Press, 1998), p. 17.

51 Brock, *Life and Death*, p. 107. Cf., Gormally, *Euthanasia, Clinical Practice and the Law*, p. 130.

52 Ibid., p. 117. For an assessment of different models of patient–carer relations see Fiona Randall and R. S. Downie, *Palliative Care Ethics: A Good Companion* (Oxford: Oxford University Press, 1996), pp. 25–39.

53 Dworkin, *Life's Dominion*, p. 222.

54 Ibid., pp. 222–23.

55 Ibid., pp. 223–24.
56 Ibid.
57 Ibid.
58 For a critique of the view that value resides not in what we decide, but in that we decide see Biggar, 'God, the Responsible Individual, and the Value of Human Life and Suffering', pp. 30–31. His critique is parallel to MacIntyre's critique of the liberal view of the self: AV, chs 2, 3.
59 Dworkin, *Life's Dominion*, p. 69.
60 Mary Warnock, *The Uses of Philosophy* (Oxford: Blackwell, 1992), pp. 22–23. James Rachels makes a parallel distinction between the 'biographical' dimension of human life and the merely 'biological' dimension: James Rachels, *The End of Life* (Oxford, Oxford University Press, 1986), p. 5. See also, Singer, *Rethinking Life and Death*, p. 80.
61 Dworkin, *Life's Dominion*, p. 228.
62 May, 'The Sacral Power of Death in Contemporary Experience', in Lammers and Verhey, *On Moral Medicine*, p. 199.
63 Ibid.
64 Derek Humphry, *Final Exit* (Eugene, OR: Hemlock Society, 1991), p. 54.
65 Ibid., p. 33.
66 By contrast, Christians countenance death each time they come before the communion table and seek to abide and lament with the dying and provide such care as is needed.
67 Banner, 'Christian Anthropology', pp. 77–82.
68 Dworkin, *Life's Dominion*, pp. 182–83.
69 *Desire*, p. 276.
70 O'Donovan, *Begotten or Made?*, pp. 3–12.
71 Hauerwas, *Naming the Silences*, p. 63. Cf., Dennis Sansom, 'Why Do We Want to be Healthy? Medicine, Autonomous Individualism, and the Community of Faith', in *On Moral Medicine*, pp. 262–66.
72 John Paul II, 'Euthanasia', pp. 652–53. See also: idem, *Evangelium Vitae*, p. 123.
73 Biggar, 'God, the Responsible Individual, and the Value of Human Life and Suffering', pp. 42–46.
74 Ibid., p. 46.
75 Ibid.
76 Gilbert Meilaender, *Bioethics: A Primer for Christians* (Grand Rapids: Eerdmans, 1996), pp. 65–66.
77 Karl Barth, *Church Dogmatics*, III: 4, trans. by A. T. Mackay, T. H. L. Parker, H. Knight, H. A. Kennedy and J. Marks (Edinburgh: T&T Clark, 1961), p. 342. For a critique of those who make the 'sanctity of life' an idol and ideology see Stanley Hauerwas, *Suffering Presence: Theological Reflections on Medicine, the Mentally Handicapped and the Church* (Edinburgh T&T Clark 1986), pp. 91–93.
78 Barth, *Church Dogmatics*, III: 4.
79 In this assessment of the Christian conception of death we put to one side the question of how different conceptions of death relate to the empirical criteria that determine when death has occurred. For a discussion of this relationship see Hauerwas, *Suffering Presence*, pp. 89–99.
80 Meilaender, *Bioethics*, p. 4.
81 Paul Ramsey, 'The Indignity of "Death with Dignity"', in *The Essential Paul Ramsey: A Collection*, p. 237. For a critique of this article see Oliver O'Donovan, 'Keeping Body and Soul Together', in *On Moral Medicine*, pp. 223–38.
82 Ramsey, 'The Indignity of "Death with Dignity"', p. 240.
83 O'Donovan, 'Keeping Body and Soul Together', p. 228.
84 Ibid., p. 226.
85 This contrasts with the theological premises that underpin the assessment of euthanasia and death in *Evangelium Vitae*. For a critique of *Evangelium Vitae* in relation to this see Oliver O'Donovan, 'Review of *Evangelium Vitae*', SCE, 9.1 (1996), 89–94.
86 O'Donovan, 'Keeping Body and Soul Together', p. 232.
87 Ibid., p. 233.

88 Banner, 'Christian Anthropology', p. 82.
89 May, 'The Sacral Power of Death in Contemporary Experience', p. 205.
90 For a philosophical critique of dualistic account of human personhood see Finnis, 'A Philosophical Case Against Euthanasia', pp. 30–33.
91 Augustine, *City of God*, i, 13.
92 Biggar may well be right to criticize Grisez for over-identifying personhood with the bodily life. However, Biggar fails to properly account for how the bodily life, while not exhaustive of nor definitive of personhood, is still a created good in and of itself. Biggar, 'God, the Responsible Individual, and the Value of Human Life and Suffering', pp. 36–39.
93 Banner, 'Christian Anthropology', p. 67.
94 Stanley Hauerwas, 'Rational Suicide and Reasons for Living', in Lammers and Verhey, *On Moral Medicine*, p. 674.
95 Cf., Barth, *Church Dogmatics*, III: 4, pp. 404–405.
96 Rogers, *Sexuality and the Christian Body*, p. 240.
97 Banner, 'Christian Anthropology', p. 60.
98 Ibid., p. 53.
99 See, for example, Peter Singer, 'Justifying Voluntary Euthanasia', in *Ethical Issues in Death and Dying*, ed., Robert Weir (New York: Columbia University Press, 1986), p. 273.
100 John Stuart Mill, *On Liberty* (Cambridge: Cambridge University Press, 1989), p. 103.
101 RMO, p. 108.
102 Ibid.
103 Ibid.
104 Barth, *Church Dogmatics*, III: 4, p. 407.
105 Meilaender, 'Euthanasia and Christian Vision', p. 660.
106 Barth, *Church Dogmatics*, III: 4, p. 425.
107 Ibid.
108 Cf., Banner, 'Christian Anthropology', p. 79.
109 While I recognize that not all who identify themselves as Christians are opposed to euthanasia I would still maintain that opposition to euthanasia is the normative Christian view.
110 DRA, p. 130.
111 For a parallel, but theological formulation of the same conception of what constitutes the good society see Barth, *Church Dogmatics*, III: 4, p. 424.
112 DRA, p. 137.
113 Benedict, *The Rule*, p. 38.
114 DRA, p. 138.
115 Ibid., p. 4.
116 Ibid., p. 5.
117 O'Donovan, 'Keeping Body and Soul Together', p. 228.
118 Ibid., p. 231.
119 Ibid., p. 235.
120 Grisez and Boyle, *Life and Death*, pp. 182–83.
121 Ibid., p. 18.
122 LCL, p. 476.
123 Ibid., p. 463.
124 Ibid., p. 464.
125 Ibid.
126 Grisez and Boyle, *Life and Death*, p. 461.
127 For a critique of Grisez's recourse to law as a way of settling disputes in a pluralistic society see John Ladd, 'Euthanasia, Liberty and Religion', *Ethics*, 93.1 (1982), 129–38.
128 For a critique of Grisez's conception of the relationship between the body and personhood see Biggar, 'God, the Responsible Individual, and the Value of Human Life and Suffering', pp. 36–39. Biggar

argues that Grisez overstates the relationship between personhood and the body and moves beyond what is theologically warranted.

129 Finnis, 'A Philosophical Case Against Euthanasia', p. 31.
130 LCL, p. 460.
131 Grisez and Boyle, *Life and Death*, p. 183.
132 Underlying the point of divergence with Grisez is the much broader question of whether it is ever appropriate for the church to rely on political authority and human law to act as the primary agents of moral perfection or *paideia* if the church itself, in its life together, is to be the paradigm for the life of the nations. However, there is not the space to address that question here.
133 Humphry, *Final Exit*, pp. 34–37.
134 For a formal definition of hospice care see: Avril Jackson and Ann Eve, eds, *Directory of Hospice and Palliative Care Services in the United Kingdom and the Republic of Ireland* (London: St Christopher's Hospice Information Service, 1998), p. iv.
135 For an assessment and definition of the term 'palliative care' see Clark and Seymour, *Reflections on Palliative Care*, pp. 80–87.
136 Cicely Saunders, 'The Hospice: its Meaning to Patients and their Physicians', *Hospital Practice* 16.6 (1981), 93–108.
137 Randall and Downie, *Palliative Care Ethics*, pp. 18–21.
138 Cicely Saunders, 'The Founding Philosophy', in *Hospice: the Living Idea* eds Cicely Saunders, Dorothy Summers and Neville Teller (London: Edward Arnold, 1981), p. 4.
139 Cicely Saunders, 'Care of the Dying. 2: The Problem of Euthanasia', *Nursing Times,* 72.27 (1976), 1049–51.
140 Nicky James, 'From Vision to System: the Maturing of the Hospice Movement', in *Death Rites: Law and Ethics as the End of Life*, eds Robert Lee and Derek Morgan (London: Routledge, 1994), p. 111.
141 Margaret Manning, *The Hospice Alternative: Living with Dying* (London: Souvenir Press, 1984), pp. 33–45. See also Stephen Connor, *Hospice: Practice, Pitfalls, and Promise* (Washington DC: Taylor & Francis, 1998), pp. 4–7.
142 Clark and Seymour, *Reflections on Palliative Care*, p. 66.
143 Manning, *The Hospice Alternative*, p. 34. See also, Jerome, 'Letter 77', in NPNF, trans. by W. H. Fremantle with the assistance of G. Lewis and W. G. Martley, ed. by Philip Schaff and Henry Wace, Second Series, 14 vols (Edinburgh: T&T Clark, 1996), VI, p. 160.
144 Miller, 'Hospital: Medieval and Renaissance History', p. 1160.
145 Ibid.
146 Pohl, *Making Room*, p. 44.
147 Manning, *The Hospice Alternative*, p. 41; Cicely Saunders, 'The Modern Hospice' (paper presented at the In Quest of the Spiritual Component of Care for the Terminally Ill – Proceedings of a Colloquium, Yale University School of Nursing, 1986), pp. 41–42.
148 There is some dispute as to whether Mary Aikenhead, founder of the Irish congregation of the Sisters of Charity, founded this hospice herself or whether it was founded after her death. Saunders believes Mother Aikenhead opened the hospice (Saunders, 'The Modern Hospice', p. 42), whereas Clark and Seymour state it was founded twenty-one years after her death (Clark and Seymour, *Reflections on Palliative Care*, p. 67).
149 Manning, *The Hospice Alternative*, p. 41.
150 G. Goldin, 'A Protohospice at the Turn of the Century: St Luke's House, London, from 1893–1921', *Journal of the Social History of Medicine and Allied Science*, 3 (1981), p. 385. Quoted in Clark and Seymour, *Reflections on Palliative Care*, p. 67.
151 James, 'From Vision to System', p. 109.
152 Margaret Manning, *The Hospice Alternative*, p. 113. For a discussion of the Christian foundations of St Christopher's Hospice see also Shirley Du Boulay, *Cicely Saunders: Founder of the Modern Hospice Movement* (London: Hodder and Stoughton, 1984), pp. 155–71.
153 Quoted in James, 'From Vision to System', p. 108.

154 Clark and Seymour, *Reflections on Palliative Care*, p. 72. See also, Saunders, 'The Modern Hospice', pp. 42–48. Against all other assessments of the movement, Connor tries to locate the foundations of hospice care in a 'philosophy of humanism'. Connor, *Hospice: Practice, Pitfalls, and Promise*, pp. 8–9.

155 Rev. 21:4.

156 Sir George Young Bt MP, 'Hospice and Health Care', in Saunders *et al.*, *Hospice: the Living Idea*, p. 3.

157 Quoted in Grisez and Boyle, *Life and Death*, p. 182.

158 Quoted from the Jackson and Eve, *Directory of Hospice and Palliative Care Services*, p. vii.

159 Ann Bradshaw, 'The Spiritual Dimension of Hospice: The Secularization of an Ideal', *Social Science and Medicine*, 43.3 (1996), p. 416.

160 James, 'From Vision to System', p. 123.

161 Samuel Klagsbrun, 'Hospice – a Developing Role', in Saunders *et al.*, *Hospice: the Living Idea*, pp. 5–8 (p. 6).

162 James, 'From Vision to System', p. 115.

163 Ibid., p. 117.

164 For a critical assessment of the future of hospice and palliative care in Britain see Clark and Seymour, *Reflections on Palliative Care*, pp. 176–87.

Conclusion

In the European imagination the Balkans is not just a geographic place. It is also a symbol for fragmentation, chaotic internecine rivalry and the violent assertion of group particularity. As Maria Todorova notes: 'A spectre is haunting Western culture – the spectre of the Balkans. ... Where is the adversarial group that has not been decried as "Balkan" and "balkanising" by its opponents?'[1] This book began with a journey to the actual Balkans and a description of a highly complex and unstable situation in which the church is both part of the problem and attempting to be part of the remedy. It was a story that highlighted the inadequacy of stigmatizing labels such as 'Balkan' with its denotation of clearly delineated tribal – and thus retrograde – differences. Moral debate between Christians and non-Christians can often seem to resemble the Balkans of our imagination. However, my initial story illustrated, in stark form, the situation of Christians in Europe and America wherein they are, for better and for worse, both like and unlike, and immersed in, the life together of their non-Christian neighbours. This book has attempted to both delineate the nature and shape of this context and offer a constructive, theological account of how Christians can engage with their neighbours within it.

The central question under consideration has been: what is the nature and basis of Christian moral thought and action and, in the contemporary context, can moral disputes be resolved with those whose thought and action is divergent to that of Christians? A related question was whether the resolution of ethical differences is affected by the contemporary context or not. Addressing these questions involved mapping the contemporary context in which Christians and non-Christians encounter each other, defining how significant are the differences between Christian and non-Christian moral judgements, and analysing the shape of relations between Christians and non-Christians. An answer to these questions emerged through a critical assessment of MacIntyre's account of how different traditions relate. The conclusion reached was that the line between Christians and non-Christians is fluid and that relations between Christians and non-Christians are not necessarily characterized by rivalry or conflict. Contrary to MacIntyre, I concluded that conflict is neither necessary nor normative in relations between Christians and non-Christians with regard to moral problems. However, contrary to Grisez, neither are they congruent by means of rational deliberation. Rather, the church is a specific community with its own criteria of moral evaluation, yet there is no clear dividing line between its life and the life of its neighbours. The analysis established an unexpected contrast: that while MacIntyre argues for the possibility of philosophical convergence, the model of practice he suggests is characterized by rivalry and conflict, whereas for O'Donovan, for whom theoretical convergence can be neither normative nor systematic, the model of practice his account gives rise to allows for a great deal of co-operation and similarity between Christians and non-Christians at the level of social practice.

The real difference between Christians and non-Christians lies in how God is present within the church and is eschatological in character. This is to say, Christians are involved in relations of simultaneous distance and belonging with their non-Christian neighbours. Such relations occur because the church is to be a people specified by its relationship with Jesus Christ, and at the same time it is to display a given culture's eschatological possibilities. Therefore, Christians cannot stand outside their culture, or against it, but must participate in their culture and the enterprises of their neighbours as those transfigured. In this age, no clear dividing lines can be drawn. Instead of clearly demarcated lines separating Christians and non-Christians, questions about what to reject and what to retain confront Christians constantly as they participate in, and bear witness to, God's transfiguration of their context.

The social practice that best embodies and bears witness to the nature of the relationship between Christians and non-Christians is hospitality. As a social practice hospitality has always been central to shaping relations between the church and its neighbours and has taken many forms in the Christian tradition. Care for the sick and the suffering-dying, hospitality to immigrants, educational initiatives, and peace-making endeavours are all examples of ways in which the church hosts the life together of its neighbours and enables that life to bear witness to its eschatological possibilities. As the last chapter argues at length, the contemporary practice of hospice care is a paradigmatic example of Christian hospitality in the contemporary context and points to how Christians can engage in moral debate in ways that are faithful to the nature of its relationship with its neighbours, ways that recapitulate the Christ-event. For the practice of hospitality, as instantiated in hospice care, takes account of both the simultaneous continuity and radical discontinuity between Christians and non-Christians.

In conclusion, when confronted with moral problems the church develops specific patterns of thought and action. However, the response of the church is not developed in isolation from the life together of its neighbours. As it develops its response, the church will be engaged with the life of those around it, who will inevitably be involved with and inform its discernment. In conjunction with the life of its neighbours, the church will also seek to establish patterns of sociality which bear witness to how a particular moral issue is transfigured by the actions of God. The patterns of thought and action that constitute the response of the church to a particular issue are constantly open to further specification in the light of who Jesus Christ is. Such specification and alignment is a constant and ever-present task. Furthermore, and as the exposition of 1 Peter clarified, some of its neighbours will participate in the church's response to the issue, some will reject it, some will ignore it, and some will actively oppose it. Mediating disputes over moral problems which confront Christians and non-Christians is not a question of accommodating each other's view, nor of compromise between two positions, nor of rivalry as one tradition seeks to vindicate its answer against the answer given by other traditions. The only criterion by which the church can accept or reject the thought and action of its neighbours is whether such thought and action accords with thought and action directed to God. Empowered by the Spirit, the only response the church can make to moral problems is to bear witness to their resolution in and through Jesus Christ. The church must either invite its neighbours to follow its witness or it must change its own pattern of life as it discerns in the life of its neighbours patterns of thought and action that bear more truthful witness to Jesus Christ. The church, following after Jesus, is both the guest and host of its neighbours and in being a good guest and a faithful host the holiness of the church is shown forth.

Note

1 Maria Todorova, *Imagining the Balkans* (Oxford: Oxford University Press, 1997), p. 3.

Bibliography

Adolf, Adam, *The Liturgical Year*, trans. Matthew O'Connell (Collegeville, MN: The Liturgical Press, 1990).
Adams, Rebecca, 'Violence, Difference, and Sacrifice: A Conversation with René Girard', *Religion and Literature*, 25.2 (1993), 9–33.
Alkire, Sabina and Black, Rufus, 'A Practical Reasoning Theory of Development Ethics: Furthering the Capabilities Approach', *Journal of International Development*, 9.2 (1997), 263–79.
Anagnastopoulos, Georgios, 'Euthanasia and the Physician's Role: Reflections on Some Views in the Ancient Greek Tradition', in *Bioethics: Ancient Themes in Contemporary Issues*, ed. Mark Kuczewski and Ronald Polansky (Cambridge, MA: MIT Press, 2000).
Appleby, R. Scott, *The Ambivalence of the Sacred: Religion, Violence, and Reconciliation* (Oxford: Rowman & Littlefield, 2000).
Aquinas, Thomas, *St Thomas Aquinas on Politics and Ethics*, trans. Paul Sigmund, (London: W.W. Norton & Co., 1988).
Aristotle, *Nicomachean Ethics*, trans. Roger Crisp (Cambridge: Cambridge University Press, 2000).
Asad, Talal, 'The Construction of Religion as an Anthropological Category', in *Genealogies of Religion: Discipline and Reasons of Power in Christianity and Islam* (Baltimore: Johns Hopkins University Press, 1993), pp. 27–54.
Augustine, *City of God*, trans. Henry Bettenson (London: Penguin, 1972).
Bailey, Kenneth, *Poet and Peasant and Through Peasant Eyes: A Literary-Cultural Approach to the Parables of Luke* (Grand Rapids: Eerdmans, 1983).
Baillie, Gil, *Violence Unveiled: Humanity at the Crossroads* (New York: Crossroad, 1997).
Banner, Michael, 'Turning the World Upside Down – and some Other Tasks for Dogmatic Christian Ethics', in *Christian Ethics and Contemporary Moral Problems* (Cambridge: Cambridge University Press, 1999), pp. 1–46.
———, 'Christian Anthropology at the Beginning and End of Life', in *Christian Ethics and Contemporary Moral Problems*, pp. 47–85.
———, ' "Who are my Mother and my Brothers?": Marx, Bonhoeffer and Benedict and the Redemption of Family', in *Christian Ethics and Contemporary Moral Problems*, pp. 225–51.
———, 'Catholics and Anglicans and Contemporary Bioethics: Divided or United?', in *Issues for a Catholic Bioethic*, ed. Luke Gormally (London: Linacre Centre, 1999), pp. 34–57.
Barbour, John, 'The Virtues in a Pluralistic Context', *Journal of Religion*, 63 (1983), 175–82.
Barry, Brian, 'The Light That Failed', *Ethics*, 100.1 (1989), 160–68.
Barth, Karl, *Church Dogmatics,* II: 2, trans. A. T. Mackay, T. H. L. Parker, H. Knight, H. A. Kennedy and J. Marks (Edinburgh: T&T Clark, 1957).
———, *Church Dogmatics*, III: 4, trans. A. T. Mackay, T. H. L. Parker, H. Knight, H. A. Kennedy and J. Marks, IV vols (Edinburgh: T&T Clark, 1961).
———, *Church Dogmatics*, IV: 3, trans. G. W. Bromiley (Edinburgh: T&T Clark, 1961).
———, *The Christian Life*, trans. G. W. Bromiley (Grand Rapids: Eerdmans, 1981).
Bartoli, Andrea, 'Forgiveness and Reconciliation in the Mozambique Peace Process', in *Forgiveness and Reconciliation: Religion, Public Policy and Conflict Transformation*, eds

Raymond G. Helmick and Rodney L. Petersen (Radnor, PA: Templeton Foundation, 2001), pp. 361–81.
Barton, Stephen, 'Christian Community in the Light of 1 Corinthians', SCE, 10.1 (1997), 1–15.
Beauchamp, Tom, ed., *Intending Death: The Ethics of Assisted Suicide and Euthanasia* (New Jersey: Prentice Hall, 1996).
Benedict, *The Rule of St Benedict*, trans. Timothy Fry (New York: Vintage Books, 1998).
Berkman, John Ross, 'The Politics of Moral Theology: Historicizing Neo-Thomist Moral Theology, With Special Reference to the Work of Germain Grisez' (unpublished doctoral dissertation, Duke University, 1994).
Berman, Marshall, *All That is Solid Melts into Air: The Experience of Modernity* (London: Verso, 1983)
Biggar, Nigel, *The Hastening That Waits: Karl Barth's Ethics*, (Oxford: Clarendon Press, 1993).
———, 'Review of The Way of the Lord Jesus, vol. 2', SCE, 8.1 (1995), 105–18.
———, 'God, the Responsible Individual, and the Value of Human Life and Suffering', SCE, 11.1 (1998), 28–47.
———, 'Karl Barth and Germain Grisez on the Human Good: An Ecumenical Rapprochement', in Biggar and Black, *The Revival of Natural Law*, pp. 164–83.
Biggar, Nigel and Black, Rufus, eds, *The Revival of Natural Law: Philosophical, Theological and Ethical Responses to the Finnis-Grisez School* (Aldershot: Ashgate, 2000).
Black, Rufus, *Christian Moral Realism: Natural Law, Narrative, Virtue, and the Gospel* (Oxford: Clarendon Press, 2000).
———, 'Introduction: The New Natural Law Theory', in Biggar and Black, *The Revival of Natural Law*, pp. 1–25.
———, 'Is the New Natural Law Theory Christian?', in Biggar and Black, *The Revival of Natural Law*, pp. 148–63.
Bonhoeffer, Dietrich, *Ethics*, trans. Neville Horton Smith (London: SCM Press, 1993).
Borg, Marcus, *Conflict, Holiness and Politics in the Teachings of Jesus*, Studies in the Bible and Early Christianity (Lampeter: Edwin Mellen Press, 1972).
Boyle, Joseph, 'Natural Law and the Ethics of Traditions', in *Natural Law Theory: Contemporary Essays*, ed. Robert P. George (Oxford: Clarendon Press, 1992), pp. 3–30.
Bradshaw, Ann, 'The Spiritual Dimension of Hospice: The Secularization of an Ideal', *Social Science and Medicine*, 43.3 (1996), 409–19.
Braun, Willi, *Feasting and Social Rhetoric in Luke 14*, (Cambridge: Cambridge University Press, 1995).
Breen, Keith, 'Alasdair MacIntyre and the Hope for a Politics of Virtuous Acknowledged Dependence', *Contemporary Political Theory*, 1.2 (2002), 181–201.
Bretherton, Luke, 'Tolerance, Hospitality and Education: A Theological Proposal', SCE, 17.1 (2004), 80–103.
Brock, Dan, *Life and Death: Philosophical Essays in Biomedical Ethics* (Cambridge: Cambridge University Press, 1993).
Brueggemann, Walter, *The Prophetic Imagination* (Minneapolis: Fortress Press, 1978).
———, *Hopeful Imagination: Prophetic Voices in Exile* (Philadelphia: Fortress Press, 1986).
———, *The Land: Place as Gift, Promise, and Challenge in Biblical Faith*, 2nd edn (Minneapolis: Augsburg Fortress Publishers, 2002).
Byrne, Brendan, *The Hospitality of God: A Reading of Luke's Gospel* (Collegeville, Minnesota: Liturgical Press, 2000).
Cartwright, Michael G., ed., *The Royal Priesthood: Essays Ecclesiological and Ecumenical* (Grand Rapids: Eerdmans, 1994).
Casey, Edward, *The Fate of Place: A Philosophical History* (Berkeley: University of California Press, 1997).

Cavanaugh, William, '"A Fire Strong Enough to Consume the House:" The Wars of Religion and the Rise of the State', *Modern Theology*, 11.4 (1995), 397–420.
———, *Torture and Eucharist: Theology, Politics, and the Body of Christ* (Oxford: Blackwell Publishers, 1998).
Chrysostom, John, 'Homily 20 on 1 Corinthians', *Epistles of Paul to the Corinthians*, in NPNF, trans. Talbot Chambers, ed. Philip Schaff, First Series, 14 vols (Edinburgh: T&T Clark, 1989), XII, pp.111–18.
———, *Homily 45 on The Acts of the Apostles*, in NPNF, trans. J. Walker and J. Sheppard, ed. Philip Schaff, First Series, 14 vols (Edinburgh: T&T Clark, 1989), XI, pp. 272–77.
Clapp, Rodney, *Families at the Crossroads: Beyond Traditional and Modern Options* (Leicester: InterVarsity Press, 1993).
Clark, David and Seymour, Jane, *Reflections on Palliative Care* (Buckingham: Open University Press, 1999).
Connor, Stephen, *Hospice: Practice, Pitfalls, and Promise* (Washington, DC: Taylor & Francis, 1998).
Constitutions of the Holy Apostles, in ANF, trans. William Fletcher, eds Alexander Roberts and James Donaldson, 10 vols (Edinburgh: T&T Clark, 1994), VII, pp. 384–508.
Cranston, Maurice, 'John Locke and the Case for Toleration', in *On Toleration*, eds Susan Mendus and David Edwards (Oxford: Clarendon Press, 1987), pp. 114–15.
Creighton, Mandell, *Persecution and Tolerance* (London: Longmans, Green & Co., 1895).
D'Costa, Gavin, 'Christ, the Trinity, and Religious Pluralism', in *Christian Uniqueness Reconsidered: The Myth of a Pluralistic Theology of Religions*, ed. Gavin D'Costa (New York: Orbis Books, 1996), pp. 16–29.
———, *Sexing the Trinity: Gender, Culture and the Divine* (London: SCM Press, 2000).
Derrida, Jacques and Dufourmantelle, Anne, *Of Hospitality*, trans. Rachel Bowlby (Stanford: Stanford University Press, 2000).
Digeser, Elizabeth, *The Making of a Christian Empire: Lactantius and Rome* (Ithaca, NY: Cornell University Press, 2000).
Docker, John, *Postmodernism and Popular Culture: A Cultural History* (Cambridge: Cambridge University Press, 1994).
Du Boulay, Shirley, *Cicely Saunders: Founder of the Modern Hospice Movement* (London: Hodder and Stoughton, 1984).
Dulles, Avery, *Models of the Church: A Critical Assessment of the Church in all its Aspects*, 2nd edn (Dublin: Gill and Macmillan, 1989).
Dunn, James, 'The Household Rules in the New Testament', in *The Family in Theological Perspective*, ed. Stephen Barton (Edinburgh: T&T Clarke, 1996), pp. 43–63.
———, *Theology of Paul the Apostle* (Edinburgh: T&T Clark, 1998).
Dworkin, Gerald, R. G. Frey and Sissela Bok, eds, *Euthanasia and Physician Assisted Suicide: For and Against* (Cambridge: Cambridge University Press, 1998).
Dworkin, Ronald, *Life's Dominion: An Argument About Abortion and Euthanasia* (London: HarperCollins, 1993).
Edelstein, Ludwig, 'The Hippocractic Oath: Text, Translation, and Interpretation', in *Cross Cultural Perspectives in Medical Ethics*, ed. Robert Veatch (Boston: Jones and Bartlett, 1989).
Ellul, Jacques, *The Meaning of the City* (Carlisle: Paternoster Press, 1997).
'Epistle of Mathetes to Diognetus', in ANF, trans. Alexander Roberts and James Donaldson, eds Alexander Roberts and James Donaldson, 10 vols (Edinburgh: T&T Clark, 1996), I, pp. 25–30.
Farrow, Douglas, *Ascension and Ecclesia: On the Significance of the Doctrine of the Ascension for Ecclesiology and Christian Cosmology* (Edinburgh: T&T Clark, 1999).
———, 'St Irenaeus of Lyons. The Church and the World', *Pro Ecclesia* 4 (1995), pp. 333–55

Fee, Gordon, *God's Empowering Presence: The Holy Spirit in the Letters of Paul* (Peabody, MA: Hendrickson, 1994).
Feldmeier, Reinhard, 'The "Nation" of Strangers: Social Contempt and its Theological Interpretation in Ancient Judaism and Early Christianity', in *Ethnicity and the Bible*, ed. Mark Brett (Leiden: E. J. Brill, 1996), pp. 241–70.
Fergusson, David, *Community, Liberalism and Christian Ethics* (Cambridge: Cambridge University Press, 1998).
———, *Church, State and Civil Society* (Cambridge: Cambridge University Press, 2004).
Finley, Moses, *The Ancient Economy*, 2nd edn (London: Hogarth, 1985).
Finnis, John, *Natural Law and Natural Rights* (Oxford: Clarendon Press, 1980).
———, 'A Philosophical Case Against Euthanasia', in Keown, *Euthanasia Examined*, pp. 23–35.
Finnis, John, Boyle, Joseph and Grisez, Germain, *Nuclear Deterrence, Morality and Realism* (Oxford: Clarendon Press, 1987).
Ford, David, *Self and Salvation: Being Transformed* (Cambridge: Cambridge University Press, 1998).
Ford, Massyngbaerde, *My Enemy is My Guest: Jesus and Violence in Luke* (New York: Orbis, 1984).
Frey, R. G., 'Distinctions in Death', in Dworkin *et al.*, *Euthanasia and Physician Assisted Suicide*, pp. 17–42.
Fuller, Michael, *Making Sense of MacIntyre* (Aldershot: Ashgate, 1998).
George, Robert, ed., *Natural Law Theory: Contemporary Essays* (Oxford: Clarendon Press, 1992).
———, 'Natural Law and International Order', in *Catholicism, Liberalism and Communitarianism: The Catholic Intellectual Tradition and the Moral Foundations of Democracy*, eds Kenneth Grasso, Gerard Bradley and Robert Hunt (London: Rowman & Littlefield, 1995), pp. 133–49.
Girard, René, 'Mimesis and Violence', in *The Girard Reader*, ed. James G. Williams (New York: Crossroad Publishing, 1996), pp. 9–19.
Goldin, G., 'A Protohospice at the Turn of the Century: St Luke's House, London, from 1893–1921', *Journal of the Social History of Medicine and Allied Science*, 3 (1981), 383–413.
Gordon-Carter, Glynne, *An Amazing Journey: The Church of England's Response to Institutional Racism* (London: Church House Publishing, 2003).
Gormally Luke, ed., *Euthanasia, Clinical Practice and the Law* (London: The Linacre Centre for Health Care Ethics, 1994).
Gray, John, 'Pluralism and Toleration in Contemporary Political Philosophy', *Political Studies*, 48.2 (2000), 323–33.
Grisez, Germain, *Contraception and the Natural Law* (Milwaukee: Bruce Publishing Company, 1964).
———, 'First Principle of Practical Reason: A Commentary on the Summa Theologiae 1–2, Question 94, Article 2', *Natural Law Forum*, 10 (1965), 168–201.
———, *Abortion: The Myths, the Realities, and the Arguments* (New York: Corpus Books, 1970).
———, *Beyond the New Theism: A Philosophy of Religion* (Notre Dame: University of Notre Dame Press, 1975).
———, *The Way of the Lord Jesus: Christian Moral Principles*, 3 vols (Chicago: Franciscan Herald Press, 1983), I.
———, *The Way of the Lord Jesus: Living a Christian Life*, 3 vols (Quincy, IL: Franciscan Press, 1993), II.
———, *The Way of the Lord Jesus: Difficult Moral Questions*, 3 vols (Quincy, IL: Franciscan Press, 1997), III.

———, 'The Christian Family as Fulfillment of Sacramental Marriage', SCE, 9.1 (1996), 23–33.
———, 'Review of "Revisions: Changing Perspectives in Moral Philosophy"', eds Stanley Hauerwas and Alasdair MacIntyre', *Theological Studies*, 45 (1984), 579–581.
Grisez Germain and Boyle, Joseph, *Life and Death with Liberty and Justice: A Contribution to the Euthanasia Debate* (Notre Dame: University of Notre Dame Press, 1979).
Grisez, Germain, Boyle, Joseph and Finnis, John, 'Practical Principles, Moral Truth, and Ultimate Ends', *American Journal of Jurisprudence*, 32 (1987), 99–151.
Grisez, Germain and Shaw, Russell, *Beyond the New Morality* (Notre Dame: University of Notre Dame Press, rev. edn, 1980).
Grisez Germain, and Shaw, Russell, *Fulfillment in Christ: A Summary of Christian Moral Principles* (Notre Dame: Notre Dame University Press, 1991).
Gunton, Colin, *The One, The Three and The Many: God, Creation and the Culture of Modernity, The 1992 Bampton Lectures* (Cambridge: Cambridge University Press, 1993).
———, *A Brief Theology of Revelation* (Edinburgh: T&T Clark, 1995).
———, 'The Church as a School of Virtue? Human Formation in Trinitarian Framework', in *Faithfulness & Fortitude: In Conversation with the Theological Ethics of Stanley Hauerwas*, eds Mark Theissen Nation and Samuel Wells (Edinburgh: T&T Clark, 2000), pp. 211–31.
Habermas, Jürgen, *Between Facts and Norms: Contributions to a Discourse Theory of Law and Democracies*, trans. William Rehg (Cambridge, MA: MIT Press, 1998).
Haldane, John, 'MacIntyre's Thomist Revival: What Next?', in Horton and Mendus, *After MacIntyre*, pp. 91–107.
Hallie, Philip, *Lest Innocent Blood Be Shed* (New York: Harper & Row, 1979).
Hanink, James, 'A Theory of Basic Goods: Structure and Hierarchy', *The Thomist*, 52 (1988), 221–45.
———, 'On Germain Grisez: Can Christian Ethics Give Answers?', in *Theological Voices in Medical Ethics*, eds Allen Verhey and Stephen Lammers (Grand Rapids: Eerdmans, 1993), pp. 157–77.
Harris, John, 'Euthanasia and the Value of Life', in Keown, *Euthanasia Examined*, pp. 6–22.
———, 'The Philosophical Case Against the Philosophical Case Against Euthanasia', in Keown, *Euthanasia Examined*, pp. 36–45.
Harvey, David, *The Condition of Post-Modernity: An Enquiry into the Origins of Cultural Change* (Oxford: Blackwell, 1990).
Hauerwas, Stanley, 'Medicine as Tragic Profession', in *Truthfulness and Tragedy: Further Investigations into Christian Ethics* (Notre Dame: University of Notre Dame Press, 1977).
———, *The Peaceable Kingdom: A Primer in Christian Ethics* (Notre Dame: University of Notre Dame Press, 1983).
———, *Against the Nations: War and Survival in a Liberal Society* (Minneapolis: Winston Press, 1985).
———, *Suffering Presence: Theological Reflections on Medicine, the Mentally Handicapped and the Church* (Edinburgh: T&T Clark, 1986).
———, *Naming the Silences: God, Medicine, and the Problem of Suffering* (Edinburgh: T&T Clark, 1993).
———, *Dispatches from the Front: Theological Engagements with the Secular* (Durham: Duke University Press, 1994).
———, 'What Could It Mean for the Church to Be Christ's Body? A Question without a Clear Answer', in *In Good Company: The Church as Polis*, ed. Stanley Hauerwas (Notre Dame: University of Notre Dame Press, 1995), pp. 19–31.
———, 'On Doctrine and Ethics', in *The Cambridge Companion to Christian Doctrine*, ed. Colin Gunton (Cambridge: Cambridge University Press, 1997), pp. 21–40.

———, 'Salvation and Health: Why Medicine Needs the Church', in Lamers and Verhey, *On Moral Medicine*, pp. 72–83.
———, 'Rational Suicide and Reasons for Living', in Lammers and Verhey, *On Moral Medicine*, pp. 671–78.
———, 'The Non-Violent Terrorist: In Defence of Christian Fanaticism', in *Sanctify Them in the Truth* (Edinburgh: T&T Clark, 1998), pp. 177–90.
———, 'No Enemy, No Christianity: Preaching between "Worlds"', *Sanctify Them in the Truth* (Edinburgh: T&T Clark, 1998), pp. 191–200.
———, *With the Grain of the Universe* (London: SCM Press, 2002).
———, *Performing the Faith: Bonhoeffer and the Practices of Nonviolence* (London: SPCK, 2004).
Hauerwas, Stanley and Pinches, Charles, *Christians Among the Virtues: Theological Conversations with Ancient and Modern Ethics* (Notre Dame: University of Notre Dame Press, 1997).
Hauerwas, Stanley with Sherwindt, Mark, 'The Reality of the Kingdom: An Ecclesial Space for Peace', in Hauerwas, *Against the Nations*, pp. 107–19.
Hauerwas, Stanley and Willimon, William, *Resident Aliens* (Nashville: Abingdon, 1989).
Hays, Richard, *The Moral Vision of the New Testament: A Contemporary Introduction to New Testament Ethics* (Edinburgh: T&T Clark, 1996).
Healy, Nicholas, 'Practices and the New Ecclesiology: Misplaced Concreteness?' *International Journal of Systematic Theology*, 5.3 (2003), 287–308.
Hibbs, Thomas, 'MacIntyre, Tradition and the Christian Philosopher', *The Modern Schoolman*, 68 (1991), 211–23.
Hill, C. S., *West Indian Migrants and the London Churches* (Oxford: Oxford University Press, 1963).
Hittinger, Russell, *A Critique of the New Natural Law Theory* (Notre Dame: University of Notre Dame Press, 1987).
———, 'After MacIntyre: Natural Law Theory, Virtue Ethics, and Eudaimonia', *International Philosophical Quarterly*, 29 (1989), 449–61.
Hoffmann, Joseph, ed., *Porphyry's Against the Christians: the Literary Remains* (Amherst, NY: Prometheus Books, 1994).
Hollenbach, David, *The Common Good and Christian Ethics* (Cambridge: Cambridge University Press, 2002).
Holy Bible, New Revised Standard Version (Oxford: Oxford University Press, 1989).
Horton, John, 'Toleration', in *Routledge Encyclopedia of Philosophy*, ed. Edward Craig (London: Routledge, 1998), pp. 429–33.
Horton John and Mendus, Susan, eds, *Aspects of Toleration: Philosophical Studies* (London: Methuen, 1985).
———, eds, *After MacIntyre: Critical Perspectives on the Work of Alastair MacIntyre* (London: Polity Press, 1994).
Howard, Michael, *The Invention of Peace: Reflections on War and International Order* (London: Profile Books, 2000).
Humphry, Derek, *Final Exit* (Eugene, OR: Hemlock Society, 1991).
Hunter, James Davidson, *Culture Wars: The Struggle to Define America* (New York: Basic Books, 1991).
Huntington, Samuel, *The Clash of Civilizations and the Remaking of World Order* (London: Simon & Schuster, 1996).
Hütter, Reinhard, 'Ecclesial Ethics, the Church's Vocations, and Paraclesis', *Pro Ecclesia*, 2 (1993), 433–50.
———, 'Hospitality and Truth: The Disclosure of Practices in Worship and Doctrine', in *Practicing Theology: Beliefs and Practices in Christian Life*, eds Miroslav Volf and Dorothy C. Bass (Grand Michigan, MI: Eerdmans, 2002), pp. 206–27.

Illich, Ivan, *Tools for Conviviality* (New York,: Harper & Row, 1973).
———, *Medical Nemesis: The Expropriation of Health* (London: Marian Boyars, 1976).
Jackson, Avril and Eve, Ann, eds, *Directory of Hospice and Palliative Care Services in the United Kingdom and the Republic of Ireland* (London: St Christopher's Hospice Information Service, 1998).
Jacobs, Alan, *A Theology of Reading: The Hermeneutics of Love* (Cambridge, MA: Westview Press, 2001).
James, Nicky, 'From Vision to System: the Maturing of the Hospice Movement', in *Death Rites: Law and Ethics as the End of Life*, eds Robert Lee and Derek Morgan (London: Routledge, 1994), pp. 102–30.
Jenson, Robert, 'The Hauerwas Project', *Modern Theology*, 8 (1992), 285–95.
Jerome, 'Letter 77', in NPNF, trans. W. H. Fremantle, G. Lewis and W. G. Martley, eds Philip Schaff and Henry Wace, Second Series, 14 vols (Edinburgh: T&T Clark, 1996), VI, pp. 157–63.
John Paul II, *Evangelium Vitae* (London: Catholic Truth Society, 1995).
———, 'Euthanasia: Declaration of the Sacred Congregation for the Doctrine of the Faith (May 5, 1980)', in Lammers and Verhey, *On Moral Medicine*, pp. 650–55.
Jones, Gregory, 'Alasdair MacIntyre on Narrative, Community, and the Moral Life', *Modern Theology*, 4 (1987), 53–69.
Jonsen, Albert, 'Criteria That Make Intentional Killing Unjustified', in Beauchamp, *Intending Death*.
Jordan, Wilbur, *The Development of Religious Toleration in England*, 4 vols (Cambridge: Cambridge University Press, 1932–40).
Just, Arthur, *The Ongoing Feast: Table Fellowship and Eschatology at Emmaus* (Collegeville: The Liturgical Press, 1993).
Kant, Immanuel, 'Perpetual Peace: A Philosophical Sketch', in *Kant: Political Writings*, trans. H. B. Nisbet, ed. Hans Reiss (Cambridge: Cambridge University Press, 1991), pp. 93–130.
Keener, Craig, *A Commentary on the Gospel of Matthew* (Grand Rapids: Eerdmans, 1999).
Kelly, Paul, 'MacIntyre's Critique of Utilitarianism', in Horton and Mendus, *After MacIntyre*, pp. 172–45.
Keown, John, *Euthanasia Examined: Ethical, Clinical and Legal Perspectives* (Cambridge: Cambridge University Press, 1995).
King, Preston, *Toleration* (London: Allen & Unwin, 1976).
Kingwell, Mark, *A Civil Tongue: Justice, Dialogue and the Politics of Pluralism* (Pennsylvania: Pennsylvania State University Press, 1995).
Klagsbrun, Samuel, 'Hospice – a Developing Role', in Saunders *et al.*, *Hospice: The Living Idea*, pp. 5–8.
Knight, Kelvin, ed., *The MacIntyre Reader* (London: Polity Press, 1998).
———, 'Guide to Further reading', in *The MacIntyre Reader*, p. 276–94.
Koenig, John, *New Testament Hospitality: Partnership with Strangers as Promise and Mission*, Overtures to Biblical Theology (Philadelphia: Fortress Press, 1985).
———, 'Two Models of Pluralism and Tolerance', in *Toleration: An Elusive Virtue*, ed. David Heyd (Princeton: Princeton University Press, 1996), pp. 81–105.
Lactantius, *The Divine Institutes*, in ANF, trans. William Fletcher, eds Alexander Roberts and James Donaldson, 10 vols (Edinburgh: T&T Clark, 1994), VII, pp. 9–223.
Ladd, John, 'Euthanasia, Liberty and Religion', *Ethics*, 93.1 (1982), 129–38.
Lammers, Stephen and Verhey, Allen, eds, *On Moral Medicine: Theological Perspectives in Medical Ethics*, 2nd edn (Grand Rapids: Eerdmans, 1998).
Levenson, Jon, *Creation and the Persistence of Evil: The Jewish Drama of Divine Omnipotence* (Princeton: Princeton University Press, 1988).

Lévinas, Emmanuel, *Ethics and Infinity*, trans. Richard Cohen (Pittsburgh: Duquesne University Press, 1985).
Lindbeck, George, *The Nature of Doctrine* (London: SPCK, 1984).
Locke, John, *An Essay on Toleration*, in *Locke: Political Essays*, ed. Mark Goldie (Cambridge: Cambridge University Press, 1997), pp. 134–59.
Loughlin, Gerard, 'René Girard (b. 1923): Introduction', in *The Postmodern God: A Theological Reader*, ed. Graham Ward (Oxford: Basil Blackwell, 1997), pp. 96–104.
MacIntyre, Alasdair, 'Can Medicine Dispense with a Theological Perspective on Human Nature', in *Knowledge, Value and Belief*, eds T. Engelhart and D. Callahan (Hastings-on-Hudson: Institute of Society, Ethics and the Life Sciences, 1977), pp. 25–43.
——, 'Patient as Agent', in *Philosophical Medical Ethics: its Nature and Significance*, eds Stuart Spicker and H. Tristram Englehardt (Dordrecht: Reidel, 1977), pp. 197–212.
——, 'Which God Ought We To Obey and Why?', *Faith and Philosophy*, 3.4 (1986), 359–71.
——, *Whose Justice? Which Rationality?* (London: Duckworth, 1988).
——, *Three Rival Versions of Moral Enquiry: Encyclopaedia, Genealogy, and Tradition* (London: Duckworth, 1989).
——, 'Incommensurability, Truth and the Conversation between Confucians and Aristotelians about the Virtues', in *Culture and Modernity: East–West Philosophic Perspectives*, ed. Eliot Deutsch (Honolulu: University of Hawaii Press, 1991), pp. 104–22.
——, 'Community, Law and the Idiom and Rhetoric of Rights', *Listening* 26 (1991), 96–110.
——, *After Virtue: A Study in Moral Theory*, 2nd edn (London: Duckworth, 1994).
——, 'How Can We Learn what *Veritatis Splendor* Has to Teach', *The Thomist*, 58 (1994), 171–95.
——, 'Natural Law as Subversive: The Case of Aquinas', *Journal of Medieval and Early Modern Studies* 26 (1996), 61–83.
——, 'Plain Persons and Moral Philosophy: Rules, Virtues and Goods', in Knight, *The MacIntyre Reader*, pp. 136–52.
——, 'First Principles, Final Ends and Contemporary Philosophical Issues', in Knight, *The MacIntyre Reader*, pp. 171–201.
——, 'Politics, Philosophy and the Common Good', in Knight, *The MacIntyre Reader*, pp. 235–52.
'Moral Relativism, Truth and Justification', in Knight, *The MacIntyre Reader*, pp. 202–20.
——, *Dependent Rational Animals: Why Human Beings Need the Virtues* (London: Duckworth, 1999).
——, 'Toleration and the Goods of Conflict', in Mendus, *The Politics of Toleration*, pp. 133–55.
——, 'Theories of Natural Law in the Culture of Advanced Modernity', in *Common Truths: New Perspectives on Natural Law*, ed. Edward McLean (Wilmington, DE: ISI Books, 2000), pp. 91–115.
Manning, Margaret, *The Hospice Alternative: Living with Dying* (London: Souvenir Press, 1984).
Markham, Ian, *Plurality and Christian Ethics* (Cambridge: Cambridge University Press, 1995).
Markus, Robert, *Saeculum: History and Society in the Theology of St Augustine* (Cambridge: Cambridge University Press, 1970).
Marx, Karl, and Engels, Friedrich, *The Communist Manifesto*, trans. Samuel Moore (London: Penguin, 1967).
Mauss, Marcel, *The Gift: The Form and Reason for Exchange in Archaic Societies* (London: Routledge, 2002).

May, William, 'The Sacral Power of Death in Contemporary Experience', in Lammers and Verhey, *On Moral Medicine*, pp. 197–209.
McClendon, James, *Ethics* (Nashville: Abingdon Press, 1986).
McDonald, Ian, *The Crucible of Christian Morality* (London: Routledge, 1998).
McInerny, Ralph, 'Ethics', in *The Cambridge Companion to Aquinas*, eds N. Kretzmann and E. Stump (Cambridge: Cambridge University Press, 1993), pp. 196–216.
McMylor, Peter, *Alasdair MacIntyre Critic of Modernity* (London: Routledge, 1994).
Meeks, Wayne, *The Origins of Christian Morality* (New Haven: Yale University Press, 1993).
Meilaender, Gilbert, *Bioethics: A Primer for Christians* (Grand Rapids: Eerdmans, 1996).
——, 'Euthanasia and Christian Vision', in Lammers and Verhey, *On Moral Medicine*, pp. 655–66.
Mendus, Susan, *Toleration and the Limits of Liberalism* (London: Macmillan, 1989).
——, ed., *The Politics of Toleration: Tolerance and Intolerance in Modern Life* (Edinburgh: Edinburgh University Press, 1999).
Milbank, John, *Theology and Social Theory: Beyond Secular Reason* (Oxford: Basil Blackwell, 1990).
Milgrom, Jacob, *Leviticus 1–16*, 3 vols, *Anchor Bible* (New York: Doubleday, 1991), III.
Mill, John Stuart, *On Liberty* (Cambridge: Cambridge University Press, 1989).
Miller, Timothy, 'Hospital: Medieval and Renaissance History', in *Encyclopedia of Bioethics*, ed. Warren Reich (New York: Macmillan, 1995), pp. 1160–63.
Moessner, David, *Lord of the Banquet: The Literary and Theological Significance of the Lukan Travel Narrative* (Minneapolis: Fortress Press, 1989).
Moltmann, Jürgen, 'The Liberating Feast', *Concilium*, 10.2 (1974), 74–84.
——, *The Church in the Power of the Spirit* (London: SCM, 1977).
Muir, Edward, *Ritual in Early Modern Europe* (Cambridge: Cambridge University Press, 1997).
Mulhall, Stephen and Swift, Adam, *Liberals and Communitarians* (Oxford: Blackwell, 1992).
Murphy, Mark, 'MacIntyre's Political Philosophy', in *Alasdair MacIntyre*, ed., Mark Murphy (Cambridge: Cambridge University Press, 2003), pp. 152–75.
Nagel, Thomas, *Equality and Partiality* (Oxford: Oxford University Press, 1991).
Navone SJ, John, 'Divine and Human Hospitality', *New Blackfriars*, 85.997 (2004), 329–40.
Nazianzen, Gregory, *Panegyric on St Basil*, in NPNF, trans. Charles Brown and James Swallow, eds Philip Schaff and Henry Wace, Second Series, 14 vols (Edinburgh: T&T Clark, 1996), VII, pp. 395–422.
New Shorter Oxford English Dictionary, CD-ROM edn (Oxford: Oxford University Press, 1996).
Newbigin, Lesslie, *The Open Secret: An Introduction to the Theology of Mission*, rev. edn (London: SPCK, 1995).
Niebuhr, Reinhold, *The Children of Light and the Children of Darkness* (London: Nisbet & Co, 1945).
——, 'The Test of Tolerance' in *Religious Pluralism in the West*, ed. D Mullan (Oxford: Blackwell, 1998), pp. 281–96.
Niebuhr, Richard, *Christ and Culture* (London: Faber & Faber, 1952).
O'Daly, Gerard, trans., *Augustine's City of God: A Reader's Guide* (Oxford: Clarendon Press, 1999).
Oden, Amy, ed., *And You Welcomed Me: A Sourcebook on Hospitality in Early Christianity* (Nashville: Abingdon Press, 2001).
O'Donovan, Oliver, 'The Natural Ethic', in *Essays in Evangelical Social Ethics*, ed. D. Wright (Exeter: Paternoster Press, 1978), pp. 19–35.
——, *Begotten or Made?* (Oxford: Clarendon Press, 1984).

——, *Resurrection and Moral Order: An Outline for Evangelical Ethics* (Grand Rapids: Eerdmans, 1986).
——, *On the 39 Articles: A Conversation with Tudor Christianity* (Carlisle: Paternoster Press, 1986).
——, 'Moral Disagreement as an Ecumenical Issue', SCE, 1.1 (1988), 5–19.
——, 'John Finnis on Moral Absolutes', SCE, 6.2 (1993), 50–66.
——, 'Christian Moral Reasoning', in *New Dictionary of Christian Ethics and Pastoral Theology*, eds David Atkinson and David Field (Leicester: Inter-Varsity Press, 1995), pp. 122–27.
——, *The Desire of the Nations: Rediscovering the Roots of Political Theory* (Cambridge: Cambridge University Press, 1996).
——, 'Review of *Evangalium Vitae*', SCE, 9.1 (1996), 89–94.
——, 'Keeping Body and Soul Together', in Lammers and Verhey, *On Moral Medicine*, pp. 223–38.
——, 'What Can Ethics Know About God?', *The Doctrine of God and Theological Ethics*, eds, Alan Torrance and Michael Banner (Edinburgh: T&T Clark, forthcoming).
Ogletree, Thomas, 'Hospitality to the Stranger: the Role of the "Other" in Moral Experience', in *Hospitality to the Stranger: Dimensions of Moral Understanding* (Philadelphia: Fortress Press, 1985), pp. 35–63.
Pavlischek, Keith, 'Questioning the New Natural Law Theory: The Case of Religious Liberty as Defended by Robert P. George in *Making Men Moral*', SCE, 12.2 (1999), 17–30.
Pellegrino, Edmund, 'The Place of Intention in the Moral Assessment of Assisted Suicide and Active Euthanasia', in Beauchamp, *Intending Death*, pp. 163–83.
——, 'Postliberal Theology', in *The Modern Theologians: An Introduction to Christian Theology in the Twentieth Century*, ed. David Ford, 2nd edn (Oxford: Blackwell, 1997), pp. 343–56
Pohl, Christine, *Making Room: Recovering Hospitality as a Christian Tradition* (Grand Rapids: Eerdmans, 1999).
Porter, Jean, 'Openness and Constraint: Moral Reflection as Tradition-guided Inquiry in Alasdair MacIntyre's Recent Works', *Journal of Religion*, 73 (1993), 514–36.
——, *The Recovery of Virtue: The Relevance of Aquinas for Christian Ethics* (London: SPCK, 1994).
——, *Natural and Divine Law: Reclaiming the Tradition for Christian Ethics* (Grand Rapids: Eerdmans, 1999)
Preston, Geoffrey, *Faces of the Church: Meditations on a Mystery and Its Images* (Edinburgh: T&T Clark, 1997).
Rachels, James, *The End of Life* (Oxford: Oxford University Press, 1986).
Ramsey, Paul, 'On (Only) Caring for the Dying', in *The Essential Paul Ramsey: A Collection*, eds Paul Ramsey, William Werpehowski and Stephen Crocco (New Haven: Yale University Press, 1994), pp. 195–222.
'The Indignity of "Death with Dignity"', in *The Essential Paul Ramsey: A Collection*, pp. 223–46.
Randall, Fiona, and Downie, R. S., *Palliative Care Ethics: A Good Companion* (Oxford: Oxford University Press, 1996).
Rawls, John, *Political Liberalism* (New York: Columbia University Press, 1993).
Roberts, Alexander and Donaldson, James, eds and trans., *Anti-Nicene Fathers* (ANF), 10 vols (Edinburgh: T&T Clark, 1996).
Rogers, Eugene, *Sexuality and the Christian Body* (Oxford: Blackwell, 1999).
Sansom, Dennis, 'Why Do We Want to be Healthy? Medicine, Autonomous Individualism, and the Community of Faith', in Lammers and Verhey, *On Moral Medicine*, pp. 262–66.

Saunders, Cicely, 'Care of the Dying. 2: The Problem of Euthanasia', *Nursing Times*, 72. 27 (1976), 1049–51.

——, 'The Hospice: its Meaning to Patients and their Physicians', *Hospital Practice*, 16.6 (1981), 93–108.

——, 'The Modern Hospice' (paper presented at the In Quest of the Spiritual Component of Care for the Terminally Ill – Proceedings of a Colloquium, Yale University School of Nursing, 1986), pp. 41–48.

Saunders, Cicely, Summers, Dorothy and Teller, Neville, eds, *Hospice: the Living Idea* (London: Edward Arnold, 1981).

Sennett, Richard, *Flesh and Stone: the Body and the City in Western Civilization* (London: Faber & Faber, 1994).

Shaw, Russell, 'Pioneering the Renewal in Moral Theology', in *Natural Law and Moral Inquiry: Ethics, Metaphysics, and Politics in the Work of Germain Grisez*, ed. Robert P. George (Washington DC: Georgetown University Press, 1998), pp. 241–71.

Singer, Peter, 'Justifying Voluntary Euthanasia', in *Ethical Issues in Death and Dying*, ed. Robert Weir (New York: Columbia University Press, 1986), pp. 268–74.

——, *Rethinking Life and Death: The Collapse of Our Traditional Ethics* (Oxford: Oxford University Press, 1995)

Smith-Christopher, Daniel, 'Between Ezra and Isaiah: Exclusion, Transformation, and Inclusion of the "Foreigner" in Post-Exilic Biblical Theology', in *Ethnicity and the Bible*, ed. Mark Brett (Leiden: E. J. Brill, 1996), pp. 117–42.

Stallybrass, Peter and White, Allon, *The Politics and Poetics of Transgression* (London: Methuen, 1986).

Stanton, Graham, *A Gospel for a New People* (Edinburgh: T&T Clark, 1992).

Stout, Jeffrey, 'Homeward Bound: MacIntyre on Liberal Society and the History of Ethics', *Journal of Religion*, 69 (1989), 220–32.

Swift, Adam and Mulhall, Stephen, *Liberals and Communitarians* (Oxford, Blackwell, 1992).

Tanner, Kathryn, *Jesus, Humanity and the Trinity* (Edinburgh: T&T Clark, 2001).

TeSelle, Eugene, *Living in Two Cities: Augustinian Trajectories in Political Thought* (Scranton: University of Scranton Press, 1999).

Thomas, Scott, 'Taking Religious and Cultural Pluralism Seriously: The Global Resurgence of Religion and the Transformation of International Society', *Millennium: Journal of International Studies*, 29.3 (2000), 815–41.

Thompson, Christopher, 'Benedict, Thomas, or Augustine? The Character of MacIntyre's Narrative', *The Thomist*, 59 (1995), 379–407.

Todorova, Maria, *Imagining the Balkans* (Oxford: Oxford University Press, 1997).

Trowell, Hugh, *Euthanasia: The Unfinished Debate on Euthanasia* (London: SCM Press, 1973).

Tugwell, Simon, *The Apostolic Fathers* (London: Geoffrey Chapman, 1989).

Vanier, Jean, *An Ark for the Poor: The Story of L'Arche* (New York: Crossroad, 1995).

Verhey, Allen, 'The Doctor's Oath – and a Christian Swearing It', in Lammers and Verhey, *On Moral Medicine*, pp. 108–19.

Volf, Miroslav, 'Soft Difference: Theological Reflections on the Relation Between Church and Culture in 1 Peter', *Ex Auditu*, 10 (1994), 15–30.

——, *Exclusion and Embrace: A Theological Exploration of Identity, Otherness, and Reconciliation* (Nashville: Abingdon Press, 1996).

Walzer, Michael, *Thick and Thin: Moral Argument at Home and Abroad* (Notre Dame: University of Notre Dame Press, 1994).

——, *On Toleration* (New Haven: Yale University Press, 1997).

Warnock, Mary, *The Uses of Philosophy* (Oxford: Blackwell, 1992).

Welker, Michael, *God the Spirit*, trans. John Hoffmeyer (Minneapolis: Fortress Press, 1992).

Wells, Samuel, *Transforming Fate into Destiny: The Theological Ethics of Stanley Hauerwas* (Carlisle: Paternoster Press, 1998).
Werpehowski, William, 'Ad Hoc Apologetics', *Journal of Religion*, 66 (1986), 282–301.
Westerman, Pauline, *The Disintegration of Natural Law Theory: Aquinas to Finnis* (Leiden: Brill, 1998).
Wilken, Robert, 'In Defense of Constantine', *First Things*, 112 (2001), 36–40.
Williams, Bernard, 'Toleration: An Impossible Virtue', in *Toleration: An Elusive Virtue*, ed. David Heyd (Princeton: Princeton University Press, 1996), pp. 19–27.
———, 'Tolerating the Intolerable', in Mendus, *The Politics of Toleration*, pp. 65–75.
Winter, Bruce, *Seek the Welfare of the City: Christians as Benefactors and Citizens* (Carlisle: Paternoster Press, 1994).
Woodill, Joseph, *The Fellowship of Life: Virtue Ethics and Orthodox Christianity* (Washington DC: Georgetown University Press, 1998).
Wright, N. T., *Jesus and the Victory of God, Christian Origins and the Question of God* (London: SPCK, 1996).
Wuthnow, Robert and Lawson, Matthew P., 'Sources of Christian Fundamentalism in the United States', in *Accounting for Fundamentalisms: The Dynamic Character of Movements*, eds. Martin Marty and R. Scott Appleby (Chicago: University of Chicago Press, 1991), pp. 18–56.
Wyschogrod, Michael, *The Body of Faith: God in the People of Israel* (San Francisco: Harper and Row, 1983)
Yeago, David, 'Messiah's People: The Culture of the Church in the Midst of the Nations', *Pro Ecclesia*, 6 (1997), 146–71.
Yoder, John Howard, 'Binding and Loosing', in Cartwright, *The Royal Priesthood*, pp. 323–58.
'A People in the World', in *The Royal Priesthood*, pp. 65–101.
———, *The Politics of Jesus*, 2nd edn (Grand Rapids: Eerdmans, 1994)
———, 'How H. Richard Niebuhr Reasoned: A Critique of *Christ and Culture*', in *Authentic Transformation: A New Vision of Christ and Culture* eds Glen Stassen, Diane Yeager and John Howard Yoder (Nashville: Abingdon, 1996), pp. 31–90.
———, *For the Nations: Essays Evangelical and Public* (Grand Rapids: Eerdmans, 1997).
Zaw, Susan Khin, 'Locke and multiculturalism: Toleration, Relativism, and Reason', in *Public Education in a Multicultural Society*, ed. Robert K. Fullinwider (Cambridge: Cambridge University Press, 1996), pp. 121–55.
Zizioulas, John, *Being as Communion: Studies in Personhood and the Church* (New York: St Vladimir's Seminary Press, 1985).

Index

Acts, Book of 136–8, 189
ad hoc commensurability 74–80, 111, 112–14
Anagnastopoulos, G. 166, 167
Aquinas *see* Thomist perspective (Aquinas)
Aristotle 15, 19, 20, 21–2, 27–8, 30, 48–9, 49–50, 66, 84, 133, 166, 167
ascension 73, 79, 81–2
Augustine 21–2, 48–9, 66–7, 111
autonomy
 and choice 45–6
 Christian approaches to 175–7
 death, suffering and good care 172–8
 and euthanasia 168–70
 see also individualism/individuality

Bailey, K. 132, 134
Bakhtin, M. 145–6
Banner, M. 56, 77, 140, 176
Barry, B. 15–16
Barth, K. 107, 108–9, 173, 175, 177, 178
basic good(s) 34, 40, 41–2, 47
 religion as 52–3
 substantive and reflexive 36, 42
 teleology 36–7, 53–4
Beauchamp, T. 161–2, 163, 163–4, 165
Benedict 140, 146, 179
Biggar, N. 35, 53, 172, 173
Black, R. 43, 46
Bland, T. (euthanasia case) 164
Boyle, J. 35, 42, 43–4, 45
 Grisez, G. and 161, 162
Bradshaw, A. 188–9
Braun, W. 132, 133
Brock, D. 162, 165, 168–9
bureaucratic rationality 9, 16–17

Calvin, J. 141
catastrophe, parable of 10
Ceighton, M. 123–4
character(s) 17, 45
choice 45–6
Christian perspectives
 on death 174–5

on hospitality 135–42
on suffering 172–3
on tolerance 121–6
see also ecclesiology; theological perspectives; Thomist perspective (Aquinas)
Christians and non-Christians 9, 30, 47, 78–80, 95–6, 196–8
 differences between 37–9, 43, 54–7, 111–12
 relations between 99–100, 101–2, 115, 126–7, 196
 resolution of moral disputes 26–30, 87–8, 101–10
 see also eschatology; euthanasia; hospice care; incommensurability; suffering-dying
Chrysostom, J. 139, 140–41, 185
The Church 101–2, 103–10
Cicero 134
Clark, D. and Seymour, J. 184–5
community
 character and 45
 individuality and 44
 politics of local 96–9, 110–11, 114, 180
 of resistance 99–100
conflicting traditions 86–7, 105–6, 106–7
Confucius 27–8
contemporary context
 attitudes to suffering 171
 conceptions of death 170–71
 incoherence of moral debates 9–17, 67–9
conversion 68–9
Corinthians, Book of 108
Cox, Dr. N. (euthanasia case) 160
creation 64–86 *passim*

D'Costa, G. 136
death
 Christian approaches to 174–5
 contemporary conceptions of 170–71
 see also suffering; suffering-dying
Derrida, J. 24, 126
dialectics 77–80

The *Didache* 138–9
divine authority in relation to tradition 72–3
doctrinal framework of hospitality 142–3
Douglas, M. 11
Dulles, A. 137
Dworkin, R. 169, 170, 171, 179

Ecclesiastes, Book of 174
ecclesiology
 'angel-ecclesiology' 74–5, 78
 and eschatology 106–7, 109, 142–3
 as fundamental category in Christian ethics 103–5
 in resolution of ethical disputes 101–10
economic order 97–8
eschatology 54–5, 73–4, 78–9, 102–3
 and ecclesiology 106–7, 109, 142–3
 hospice care 188
 and nature of Christian distinctiveness 110–14
 and teleology 81–5, 86
ethics
 evangelical 64–74
 foundation and nature of 39–43, 51–4
 and theology 54–6
 tradition-situated *vs.* tradition-guided 75–7
 see also entries beginning moral; morality
euthanasia
 defining 161–5
 philosophical defences of 168–71
 practice of medicine and 165–8
 and theological account of good care 172–8
 see also suffering-dying
evangelical ethics 64–74

The Fall 68, 82
Farrow, D. 82
feasting 128–9
 and fasting 143–6
 Great Banquet parable 131–5
Fergusson, D. 78, 79, 80, 83, 105, 124
Finnis, J. 35, 38, 45, 56, 161, 163
Ford, D. 144
fragmentation of traditions 9, 17, 34
Frey, R.G. 168
Fuller, M. 27

George, R. 40
Gifford, A. 11

Girard, R. 132
goods *see* basic good(s)
Gray, J. 126
Great Banquet parable 131–5
Grisez, G. 34–60 *passim*, 167, 180–83
 and Boyle, J. 161, 162
 and MacIntyre, A. 34–6, 39–50, 196
Gunton, C. 76

Haldane, J. 36
Hanink, J. 34
Harris, J. 161, 163
Hauerwas, S. 81, 86, 87, 105–7, 171, 176
Healy, N. 107–8
Hippocratic Oath 166–7, 168
history
 conceptions of 12, 82, 83, 85, 86
 of hospice movement 184–5
 of rival traditions 28–9
Hittinger, R. 52–3
Hollenbach, D. 147
The Holy Spirit 73–4, 75–6, 78–9
 ecclesiological perspective 102, 103–4, 106, 107, 108, 109, 110
 encounter between Peter and Cornelius 136–8
 at Pentecost 104, 111–12, 142–3, 149, 188
Homer 19
Horton, J. 122
hospice care 180–81, 182–9
 as Christian hospitality 185, 186–8
 defining 183–4
 future developments 188–9
hospice movement, history of 184–5
hospitality
 Christian and non-Christian relations 126–7
 hospice care as 185, 186–8
 theologically specific account of 128–46
 and tolerance 121–6, 147–50
 within Christian tradition 138–42
House of Lords' Select Committee on Medical Ethics 160, 161
human nature 12, 42
Humphry, D. 170, 183
Hütter, R. 138

immigration issue 148–9
incoherence of contemporary moral debates 9–17, 67–9
incommensurability 26–30

and *ad hoc* commensurability 74–80, 111, 112–14
critiques 37, 47–8, 69–74, 87–8
individualism/individuality 9, 16, 17
and community 44
and privatization of morality 62–3
see also autonomy; liberalism
institutionalization of practices 18–19, 99, 140–41

James, N. 184, 189
Jeremias, J. 128–9
John Paul II 172
Jonsen, A. 165–6, 168
justice 9, 10, 13–15, 25–6, 34–6, 85, 97
justification and predestination 83–4

Kant, E. 126–7
Keener, C. 131
Klagsbrun, S. 189
Knight, K. 27

Lactantius 122, 123, 134, 149–50
language
of rival traditions 28, 43–4
of science and morality 10
legislation relating to euthanasia 160, 187
Leviticus, Book of 138
liberalism 9, 14–17, 34, 63–4
see also autonomy; individualism/individuality
Locke, J. 124, 148, 149
Luke, Book of 128, 129, 131–5

MacIntyre, A. 9–33 *passim*
commentators on 77–8, 79–80
conception of relations between Christians and non-Christians 99–100, 105, 196
critique of liberalism 14–17
critique of modern state 124–5
euthanasia debate 160, 166, 167, 168, 178–80, 182
and Grisez, G. 34–6, 39–50, 196
and Kant, E. 126–7
and O'Donovan, O. 61–4, 65–9, 77, 80, 81–8, 95–6, 101–2, 107, 127, 196–7
politics of local community 96–9, 110–11, 114, 180
Manning, M. 184, 185, 186
Markham, I. 147–8, 149
May, E. 170
medicine, practice of, and euthanasia 165–8

Meilaender, G. 173, 178
Mendus, S. 125
metaphysics and practical rationality 36, 37, 39
Milbank, J. 77–8, 86, 87
Mill, J.S. 125, 177
misericordia, virtue of 98, 127
modernity
apostate child of Christianity 61–4
privatization of morality 62–3
resistance to 96, 99–100
see also individualism/individuality; liberalism
Moessner, D. 135, 138
Moltmann, J. 145
moral debates, incoherence of 9–17, 67–9
moral disputes, resolution of 26–30, 87–8, 101–10
moral knowledge 37–9, 43, 54–7, 69–70
moral 'ought' *vs.* theoretical/factual 'is' 49–50
moral reasoning 12–13, 17–20, 48–9, 62, 167–8
morality
language of science and 10
privatization of 62–3
strength as determining factor in 13–14
Mulhall, S. and Swift, A. 19

natural and evangelical knowledge 64–7
natural law 25–6, 34, 35, 36
see also 'new natural law theory'
nature and tradition, authority of 70–72
'new natural law theory' 36–9, 42–4, 45, 48–9
critique 51–6
New Testament 19, 109, 128–9, 185
Acts 136–8, 189
Corinthians 108
Luke 128, 129, 131–5
Peter 113–14, 141–2
Romans 75, 144–5, 174
Newman, J. 124
Niebuhr, R. 124
Nietzsche, F. 12–13, 24
Nozick, R. 15

O'Donovan, O. 38, 55, 56, 102–7 *passim*, 142, 171–80 *passim*
and MacIntyre, A. 61–4, 65–9, 77, 80, 81–8, 95–6, 101–2, 107, 127, 196–7

Old Testament 129, 130
   Ecclesiastes 174
   Leviticus 138

parables
   of catastrophe 10
   Great Banquet 131–5
Paul 108, 174
Pavlischek, K. 35
Pellegrino, E. 163
Pentecost 104, 111–12, 142–3, 149, 188
perverted will 22
Peter, Book of 113–14, 141–2
philosophical defences of euthanasia 168–71
Placher, W. 105
Plato 34, 166, 167
Pohl, C. 131
politics
   hospitality as political practice 126–7
   of local community 96–9, 110–11, 114, 180
Porphyry 149, 150
Porter, J. 36
'post-Humean fact-value distinction' 35, 36, 49–50
Powell, E. 148
practical knowledge, self-evidence of 40, 41–2
practical rationality/reason
   first principle of 40
   metaphysics and 36, 37, 39
   vs. theoretical reason 40–41, 51–4
practical truth 41
practice(s)
   of hospitality 98, 121–59
   institutionalization of 18–19, 99, 140–41
   of medicine and euthanasia 165–8
   social 110, 112–14
   and virtues 18–19, 20, 45–7
   see also tradition(s)

Raglan, Lord 187
Ramsey, P. 160, 161, 164
rationality 9, 10, 14–15, 16
   bureaucratic 9, 16–17
   tradition and 20
   see also moral reasoning; practical rationality/reason; truth
Rawls, J. 15–16
reflexive goods 36, 42
refugee issue 148–9

relativism 77–8
religion as basic good 52–3
resistance to modernity 96, 99–100
resurrection 54–5, 66, 81–2, 174–5
rhetoric of rights 13–14
Rogers, E. 176
Romans, Book of 75, 144–5, 174
The Rule of St Benedict 140, 146, 179

Saunders, Dame C. 184, 185, 186
science 10, 13, 62
   practice of medicine and euthanasia 165–8
self-evidence of basic goods 53–4
self-evidence of practical knowledge 40, 41–2
Sidgwick, H. 11
sin
   concept of 22
   impact of 51
   and inherent disarray of moral discourse 67–9
Singer, P. 164
social practices 110, 112–14
   see also practice(s)
strength, in contemporary morality 13–14
substantive goods 36, 42
suffering
   Christian approaches to 172–3, 178
   contemporary attitudes to 171
suffering-dying 160, 161, 178–80, 180–83
   as vulnerable strangers 172, 178
   see also euthanasia

taboo 10, 11–12, 13
   death as 170
Tanner, K. 84
technology 62
teleology 19
   basic goods 36–7, 53–4
   eschatology 81–5, 86
   loss of, in moral reasoning 12–13, 48–9, 62, 167–8
   practice of medicine 167
   truth as 20–21, 24–5, 26
Tertullian 123
theological perspectives 54–6, 64–9, 80–87, 128–46
   see also Christian perspectives
theoretical *vs.* practical reason 40–41, 51–4
Thomist perspective (Aquinas) 14, 15–16, 19, 34–6

on hospitality 122, 127
Thomist Aristotelianism 30, 49–50, 84
on truth 21–5
Todorova, M. 196
tolerance and hospitality 121–6, 147–50
tradition(s) 19–20
  authority of nature and 70–72
  conflicting 86–7, 105–6, 106–7
  different conception of role of 43–5, 47
  divine authority in relation to 72–3
  fragmentation of 9, 17, 34
  -situated *vs.* -guided ethics 75–7
  and truth 22–4, 27
  virtues and recovery of moral reason 17–20
  see also Christian perspectives; Christians and non-Christians; incommensurability
truth
  practical 41
  Thomist perspective 21–5
  and tradition 22–4

Veritatis Splendor 24

Verhey, A. 166–7
virtue(s)
  of *misericordia* 98, 127
  practices and 18–19, 20, 45–7
  tradition and recovery of moral reason 17–20
Volf, M. 79, 112–13, 114
vulnerable strangers 139–40, 141–2, 148, 149
  suffering-dying as 172, 178

Walzer, M. 27
Warnock, M. 169
Weber, M. 16–17
Wesley, J. 139
Westermann, P. 35, 53
Wilken, R. 149
Williams, B. 124, 125
Word of God 55–6, 108–9
Wright, N.T. 129, 130

Yoder, J.H. 109–10

Zizioulas, J. 82, 101